British Fascism, the Labour Movement and the State

British Fascism, the Labour Movement and the State

Edited by

Nigel Copsey
Senior Lecturer in History, University of Teesside, UK

and

David Renton
Research Associate, Rand-Afrikaans University, South Africa and University of Sunderland, UK

First published in 2005 by
PALGRAVE MACMILLAN
Houndmills, Basingstoke, Hampshire RG21 6XS and
175 Fifth Avenue, New York, N.Y. 10010
Companies and representatives throughout the world.

PALGRAVE MACMILLAN is the global academic imprint of the Palgrave
Macmillan division of St. Martin's Press, LLC and of Palgrave Macmillan Ltd.
Macmillan® is a registered trademark in the United States, United Kingdom
and other countries. Palgrave is a registered trademark in the European
Union and other countries.

ISBN-13: 978–1–4039–3916–6
ISBN-10: 1–4039–3916–0 hardback

This book is printed on paper suitable for recycling and made from fully
managed and sustained forest sources.

A catalogue record for this book is available from the British Library.

Library of Congress Cataloging-in-Publication Data

British fascism, the labour movement, and the state / edited by
Nigel Copsey, David Renton.
p. cm.
Includes bibliographical references and index.
ISBN 1–4039–3916–0
1. Fascism – Great Britain – History – 20th century. 2. Great
Britain – Politics and government – 20th century. 3. Labor
movement – Great Britain – History – 20th century. 4. Anti-fascist
movements – Great Britain – History – 20th century. 5. Working
class – Great Britain – Political activity – History – 20th century.
I. Copsey, Nigel, 1967– II. Renton, Dave, 1972–

DA566.7.B665 2005
335.6′0941′0904—dc22   2004059163

10 9 8 7 6 5 4 3 2 1
14 13 12 11 10 09 08 07 06 05

Printed and bound in Great Britain by
Antony Rowe Ltd, Chippenham and Eastbourne.

Contents

Notes on Contributors

Nigel Copsey is Senior Lecturer in Modern and Contemporary History at the University of Teesside. Dr Copsey is the author of *Anti-Fascism in Britain* (Palgrave-Macmillan, 2000) and *Contemporary British Fascism: The British National Party and the Quest for Legitimacy* (Palgrave-Macmillan, 2004). He has also published several book chapters and journal articles in the field of right-wing extremism, fascism and anti-fascism.

Philip Coupland completed his PhD in the Department of History at the University of Warwick in 2000. From 2001 to 2004 he worked as a researcher for the European Commission funded project 'The Churches and European Integration' in the Department of History at the University of Glasgow. Dr Coupland has written on British fascism and other topics of British political history in the *Journal of Contemporary History, Twentieth Century British History, Journal of British Studies* and elsewhere. Currently he is writing a monograph for Palgrave-Macmillan about British Christians, national identity and European integration.

Julie V. Gottlieb was educated at McGill University and Cambridge University, and was a post-doctoral fellow at the University of Toronto. She has taught at the University of Manchester, University of Bristol and is currently a lecturer in Modern British History at the University of Sheffield. Her publications include *Feminine Fascism: Women in Britain's Fascist Movement, 1923–1945* (I.B. Tauris, 2000/2003) and *The Culture of Fascism: Visions of the Far Right in Britain* (I.B. Tauris, 2004, co-edited with Thomas Linehan), and she is currently working on a project on 'British Women and Foreign Policy between the Wars'.

Thomas Linehan is a Lecturer in History at Brunel University. He is the author of *British Fascism, 1918–1939: Parties, Ideology and Culture* (Manchester University Press, 2000), *East London for Mosley: The British Union of Fascists in East London and South-West Essex 1933–1940* (Frank Cass, 1996), and a co-editor, with Dr Julie Gottlieb, of *The Culture of Fascism. Visions of the Far Right in Britain* (I.B. Tauris, 2004). Dr Linehan is currently working on a book on the interwar British Communist Party.

Graham Macklin completed his PhD on post-war British fascism at the University of Sheffield in 2002 before taking up his current position as Reader Advisor at the National Archives, Kew, London. He has published several articles on British fascism, including contributions to *Patterns of Prejudice, Totalitarian Movements and Religious Politics* and the *BBC History Magazine*. His book on Oswald Mosley and post-war British fascism will be published in 2005 by I.B. Tauris.

Richard Maguire is Tutor in Modern British History at the University of East Anglia, Norwich. His major research interest is the history of the state, particularly focusing on British, German and Russian history. His most recent publication in this area was 'Reassessing the British Government's Emergency Organisation on Red Friday, 31 June 1925' *Contemporary British History* 18/1 (2004) and he is currently working on a comparative history of the state in the 'Long' Cold War between 1917 and 1990.

Lewis Mates finished his PhD thesis, entitled 'The United Front and the Popular Front in the North-East of England, 1936–1939' in 2002. He has recently published articles on the Communist Party in the north-east of England in the 1930s and the Tyneside foodship and the popular front. He is currently working at the University of Northumbria on an ESRC-funded project examining post-war activism in the Labour Party.

David Renton is a Research Associate of the Rand-Afrikaans University and of the University of Sunderland. He is also an Equality Support Official for the lecturers' union NATFHE and is a member of the steering commit-tee of the anti-fascist organisation Unite Against Fascism. Dr Renton is the author of numerous books including *Fascism: Theory and Practice* (Pluto, 1999) and a forthcoming history of the Anti-Nazi League (New Clarion Press, 2005).

Richard Thurlow is a Senior Lecturer in History at the University of Sheffield. He is the author of *Fascism in Britain* (Blackwell, 1987), *The Secret State* (Blackwell, 1994) and *Fascism in Modern Britain* (Sutton, 2000), and several articles on the political surveillance of the Communist Party of Great Britain and the British Union of Fascists.

Introduction

Nigel Copsey and David Renton

The past thirty years have seen an extraordinary growth in the literature on fascism, including British fascism. The leaders of small parties have found themselves the subject of major biographies.[1] Oswald Mosley, the leader of the interwar British Union of Fascists, a party that never gained any representation in Westminster, has been the subject of a major Channel Four drama series.[2] Consideration has been given to patterns of support[3] and ideology[4] and to explanations for the failure of British fascism.[5] More recently, attention has turned to the cultural values of Britain's fascists.[6] In the meantime, the electoral success of the British National Party from 2001 onwards has demonstrated that Britain's contemporary extreme right has hardly gone away.[7]

In seeking to understand the nature of British fascism, interest has tended to focus on the leaders of fascist parties, the character of fascist ideas and the nature of their support. Considerable attention has also been paid to the violence and racism of British fascism. Less interest, however, has been devoted to the context in which fascist parties have operated. For that reason, the focus of this volume is on the relationship between British fascism, the labour movement and the state.

Significantly, by the time that fascism emerged in Britain, the Italian left had already been destroyed. From the very outset, the left and the right responded to each other as antagonists. In the popular consciousness, the story was about fascism and anti-fascism; and historians have slowly begun to catch up with the latter as well.[8] Where have different anti-fascist traditions come from? Throughout its history, British fascism has experienced waves of growth. Sometimes these have coincided with periods of national or local Labour government. How have Labour Party-controlled institutions responded to the rise of fascism? Was there a difference in police and Home Office policies towards fascism between

1

1936 and 1948, or indeed between 1958 and 1977? And what has been the relationship between local labour cultures and fascism? Is it true, for example, that the working-class cultures of northern England provided an impenetrable barrier to fascism?

Alternatively, did the far-right parties develop strategies to relate to areas of trade union and labour strength? Have there been times when supporters of the labour movement were sympathetic to specific demands put forward by far-right groups? What has been the role of women or migrant communities who identified with the left: has their activity led to the adoption of distinct anti-fascist strategies? What about labour movement traditions outside the Labour Party? What tensions have there been in local and national labour movement responses to fascism? These were the sort of questions that encouraged the writing of this book.

Several of the chapters in this volume refer to episodes when previous waves of fascism came into contact with the British State. The book opens with Richard Maguire's study of the relationship between the British Fascists (BF), the General Strike and the Home Secretary, Joynson-Hicks. Maguire argues that senior Conservative politicians were able to justify co-operating with groups such as the BF, provided that the latter were not deemed to have over-stretched the limits of constitutional politics. Whereas Maguire tends to emphasise the coercive instincts of British constitutional politics, Richard Thurlow takes the opposite approach, portraying MI5 and Special Branch as a set of disinterested pragmatists responding cautiously to the parallel manoeuvres of left- and right-wing extremists. Meanwhile, Graham Macklin's study of policing in the immediate post-war years, addresses the charge of collusion with fascism that was frequently laid at the time against the officers of the Metropolitan Police.

The chapters that appear in the middle of this volume are concerned with forces outside the state. Julie Gottlieb studies the intellectual and artistic impact of interwar British women on the struggle against fascism, including the radical Labour MP Ellen Wilkinson, the peace activist Winifred Holtby and the writer Virginia Woolf. Gottlieb is concerned with telling the story of feminist anti-fascism, a subject much neglected by historians.[9] Philip Coupland's chapter addresses several examples of interwar fascists who were recruited to the far right by the promise of revolutionary or egalitarian politics. Such individuals may have attended an individual speech by Oswald Mosley or some other prominent fascist orator. Joining the movement, they were then shocked to discover the elitism of the fascists, their antipathy to any form of reformist programme. Very quickly, the 'left-wing' fascists were driven out. The contradictions suffered by Coupland's temporary fascists arose from a deep ambivalence within their own heads. Did they see the British labour movement itself (trade unions, co-operatives, peace movements, political parties and their allies) as a source of strength? Could unions deliver the justice in which they believed? Insofar as working-class people continued to identify with their trade unions, they could not remain easily within the political space of fascism and the British extreme right.

In another chapter with a pre-1939 focus, Lewis Mates offers us a study of the Aid Spain campaigns that emerged in the north-east of England, a region characterised by a strong, yet traditionally moderate, labour movement. He demonstrates how the defeat of domestic fascism in the region did not weaken anti-fascist activity. On the contrary, he shows how Spain galvanised many. For the majority of those involved, the key factor was a desire for humanitarian relief. Mates makes a case for seeing campaigners' appeals to humanitarianism as diverting from a fully fledged anti-fascism. More precisely, Mates draws our attention to the leadership of the movement and the ambiguous role played by the Communist Party. Nonetheless, it is clear that the labour movement has done more than any other organisation to train a significant number of people in anti-fascist politics. David Renton's study of trade unionists in the 1970s Anti-Nazi League describes some of the mechanisms involved, including national campaigns, local branch meetings, and all the other processes in between. Renton is markedly sceptical about the Labour Party's national response to the threat posed by the National Front and emphasises the tactical gap between the instincts of the Labour leadership, and the movement's rank and file.

In Thomas Linehan's chapter, we see the extent to which British fascism has gathered support from the working-class. He suggests that owing to distinct socio-structural and political change, today's right-wing extremists can make significant inroads into working-class constituencies. Linehan strikes a pessimistic note and takes issue with the 'anti-fascist' practice of the Blair government. The most alarming feature of New Labour, he argues, is its reluctance to use any language of class. This contrasts with some of the activities of the British National Party, and in particular with the fascists' disingenuous claim that racist voting will result in a redistribution of resources to the white working class. The institutions and traditions of the labour movement, which in 1930s Britain existed both inside and outside the Labour Party, are found much more often these days outside than in.

New Labour also features in the final chapter of this volume. Nigel Copsey considers the response of the Labour Party to the 1970s National Front and to the British National Party. He covers the period from the early 1970s through to the European and local elections in 2004. At the national level, reflecting the change from old Labour to New Labour, Copsey shows how the nature of Labour's response to contemporary British fascism has differed significantly. He also provides a local case study of Labour's response to the British National Party in Burnley, a town that became notorious as a right extremist base, in 2002 when the BNP captured three seats on Burnley council.

This volume began life as a conference organised by the Society for the Study of Labour History and the School of Continuing Education at the University of Leeds. The conference took place in November 2003, when Nick Griffin's British National Party had seventeen elected councillors and was achieving an average of around 20 per cent of the vote in by-elections. For several of the contributors, the purpose of reviewing the history of British fascism and its relationship to the labour movement and the state was no mere historic curiosity, they were motivated as much by a desire to contribute to the forces that could push back present-day fascism.

Yet it would be false to pretend that the book represents any consensus of historians in favour of present-day activism. Rather, this collection is a representative set of diverse essays, containing a plurality of views and politics. Points of difference can frequently be traced between one essay and the next. For both radical and liberal scholars this diversity of opinion is no weakness but a strength. It is a sign of our continuing belief in values such as mutual tolerance and respect, in contrast to the narrow unanimity of thought championed by fascist parties in the past and today.

Notes

1. Robert Skidelsky, *Oswald Mosley* (London: Macmillan, 1975); Nicholas Mosley, *Rules of the Game* (London: Secker & Warburg, 1982) and *Beyond the Pale* (London: Secker & Warburg, 1983); Francis Selwyn, *Hitler's Englishman* (London: Routledge, 1987); Peter Martland, *Lord Haw Haw: The English Voice of Nazi Germany* (London: The National Archives, 2003); Mary Kenny, *Germany Calling* (Dublin: New Island Books, 2003); David Baker, *Ideology of Obsession: A. K. Chesterton and British Fascism* (London: I.B. Tauris, 1996).
2. Screened in 1998 to mixed reviews. It was written by Laurence Marks and Maurice Gran with the help of Nicholas Mosley.
3. Gerry. C. Webber, 'Patterns of Membership and Support for the British Union of Fascists', *Journal of Contemporary History* 19, 4, 1984, pp. 575–606;

John D. Brewer, *Mosley's Men: The British Union of Fascists in the West Midlands* (Aldershot: Gower, 1984); Thomas P. Linehan, *East London for Mosley* (London: Frank Cass, 1996); Julie V. Gottlieb, *Feminine Fascism* (London: I.B. Tauris, 2003); Michael Billig, *Fascists: A Social Psychological View of the National Front* (London: Harcourt Brace Jovanovich, 1981); Stan Taylor, *The National Front in English Politics* (London: Macmillan, 1982); Chris T. Husbands, *Racial Exclusionism and the City* (London: Allen & Unwin, 1983).

4. David S. Lewis, *Illusions of Grandeur* (Manchester: Manchester University Press, 1987); Richard Thurlow, *Fascism in Britain: From Oswald Mosley's Blackshirts to the National Front* (London: I.B. Tauris, 1998) and *Fascism in Modern Britain* (Stroud: Sutton, 2000); Thomas P. Linehan, *British Fascism 1918–1939: Parties, Ideology and Culture* (Manchester: Manchester University Press, 2000).

5. Mike Cronin (ed.), *The Failure of British Fascism: The Far Right and the Fight for Political Recognition* (Basingstoke: Macmillan, 1996).

6. Julie V. Gottlieb and Thomas P. Linehan (eds), *The Culture of Fascism: Visions of the Far Right in Britain* (London: I.B. Tauris, 2004).

7. Nigel Copsey, *Contemporary British Fascism: The British National Party and the Quest for Legitimacy* (Basingstoke: Palgrave, 2004).

8. David Renton, *Fascism: Theory and Practice* (London: Pluto, 1999), *Fascism, Anti-Fascism and Britain in the 1940s* (Basingstoke: Macmillan, 2000) and *This Rough Game: Fascism and Anti-Fascism* (Stroud: Sutton, 2001); Nigel Copsey, *Anti-Fascism in Britain* (Basingstoke: Macmillan, 2000).

9. Notable exceptions are Martin Durham, *Women and Fascism* (London: Routledge, 1998); Julie V. Gottlieb, *Feminine Fascism: Women in Britain's Fascist Movement, 1923–1945* (London: I.B. Tauris, 2000); and David Renton, 'Women and Fascism: A Critique', *Socialist History*, 20, 2001, pp. 72–83.

1

'The Fascists ... are ... to be depended upon.' The British Government, Fascists and Strike-breaking during 1925 and 1926

Richard Charles Maguire

On 31 July 1925, or 'Red Friday' as it came to be known, Stanley Baldwin's Conservative government intervened in an industrial dispute in the British coalfields, offering to provide an extremely costly subsidy to the coal industry while a Royal Commission examined its economic circumstances. This step averted a national lockout of miners by colliery owners, which would have led to widespread sympathetic industrial action by the members of other British trade unions. Nine months later the failure to find a mutually acceptable solution to the difficulties in the coal industry resulted in the General Strike. At the time, the Red Friday decision was fiercely attacked by many. Yet, the dominant interpretation of this action in recent years has been to see it in the context of what Philip Williamson calls Baldwin's 'appeal for industrial peace': a final attempt at mediation in which, after 'unsuccessful attempts during July 1925 to reconcile coal owners' and miners' leaders, and in the face of threatened strikes by transport unions in support of miners, he [Baldwin] took the large political risk of offering a temporary Government subsidy and a Royal Commission of Inquiry'.[1] This reading of Red Friday sits comfortably with the dominant conception of British governance in this and other eras, which emphasises a culture of minimal force, consensus and dialogue. It is a view that distinguishes the leaders of Baldwin's Conservative Party and the success of his brand of conservatism from the party's so-called extreme 'right', which, it is alleged, remained impotent.[2] Crucial to the idea of Baldwinian compromise has been an agreement that fascism was part of this defeated extremism. This agreement is based on an assessment that fascist views had little purchase on the British imagination, as demonstrated by Richard Thurlow's assertion that the British practitioners of fascism in this period were regarded by their contemporaries as 'highly eccentric' and, consequently, unimportant. Similar perspectives run though Roger Griffin's argument that fascism failed as a consequence of the 'irreducible pluralism' of British society, or David Baker's assertion that 'Nationalism, patriotism, militarism, anti-alienism, anti-socialism, all highly successful forms of propaganda in Germany, failed to add up to a political ideology of sufficient power to undermine British Conservative Party propaganda, or to make Labour appear as a threat to freedom'. Consequently, writers such as Thomas Linehan have characterised the British Fascists of the 1920s as a 'marginal' movement of little impact that was destined for inevitable obscurity.[3]

While some historians, including Kenneth Lunn and John Hope, have questioned this interpretation, the idea that British fascism was a peripheral peculiarity of little note has dominated the manner in which most have reflected upon fascism, the labour movement and the British government in the period around the General Strike.[4] For example, historians of the strike have generally assigned minimal importance to incidents such as the armed hijacking by fascists of a *Daily Herald* delivery van in October 1925, a crime dealt with by the Director of Public Prosecutions as a breach of the peace. For Robert Benewick this exploit was important only to indicate how the British Fascists gained 'a certain notoriety as a result of the pranks of its members'.[5] Similarly, the contrast with the treatment of communist leaders, arrested in October 1925 and later imprisoned for periods of up to one year for sedition, has elicited little attention. Margaret Morris merely noted how 'The Government took no action to curb the Fascists' while deciding, 'to shackle the Communists'.[6]

Equally, the well-established fact that a significant number of members of the British Fascists joined the Organisation for Maintenance of Supplies (the OMS) over this period has drawn minimal consideration. The OMS was formed in the months after Red Friday and was described by its leaders as an apolitical 'association of loyal citizens' whose purpose was to provide a pool of volunteers for the Government's emergency organisation, if required.[7] Senior officials, like Sir William Mitchell-Thompson, had detailed meetings with the leadership of the OMS throughout the coal emergency, yet the migration of fascists into the ranks of the OMS has elicited very little comment.[8] Anthony Mason discussed the organisation at length without mentioning the fascists, while Patrick Renshaw dismissed this osmosis with a cursory note that

'the Fascists merged with the OMS and the Government organisation'.[9] In contrast, much has been made of the information that in April 1926 the Home Secretary, Sir William Joynson-Hicks, threatened to resign as vice-president of the National Citizen's Union (NCU) if the fascists were allowed to join it without changing their constitution.[10] Consequently, Gerry Webber could argue that the subsequent entry of fascists into the OMS was unimportant, as in order to be allowed to assist the Government the leadership of the British Fascists had been forced to 'commit itself to parliamentary democracy'.[11]

However, on 1 September 1925, one month after Red Friday, and seven months before he apparently found contact with the British Fascists unacceptable, Joynson-Hicks sent a letter to Baldwin covering a copy of a detailed memorandum he had written to Sir John Anderson. Joynson-Hicks wanted Anderson to take command of the Supply and Transport Organisation, the Government's emergency machinery for dealing with any nationwide industrial unrest. In the letter, Joynson-Hicks described the groups he expected to provide volunteers to for the emergency organisation in any strike. He stated:

> There exist the Fascists, the Crusaders, and the Organisation for the Supply of Material Services. One need say nothing about the first two – they are well known, and, I think to be depended upon. I have seen their leaders several times.[12]

This letter implies that Joynson-Hicks was in close contact with fascists during this period and raises no doubts about their suitability as governmental allies. There is no indication in the Baldwin Papers of disquiet over this statement, nor is there any indication of dissent in Anderson's papers.[13] This apparently unthinking acceptance of the usefulness of fascists by some of the British government's most powerful figures demands further consideration, for it seems unlikely that ministers and officials were unaware of the violent activity of fascists in the period before and after Red Friday. There had been widespread newspaper coverage of street battles between fascists and communists as well of the fascist violence in Italy, while the rhetoric of the British Fascists was laced with metaphors based upon violence, as their leader General Blakeney explained, their message was that 'force must be opposed by force'.[14] Questions were asked in Parliament about fascist activity, while Hilda Chamberlain expressed concern about it to her brother Neville.[15] The police had to deal with investigations such as the stabbing of the former Communist Party member Max Adler during an attack by a gang, alleged to be fascists, and kept Home Office officials fully briefed on progress in these cases.[16] With this in mind, how can we square Joynson-Hicks' comment with the received wisdom that the fascists were unacceptable, that Baldwin and his colleagues could not work with them and that the British government, and the British political system more generally, was characterised by moderation and restraint?

The answer provided here will not involve any suggestion that these men were fascists, or that the Conservative Party was secretly intent upon following Italian methods in dealing with the General Strike; nor will it be suggested that any of these men were anti-Semitic.[17] But that which will be proposed is that the apparently nonchalant use of the term 'fascist' in correspondence among members of the Cabinet suggests an understanding of British governance and political life very different from that which has tended to dominate views of the era of Baldwin. This will be done through consideration of the discussions that took place in the period between Red Friday and the General Strike, which will be referred to as 'the coal emergency'. What this examination appears to reveal is that ministers and many civil servants understood that the fascist movement attracted thugs and was inherently violent, but viewed this as an acceptable 'downside' to a group that was, by no means, outside the cultural mainstream. It will be suggested that the reason for this acceptability lay not in any widespread anti-Semitism, but in an understanding that the fascists shared other values with ministers, many civil servants and a substantial portion of British citizens.

The 'community'

The epithet used here to explore this set of values is 'the community', a term which was used throughout the coal emergency by ministers, civil servants, industrialists, union leaders and journalists. It appears to relate to the notion that there existed an identifiable section of humanity within the British Isles who could be considered to form a coherent unitary group. In that sense it seems to have been used interchangeably with another term: the 'public'. For example, in August 1925 an article in the Norwich *Eastern Evening News* explained that the subsidy decision had been taken 'In order to save the community from the disaster of a stoppage of the coal mines and a sympathetic action on the part of other workers.' It then went on to use the term 'the public' in the same context, suggesting homogeneity between the terms, which it appears the reader was expected to understand without explanation.[18] Some historians, for instance Ross McKibbin, have already examined the term 'the public' in the interwar era. For McKibbin it is an appellation used by 'the not-working class who behave differently to the working class'. His proposal is that from 1918 onwards 'middle-class' Britain was dominated by an 'acute hostility to working class politics' among those who thought of themselves as 'the public'.[19] The main beneficiary of this was the Conservative Party, which he argues 'devised an anti-inflationary political rhetoric' that allowed its members to monopolise this anti-socialist voting base and dominate interwar politics as the party of 'the public'.[20]

Philip Williamson approaches the term in a different manner, highlighting how the notion of the 'public' played an important role in the 'socially inclusive' rhetoric of Baldwin, which identified conservatism with all sectors of the population, 'including trade unions understood in their "acceptable" form'.[21] There is a significant difference between the interpretations of McKibbin and Williamson in this instance. McKibbin seems to suggest that the Conservative leadership did not subscribe fully to the 'conventional wisdoms and "common sense" economics' integral to the idea of the public, arguing that the leadership had to 'capitulate, whatever it thought' in matters of economic policy and industrial relations.[22] In contrast Williamson sees Baldwin's rhetoric as fundamental, allowing an insight into the real beliefs of the man, and he seems to accept that for Baldwin, the public was a reality. This latter approach is continued here, where it is argued that the emotional currents swirling around the notions of 'public' and 'community' were critically important factors, which have to be understood if we are to reach an awareness of the relationship between fascism, the government and the labour movement.

One of the most consistent users of this term during the coal emergency was the Prime Minister. For example, in his speech to Parliament during the debate on the coal subsidy on 6 August 1925 he averred,

> The community will always protect itself, for the community must be fed, and it will see that it gets its food. And let me just say this too: I am convinced that, if the time should come when the community has to protect itself, with the full strength of the government behind it, the community will do so, and the response of the community will astonish the forces of anarchy throughout the world.[23]

In this speech, made less than one week after Red Friday, the concept of 'the community' was a central idea and means of justification. Baldwin made it quite clear that, for him, this body was the centre of an entire intellectual prospect, and played a key role in a value structure everyone was expected to understand. The community was seen to possess an inclusive character and a natural aspect. Furthermore, it was presented as, in very important ways, a coherent body, having an overall cohesion of mind that allowed it to 'feed' and 'protect' itself. For Baldwin it exemplified order, disorder was defined against it and was decried as 'anarchy' to be faced and defeated by a unified community supported by 'the government'.

This understanding was not merely an idiosyncratic aspect of Baldwin's rhetoric; nor was it peculiar to the rhetoric of Conservative politicians. Certainly, Conservatives had a vision of community that related to their ideology; Leo Amery argued that 'the Conservative regarded the union between the individual and the community as something essential and inherent in the sense that neither could succeed without the other'.[24] Likewise Joynson-Hicks justified the augmentation of the Supply and Transport Organisation by suggesting that it had been formed 'not for the purpose of breaking the Strike, but to protect the interests of the community'.[25] Nevertheless, it was used by a wide variety of citizens in 1925 and 1926. Home Office officials despatched documents to volunteers in the Supply and Transport Organisation explaining that 'The function of the Emergency Organisation will in general terms be to deal with the preparation and operation of schemes for maintaining the supply of the essentials of life to the community and to deal generally with the situation during Strikes, Lock-outs and similar emergencies.'[26] Similarly, Lord Lieutenants were advised that everyone who wished to assist in the protection of the community would be welcome: 'Should a serious emergency arise every person wishing to assist in maintaining services essential to the life of the community will have ample opportunity to volunteer.'[27] Industrialists used the idea with regularity. Sir Adam Nimmo, the President of the Scottish Coalowners' Association, told a meeting of the National Union of Manufacturers that the coal industry employers were 'willing to have their policy and proposals examined from the point of view of the interest of the community, and from that point of view only'.[28]

Moreover, the term was used by socialists like J. H. Thomas, who in August 1925 told members of Parliament that the trade unions had not taken action in July 1925 'as a challenge to the community, because they recognise that in a fight against the community, the community must win'.[29] Thomas was not speaking from the perspective of Conservative-style individualism; nevertheless he seems to have had an idea of the community that shared the common themes identified in the words of Baldwin and others. Similarly, in May 1926 Ernest Bevin attempted to counter criticisms of the proposed industrial action by stating 'Neither the General Council nor the miners has any quarrel with the people. We are not declaring war on the community.'[30] Therefore, it would seem that an argument that the term was purely class-based would be in danger of simplifying its significance. All those using this term seemed to share assumptions similar to those of Baldwin, the most obvious being the idea that a group called 'the community' or 'the public' existed and that its interests could be defined. There is also the implication, evident in the words of Nimmo, that this group needed to be defended and that it had some ability, and right, to decide upon the outcome of the dispute. Indeed the implication is that the decision of the community was binding; there could be no argument against such a primal phenomenon. The wide degree to which the term was used without any explanation implies a shared confidence of complete understanding on the part of the reader. However, an attempt to unravel this notion's meaning reveals that, far from being an inherently positive idea, it was one wherein there lurked significant potential for discord, a capacity that was deeply significant in the relationship of fascism to the government.

The critical issue regarding the concept of the community was that, although widely used, it lacked precision. The closest any authors came to an exact rendering was in the rather basic image of those citizens who needed to utilise public services. One writer in Norfolk explained the crucial importance of 'the public well-being, as regards food supplies, light and heat, facilities to get to and from work, etc.' in any decisions taken during 1925 and 1926.[31] Likewise the leaders of the OMS in Norwich argued that their actions were directed at the protection of the 'well-being' of the 'general community' through 'the maintenance of Law and order and the essential Public Services: – Food, Heat, Light, Power, Transport, Sanitation, etc.' They argued that the weakest members of this community 'children, the infirm and the aged' along with the 'poorest class of the population' would be most at risk in any disruption.[32] Moreover, they also stressed the organisation's social inclusiveness: their description of the meeting at which the Norwich branch was founded, stated that the social mix of those involved was 'large and very representative'.[33] Therefore, the general sense of community being used would appear to have meant the entire population, acting together to protect their weakest citizens, a statement with which few could disagree.

However, the lack of any clear characterisation of, what appeared to be, a uniformly benevolent notion meant that the use to which it could be put was, potentially, problematic. For some who employed it as the bedrock of their explanation there was an uncompromising undercurrent: that membership of this group was predicated upon the acceptance of certain rules. While the advertising of the OMS proclaimed that the movement 'is neither Political nor Aggressive' being 'a non-political, non-party organisation' that aimed to protect the general community, other data complicates this portrayal of communal membership crossing social boundaries.[34] OMS leaders appear to have been certain that they did not want the members of some social groups to join their organisation. On 13 March 1926 organisers were instructed 'not to recruit farm labourers'.[35] No written explanation was provided, but it may be that agricultural labourers were not considered sufficiently trustworthy, possibly because of the history of organised union activity amongst them in Norfolk. It seems that, in Norwich at least, membership of the community involved the acceptance of certain ideas that such people could not be relied upon to embrace.

This interpretation seems to be supported by comments made by senior Conservative figures. Amery stated that socialists were of dubious reliability because socialism 'thought of the national organisation only from the point of view of one class'.[36] Baldwin illustrated why these ideas were problematic in the context of the community. This was because industrial relations within this framework were characterised by an 'old constitutional attitude' where 'negotiations, keeping promises made collectively, employing strikes where negotiations failed' was the norm. For him trade unions were 'great movements' but only if they acted in a specific manner, one where strikes were 'the last resort in an industrial struggle'. However, the 'sympathetic strike' was increasingly the 'first resort in a struggle that was becoming more political than it was industrial'. This 'alien and foreign heresy' was now being used as 'an engine to wage what was beginning to be called class warfare'. These aims made a general strike 'the supreme instrument by which the whole community could be either starved or terrified into submission to the will of its promoters'.[37]

Williamson argues that with such ideas Baldwin 'described practices and ideals familiar to business and trade union leaders because he was defending a well-tried industrial relations system dating from the 1890s'.[38] Whilst this may be the case, this characterisation tends to ignore questions of the balance of power in this system and, crucially in this instance, the latent ideas that underpinned it. The critical issue in the context of the community was the absolute demand implicit within this system – adherence to its norms and rules. Industrial action by workers that affected only their employers was acceptable, if not desirable, as the idea of the need to protect the community 'in no way impugns the right to strike'.[39] However, it was quite unacceptable that industrial action might damage the community. According to a leader writer in the *East Anglian Daily Times*, the question was 'whether any body of workers who are dissatisfied with the conditions under which they are employed should have the right to down tools at the order of their trade union, thereby inflicting grievous injury upon an entirely innocent community outside'.[40] The material idea here was that of victimisation of the community. Any form of action that affected the community in general was not permissible and could not be tolerated: 'it is quite impossible to maintain such an attitude in a stoppage which is designed to bring the whole life of the community to a standstill'.[41] As the most senior element in the social order, the 'entirely innocent community' was always in the right when affected by such action. Consequently, it appears that a combination of the incoherence of the idea of the community and its emotional potency imbued it with the capacity to inflame industrial discord. The understanding of the notion of community among many officials and politicians, at all levels, was inimical to certain contemporary concepts of industrial solidarity; therefore, acceptance of the idea of community would appear to have placed the government and the labour movement in antagonistic positions.

Defeating industrial action

The unspoken implication was that breaking these rules would result in severe penalties and serious action could be taken against those who failed to conform. The language used to describe the consequences was unequivocal; this was a conflict between those who stood to protect a good society against those who sought to destroy it. As one writer stated in May 1926 'The Trade Union Congress having declared war on the community, the Government must take up the challenge.'[42] One crucial outcome of this was that all action taken to mitigate the effects of sympathetic strikes was morally justified. Home Office officials advised local officers that 'It should be made clear that men and women are recruited under this scheme in the interests of the community and not for the purpose of acting as strike-breakers.'[43] It would appear that while the old system of industrial bargaining described by Baldwin had frowned upon 'strike-breaking' in general, threats to the community changed the context of such activity. Commentators explained this alteration in approach by reference to the danger being faced, stating it was 'impossible to maintain such an attitude in a stoppage which is designed to bring the whole life of the community to a standstill'.[44]

Furthermore, the framework of the community made it difficult to comprehend alternative views. An integral part of the preparation after Red Friday was the dissemination of Circular 636 to local authorities to explain how the emergency apparatus would work if mobilised. Members of the Supply and Transport Committee noted that there was general agreement with the circular except in South Yorkshire, South Wales and some London Municipalities. The Home Secretary appeared perplexed at this response, commenting that 'the Circular appears to have been regarded generally from a political point of view'.[45] It was perplexing for officials because the action was taken to defend the community and so, in their minds, could not be political. As Arthur Steel-Maitland explained, government preparations were, 'compelled by the latent intention in every community to protect itself'.[46] In these circumstances to criticise government activity was to be 'partisan' because it was also to censure the community on whose behalf the government was acting. Jeffery and Hennessey have argued that the provision of 'essential public services' is an absolute duty in any emergency planning, although the provision of these services almost inevitably involves 'strikebreaking'.[47] This was the view of officials, who explained that 'It is not proposed to substitute new machinery for that ordinarily existing to meet the essential needs of the community', the belief was that the emergency apparatus was merely to ensure the community that it could obtain its basic supplies.[48] However, this approach needs further consideration, rather than being granted an automatically value-neutral status. While essential services need to be provided, the means by which they may be supplied is one of political choice. In May 1926 ministers would not agree to an offer from trade union leaders to distribute basic supplies, because officials felt that the government could not delegate this role.[49] Whether one accepts the validity of this decision or not, it was taken in the context of specific emotional and cultural attitudes and should therefore not be seen as completely impartial.

The idea of community would appear to have contained the potential to place those who failed to adhere to its norms outside its realm. Any alternative approach to the norm was seen as an aggressive activity, an attack upon the community, and placed the persons involved not only outside the community, but also outside the protection of that concept. In these circumstances Baldwin had no hesitation that it was the duty of the government to oppose and defeat organised labour, 'What then is the issue for which the Government is fighting? It is fighting because while negotiations were still in progress the Trade Union Council ordered a general strike, presumably to try to force Parliament and the community to bend to its will.'[50] In this emotional and cultural framework the danger posed by socialist ideas was elemental, they threatened the very fabric of the community, of social organisation as many in the government apparatus understood and desired, and consequently had to be defeated.

What becomes clear is that many officials were bent on routing such radicalism. In December 1925 Lionel Lindsay, the Chief Constable of Glamorgan, was unambiguous, 'I am sure that the vast majority of the population are sick of Labour tyranny and are ready to put it down the moment they can feel confident that their Government is going to lead them, but they must have proof that their Government will lead them before they show their hands.'[51] For Lindsay the community was waiting for leadership to be provided by the Government; when this was given, the enemy could be defeated. Conservative supporters were also desperate for these matters to be dealt with: Joynson-Hicks noted that 'our own people are getting so savage thinking that nothing is being done – I had a private deputation last week from the Association of Chambers of Commerce'.[52]

That 'savage' attitudes were permeating the, generally moderate, Chambers of Commerce suggests that the emotional spectrum being drawn upon by the notion of community could result in a belief that strong action was necessary and justified. This in turn requires a re-evaluation of our understanding of the perception of the threat posed by socialism and industrial unrest in this period. Some historians have been dismissive of the apocalyptic warnings of 'revolution' made in this period, for example, Webber argued the General Strike 'seemed to most more like a pathetic postscript to the troubles of the early twenties' than any real revolutionary threat.[53] Similarly, Baker asserts that 'relatively few members of the middle classes in Britain were afraid that Bolshevism would spread rapidly to the end of the Northern Line, or that the Labour Party was simply a Trojan horse for the Bolsheviks' imminent take-over'.[54] Yet, these interpretations appear to be based upon a particular view of the perceived threat and of statements made by ministers, which downplays seemingly aggressive statements made by men such as Winston Churchill. For example, in September 1925 in a letter discussing the results of the TUC conference, Churchill suggested that the Parliamentary Labour Party was 'utterly powerless' in the face of Labour's 'more violent supporters'. He was candid in his assessment of the issue that had to be faced, 'It is with the ugly menace of revolutionary Socialism that the nation will have to deal.'[55] Likewise J. C. C. Davidson had no hesitation that it was the duty of the government to oppose and defeat extremists, arguing that 'with the hearty and cohesive support of the public' the Government would show that 'it is impossible to tolerate the illegal and tyrannical attitude of some of the leaders of the Trade Union movement today'.[56] Cuthbert Headlam noted how in a conversation on 3 August with Baldwin 'I asked him whether he meant to fight Trade Union domination when the issue was a straight one – he said he certainly meant to do so – so there it is.'[57] Similarly, two days later, Tom Jones noted that Baldwin 'must make it plain that the Government were prepared to fight the extremists'.[58] The idea that the fear of certain types of socialist action was not real and genuine does not withstand exposure to the letters and diaries of ministers, who appear to have been seriously concerned. Their beliefs may have been erroneous, but they were genuine.

Furthermore, the ideas of community increased their disquiet. As authors such as Morgan have shown, the use of 'one-nation' rhetoric by Baldwin and others may be seen as ambivalent in effect and meaning and Townshend has emphasised the problematic nature of the ideas of the rural idyll that float through much of Baldwin's imagery.[59] Because the perception of danger was set against an ideal image of the community, it had the potential to be all the more terrifying. The threat to the community feared by ministers and officials was not necessarily one of another Bolshevik Revolution; instead they dreaded a peril that could manifest itself in tiny ways that would cause immense harm to the community even without full-scale street fighting. In many ways the fear was of a form of industrial terrorism, exemplified in a minor entry in the Cabinet minutes of April 1926 where it was suggested, '(f) That the Home Secretary should warn the Minister of Transport of the risk of sabotage (e.g. by dropping a spanner or other instrument in some delicate part of machinery) by electrical workers immediately before leaving work, which might dislocate the Government's emergency arrangements.'[60] The fear was that radical workers could seriously damage the community through attacks upon the infrastructure of industrial society. No such attacks took place, but the dread grew from the idea that those workers on strike were outlaws who had placed themselves beyond the community but continued to live within its homeland, from where they could attack its very heart.

This view was not completely logical, but it was very real. Ministers were authentically alarmed at the prospect of a challenge to a way of life in which they believed wholeheartedly. The emotional potency of the idea of community was such that workers engaging in industrial action that affected public services were seen as a serious danger and in an important sense ceased to be part of the community. The consequence was that when defending the community against these threats any level of force could be justified. A revealing comment was made by Davidson on events in Leeds during the General Strike: 'The Chief Constable', he wrote, 'broke 32 truncheons and a vast number of the right heads the first night of the strike', ensuring that no trouble occurred during the period. He contrasted this with Middlesborough and Ipswich where, he said, events 'got completely out of hand because the Chief Constable and the Local Authorities were both weak'.[61] The nonchalance with which Davidson regarded this violence is indicative of the mentality created by the emotional framework of 'the community'. Furthermore, it was a nonchalance reflected throughout officialdom. In Horwich, Lancashire, the Chief Constable reported how local police, confronted with a 'large body of strikers … drew their truncheons and rushed them, and completely routed the mob'.[62] There was no discussion of casualties, not even a thought to mention that there were none, the 'mob' threatening the community had to be dealt with. Throughout these discussions there was no concern at the use of violence: the community had to be safeguarded.

'Fascists', 'the community', 'the government'

It is in this context, where violence in defence of the community was condoned, that the uncontroversial use of the term 'fascist' by ministers and senior civil servants may be understood. It was a term indicative of a shared appreciation that aggressive action against the enemies of the community was acceptable. With its patriotic, anti-left overtones fascism was just one more element of the more muscular methods of defence. Unlike socialists, fascists were not outside the community because they did not seem to challenge its underlying concepts. Benjamin Alpers has argued that for many Americans in this period fascism was a perfectly acceptable movement for exactly the same reasons; it had produced a strong leader in Mussolini, who defended order. Those who admired Mussolini were fully aware of the violence inherent in these beliefs – the murder of Giacomo Matteotti in 1924 exemplified this – but accepted them nevertheless.[63] Such attitudes are illustrated by the robust comments of the Chair of the Manchester Watch Committee, James Johnson, after the *Manchester Guardian* had reported that the local Chief Constable had refused an offer of help from the British fascists. Johnson told Home

Office officials that he resented 'the altogether gratuitous complexion sought to be put on our actions' and that the situation was quite different from that reported. He explained how 'the action of our Chief Constable was not intended as any "Rebuff to British Fascists" as described in the Guardian'. On the contrary, it had been explained to the press that the Chief Constable would be willing to appoint 'any respectable person' as a Special Constable, but only if that person 'applied in his individual capacity'.[64]

The reality appears to have been that, for officials in the localities and the centre, fascist organisations were sometimes problematic, not because of their violence, but because they claimed a role that was not theirs, to act for the community in defeating unacceptable worker activity by organised force if required. As the Chief Constable of Birmingham argued, 'the Fascisti is a body organised to oppose the Communist Party by force, which it is not their business to do'.[65] This helps us to understand Joynson-Hicks' threat to resign from the NCU if the fascists were allowed to join it. The problem was not the fascists' views, but their claim to be a paramilitary opponent to socialism. Blakeney explained that the difficulty was that, 'the Home Secretary informed the president that he could not recognise them in any work for the Government so long as they retained their semi-military organisation, and so long as they claimed to act in any sense in contradistinction to the work of the Executive Government'.[66] This approach mirrored that of officials, who accepted that the fascists had a role as spear-carriers in the fight against disorder. The important action the fascists had to take to allow them to take up this role was to abandon their own organisations, however temporarily, and accept those authorised by the government. When the fascist Colonel Seymour contacted the Home Office to offer the services of an organised group of fascists he was advised they should join as Special Constables on an individual basis.[67] Likewise, the Chief Constable of Wolverhampton, D. Webber, told officials that local fascist leaders had agreed that their members would have to resign from the movement before they could become Special Constables, to allow them to be put 'on a proper and sound basis, with proper control'. Having reached this understanding Webber stated that he proposed to use such recruits in the event of an emergency. At the Home Office officials were relaxed about the proposal, noting 'I think that the C C's action will be correct. C C's may land themselves in some trouble if they enlist fascists as "organised" bodies, but as specials, working individually under the orders of the police, they should be eligible recruits.'[68]

This acceptance of their suitability for service in the protection of the community appears to have allowed the fascists to play a significant role in the government's emergency organisation during the General Strike. The *Fascist Bulletin* reported that fascists worked on the docks, in transportation, on the railways, in the Civil Constabulary Reserve and as Special Constables.[69] It is also apparent that fascists were involved in the emergency organisation in the localities, such as in Poole, where the local Voluntary Service Committee, responsible for the registration and recruitment of the volunteer workforce, included fascists in its membership.[70]

Here one may return to the attitude to fascism at the most senior levels of government. Joynson-Hicks has often been cast as an extremist and, therefore, a letter from him mentioning the fascists with approval might be seen as insufficient basis for an assessment of the attitude to fascists within the Cabinet as a whole.[71] However, this assessment of him has been challenged by authors such as Middlemass and Barnes, as well as by Rubinstein, and it is clear that the fascists did not regard the Home Secretary as an automatic ally and made strong criticisms of some of his policies.[72] Nevertheless, it would be quite correct to question any suggestion that all members of the Cabinet found the fascist an acceptable associate if the only piece of evidence for this assertion was one letter from Joynson-Hicks. This is not the case, for a crucial excerpt also exists in the Cabinet minutes. On 13 October 1925, during the Cabinet discussions about methods of recruitment, ministers had considered the potential sources of volunteers. The minutes record that they were told,

> Various unofficial organisations, however, had been founded for this purpose, including the OMS, the chambers of commerce, the Fascisti, and the Crusaders, and it was understood that the persons who volunteered under these unofficial organisations would, in the case of an emergency, be at the disposal of the Government.

This is not a letter from a 'die-hard', but a secretarial note of Cabinet discussion and appears to provide clear evidence that the use of fascists as members of the emergency organisation was discussed at ministerial level on at least two occasions in this period. There is no evidence that, on either occasion, the idea caused any difficulty for those involved; furthermore there is no record of any discussion about their suitability. Instead, discussion on 13 October focused on the choice of recruiting these civilians directly or through 'private organisations', not on whether some of those recruits should be fascists.[73]

Therefore, the term 'fascist' may be seen as one that illuminates an emotional and intellectual framework among officials of all ranks, based upon the idea of a community, which led to a determination to defeat any threat to the existing system of constitutional and social organisation. This framework of community justified, both in private consideration and public utterance, any action to achieve that end and saw the government apparatus as the organisation chosen by the community to carry out the actions needed to defend its position. In this sense the fascists were not a marginal political group, whose attitude to violence developed from their embrace of 'hypermasculinity', but one whose views lay firmly in the mainstream of British life.[74] The concept of the community fed into discussions of the use of force, like those held in March 1926, which decided that force could be used to prevent attacks on vulnerable points, 'such as destruction of a power house' but was not justifiable in a case of passive resistance.[75] Serious consideration was therefore being given to the possibility of attacks upon vulnerable points and it was agreed that violence could be used to deal with these incidents. That this force might be lethal appears to have been an option accepted by all those concerned, as later that month police liaison officers reported that 'there was little or no occasion for further supply of arms on loan to the police. Most forces probably had sufficient weapons-in-hand for all requirements.' While Dixon reminded them that the 'Police is not an armed force' he added the caveat that officers could be provided with arms if engaged on 'specially dangerous duties'.[76] The potential lengths to which this approach might lead are illustrated by the preparations of the military for the General Strike. In early 1926 naval supply officers were authorised to equip naval ratings to protect vulnerable points in any strike. Naval personnel were to be equipped with the full panoply of modern fighting equipments, including rifles, bayonets and, most remarkably machine guns – 115 Savage Lewis guns were to be made available to naval detachments.[77] It is the mundane nature of these orders that is revealing; officials appeared unconcerned that the implication of supplying this equipment was that, if the situation arose, machine guns were available for use on civilians. Furthermore, there seems little doubt that the will existed, troops were deployed to protect at least forty-one locations across the country.[78]

The suggestion made here is that historians may have failed to appreciate the impact of the emotional and cultural framework of officials, ministers and others adhering to the idea of 'community'. Rather than being a force for moderation, which is the general interpretation of this emotional milieu, it appears to have been laden with the potential for conflict. For many, including those in positions of authority, the community was to be vigorously defended, however, while the idea was used widely by citizens in this period, there was no definitive understanding of it other than as an indeterminate group of people in the British Isles who shared services and who were linked by unspecified social interactions. Nevertheless, this amorphous notion held enormous emotional significance for those using it, in the sense that they firmly believed that the community was a central entity in the social order, that it had immense moral weight and that it was in its very nature 'good'. In the circumstances of the coal emergency many using the term believed, genuinely, that the organised industrial action proposed in 1925 and 1926 was a serious threat and that socialists were a danger to the community, while the fascists were its defenders. They were, therefore, driven towards a position of conflict with the members of the labour movement, and an acceptance of the use of force in such a conflict. Their fear was enhanced because those in the labour movement failed to appreciate that their approach was so discomfiting. Furthermore, because the concept was at once vague and felt deeply, it was extremely difficult for those who proposed to engage in industrial action to show that they were not acting against the community. In this instance fascism was not an extreme and unrepresentative set of ideas, but a manifestation of widely held anti-socialist feeling that contributed, in conjunction with the actions and ideas of socialists, to a moment of real antagonism. Therefore, British fascists can be considered to be Conservatives 'with knobs on', as Arnold Leese asserted, but the significance of this status is different to that normally attributed to this remark.[79] For, as such, they were one manifestation of a widespread potential for violent antagonism to socialism, in anything but a limited form, that existed in wide areas of British society. These feelings were held not only by those Conservative ministers who have been characterised as members of the 'radical right', but by men such as Baldwin. The consequence of this sentiment was perhaps, best expressed by Baldwin himself, one month after the General Strike, 'Given the preparation for that conflict, given the propaganda of the last twenty years, given the conditions of industry since the war, given the delusions that followed the war – in my view what occurred was inevitable.'[80]

Notes

1. P. Williamson, *Stanley Baldwin. Conservative Leadership and National Values* (Cambridge: Cambridge University Press, 1999), pp. 9, 35.

2. G. C. Webber, *The Ideology of the British Right 1918–1939* (London: Croom Helm, 1986), p. 4.
3. R. Thurlow, *Fascism in Britain: From Oswald Mosley's Blackshirts to the National Front* (London: I.B. Tauris, 1998), p. 31; Roger Griffin, 'British Fascism: The Ugly Duckling', in M. Cronin (ed.), *The Failure of British Fascism. The Far Right and the Fight for Political Recognition* (Basingstoke: Macmillan, 1996), p. 162; D. Baker, 'The Extreme Right in the 1920's: Fascism in a Cold Climate, or "Conservatism with Knobs on"?', in Cronin, *Failure*, p. 22; Thomas Linehan, *British Fascism, 1918–1939: Parties, Ideology and Culture* (Manchester: Manchester University Press, 2000), p. 69.
4. K. Lunn, 'The Ideology and Impact of the British Fascists in the 1920's', in T. Kushner and K. Lunn (eds), *Traditions of Intolerance. Historical Perspectives on Fascism and Race Discourse in Britain* (Manchester: Manchester University Press, 1989), pp. 143–4; J. Hope, 'British Fascism and the State 1917–1927: A Re-examination of the Documentary Evidence', *Labour History Review*, 57, 3, 1992, pp. 72–83.
5. R. Benewick, *The Fascist Movement in Britain* (London: Allen Lane, 1972), pp. 33–4. This incident is discussed in detail in N. Copsey, *Anti-Fascism in Britain* (London: Macmillan, 2000), p. 11.
6. M. Morris, *The General Strike* (London: The Journeyman Press, 1980), pp. 161–2.
7. Norfolk Record Office (hereafter NRO) MC/335/BUL/16/76, Pamphlet C.P./1/C.
8. Public Record Office, Kew (hereafter PRO) MAF/60/515, 30 November 1925 and minutes of a meeting with fascist leaders, 7 December 1925.
9. A. Mason, 'The Government and the General Strike', *International Review of Social History*, XIV, 1969, pp. 18–20; P. Renshaw, *The General Strike* (London: Eyre Methuen, 1975), p. 133.
10. B. Storm-Farr, *The Development and Impact of Right Wing Politics in Britain 1903–1932* (New York: Garland, 1987), pp. 58–60; D. Baker, 'Extreme', p. 19.
11. G. Webber, 'Intolerance and Discretion: Conservatives and British Fascism, 1918–1926', in T. Kushner and K. Lunn (eds), *Traditions*, pp. 157–8.
12. The Baldwin Papers, Cambridge University Library (hereafter BP), Volume 2, Sir William Joynson-Hicks to Stanley Baldwin, 1 September 1925.
13. Joynson-Hicks' papers contain no replies. My thanks to the Fourth Viscount Brentford for granting me access to these papers for my work and his hospitality while doing so.
14. *The Morning Post*, 24 April 1926; *The Manchester Guardian*, 7 and 8 October 1925 and Norwich's *Eastern Evening News*, 5 October 1925; *The Fascist Bulletin*, 13 June 1925.
15. PRO/HO/144/19069, Cutting from *Daily Herald*, 28 April 1926; Neville Chamberlain Papers, Birmingham University Library, NC/18/2/458, Letter from Hilda Chamberlain, 26 June 1925.
16. PRO/MEPO/3/354, Statement of Max Adler, 18 September 1925.
17. David Cesarani has suggested Joynson-Hicks was hostile to Jews, see D. Cesarani, 'The Anti-Jewish Career of Sir William Joynson-Hicks Cabinet Minister', *Journal of Contemporary History*, 24, 1989, pp. 469–82. However, there is no evidence of this in his personal papers. Serious dissent with Cesarani's suggestion may be found in W. D. Rubenstein, 'Recent Anglo-Jewish Historiography and the Myth of Jix's Anti-Semitism', a two part article

in *Australian Journal of Jewish Studies*, 7, 1, 1993, pp. 41–70 and 7, 2, 1993, pp. 23–45.

18. *Eastern Evening News Norwich*, 1 August 1925.
19. R. McKibbin, *The Ideologies of Class. Social Relations in Britain 1880–1950* (Oxford: Clarendon Press, 1994), pp. 267–75.
20. R. McKibbin, *Ideologies*, p. 282.
21. P. Williamson, *Baldwin*, p. 200.
22. R. McKibbin, *Ideologies*, pp. 274, 285–6.
23. *Parliamentary Debates Official Reports Fifth Series Volume 187*, Debate on Temporary Subvention, H.C.Deb.5s., 6 August 1925, p. 1591.
24. Leo Amery at Overstone Park, Northampton, 24 April 1926; *The Times*, 26 April 1926.
25. Joynson-Hicks Papers, J1-A7-f, undated note entitled 'The General Strike'.
26. PRO/HO/317/73, Appendix to Memorandum No. 1, 20 January 1924.
27. PRO/HO/317/73, Note for Circulation to Lord Lieutenants in England and Wales.
28. Sir Adam Nimmo at the Westminster meeting of the National Union of Manufacturers. *The Times*, 18 February 1926.
29. *Parliamentary Debates*, H.C. Deb.55, 6 August 1925.
30. *Daily Herald*, 3 May 1926.
31. *East Anglian Daily Times*, 29 March 1926.
32. NRO/BR/254/68/1-7, OMS to D. Wilson, 5 March 1926 and undated OMS handbill.
33. NRO/BR/254/68/1-7, Letter to D. Wilson, 5 March 1926.
34. NRO/BR/254/68/1-7, OMS to W. D. Stocking, February 1926.
35. NRO/MC/335/BUL/16/76, Journal, 6 March 1926.
36. Amery at Overstone Park, *The Times*, 26 April 1926.
37. 'The Citizen and the General Strike. Extract from a Speech Delivered at a Meeting at Chippenham, 12 June 1926', in Stanley Baldwin, *Our Inheritance. Speeches and Addresses* (London: Hodder, 1928), pp. 217–24.
38. P. Williamson, *Baldwin*, p. 193.
39. NRO/BR/254/68/1-7, Letter to D. Wilson, 5 March 1926.
40. *East Anglian Daily Times*, 27 July 1925.
41. *The Nation and Athenaeum*, 21 November 1925.
42. *East Anglian Daily Times*, 4 May 1926.
43. PRO/HO/317/73, *Notice regarding volunteers*.
44. *The Nation and Athenaeum*, 21 November 1925.
45. PRO/CAB/27/261/C.P.81(26), Home Secretary's Progress Report, 22 February 1926.
46. PRO/CAB/24/175/C.P.457(25), Memorandum from the Minister of Labour, 6 November 1925.
47. K. Jeffery and P. Hennessey, *States of Emergency. British Governments and Strikebreaking Since 1919* (London: Routledge & Kegan Paul, 1983), pp. 263–7.
48. PRO/HO/317/73, Memorandum to Chairmen of Voluntary Service Committees, undated but stated to be replacing those of June 1922 and December 1925.
49. PRO/CAB/26/260, Supply and Transport Committee minutes, 1 May 1926.
50. BP, Volume 2, Prime Minister's message to the nation, 8 May 1926.

51. PRO/HO/144/6116, Letter from Chief Constable of Glamorgan, 23 December 1925. Lindsay's activities in this period and other disputes have been examined in some depth in J. Morgan, *Conflict and Order – The Police and Labour Disputes in England and Wales, 1900–1939* (Oxford: Clarendon Press, 1987), pp. 192–5.

52. PRO/MAF/60/512, Joynson-Hicks to Cunliffe-Lister, 7 September 1925.

53. G. C. Webber, *Ideology*, p. 26.

54. D. Baker, 'Extreme', p. 23. Similarly, John Charmley describes ministerial belief in a Communist plot, and of others on 'the other side' that the Government wanted confrontation, as 'equally barmy'. J. Charmley, *Churchill the End of Glory. A Political Biography* (London: Hodder and Stoughton, 1993), p. 217.

55. Churchill Archive, Churchill College, Cambridge, CHAR/2/142/35, W. S. Churchill to S. Hammersley, 14 September 1925.

56. Davidson Papers, House of Lords Record Office (hereafter JCC), DAV/171, Davidson to T. Hickman, 3 August 1925.

57. S. Ball (ed.), *Parliament and Politics in the Age of Baldwin and MacDonald. The Headlam Diaries, 1923–1935* (London: Historians' Press, 1992), p. 70.

58. K. Middlemass (ed.), *Thomas Jones Whitehall Diary Volume I* (London: Oxford University Press, 1969), p. 325.

59. J. Morgan, *Conflict*, pp. 110–229. Charles Townshend, *Making the Peace. Public Order and Public Security in Modern Britain* (Oxford: Oxford University Press, 1993), pp. 97–8.

60. PRO/CAB/23(52), Meeting, 30 April 1926.

61. JCC/DAV/173, 14 June 1926.

62. PRO/HO/144/6896, Chief Constable of Lancashire to A. Dixon, 11 May 1926.

63. Benjamin L. Alpers, *Dictators, Democracy, and American Public Culture. Envisioning the Totalitarian Enemy, 1920's–1950's* (Chapel Hill and London: University of North Carolina Press, 2003), pp. 15–16.

64. PRO/HO/144/6896, Letter from James Johnson, 8 October 1925.

65. PRO/HO/45/24860, Chief Constable of Birmingham to A. Dixon, 23 April 1926. Similarly, John Hope argues that it was the fascists' claim to independence that was of concern to the Government, rather than their policies, J. Hope, 'Fascism and the State in Britain: The Case of the British Fascist 1923–31', *Australian Journal of Politics and History*, 39, Part 3, 1993, p. 369.

66. PRO/HO/144/19069, *The Times*, 28 April 1926.

67. PRO/HO/144/19069, Telephone Note between Mr Boyd and Col. Seymour, 7 May 1926.

68. PRO/HO/45/24860, Minute by A. Dixon, 27 July 1925.

69. *The Fascist Bulletin*, 22 May 1926.

70. *The Dorset County Chronicle*, 6 May 1926. For details of how this organisation was intended to work see PRO/CAB/27/26, Report by the Home Secretary, 6 August 1925.

71. Joynson-Hicks remains an under-researched politician, with most attitudes to him still reflecting the vilification by Blythe in 'The Salutary Tale of Jix', in R. Blythe, *The Age of Illusion. England in the Twenties and Thirties. 1919–1940* (London: Penguin, 1963), p. 31.

72. Keith Middlemass and John Barnes, *Baldwin – A Biography* (London, 1969), p. 283. Rubenstein argued that Joynson-Hicks 'never left the British political

mainstream', Rubenstein 'Recent Part II', pp. 27–33. *The Fascist Bulletin,* 17 October 1925.
73. PRO/CAB/23/51/47(25), Meeting, 7 October 1925.
74. Matthew Hendley, 'Women and the Nation: The Right and Projections of Feminised Political Images in Great Britain, 1900–18', in J. V. Gottlieb and T. P. Linehan (eds), *The Culture of Fascism. Visions of the Far Right in Britain* (London: I.B. Tauris, 2004), pp. 13–14.
75. PRO/MAF/60/515, Meeting, 9 March 1926.
76. PRO/MAF/60/515, Meeting, 18 March 1926.
77. PRO/ADM/116/3443, Regulations governing the conduct of Civil Servants and the armed forces, Ref.371/0350.
78. PRO/HO/45/24819, Ref.455/395/28.
79. Quoted in D. Baker, 'Extreme', p. 26.
80. S. Baldwin 'The Citizen and the General Strike. Extract from a speech delivered at a meeting at Chippenham, 12 June 1926', in S. Baldwin, *Our Inheritance. Speeches and Addresses* (London: Hodder, 1928), p. 214.

2
The Security Service, the Communist Party of Great Britain and British Fascism, 1932–51

Richard C. Thurlow

In the often dramatic story of the confrontations between the labour movement and British fascism from the 1930s until the early Cold War, there is a tendency to forget the role played by a third player in the proceedings, the state authorities, particularly the security service and the various police forces around the country. Yet although the state saw its role as being that of an impartial umpire between the combatants, there was a significant difference in the attitude adopted towards the two parties: the labour movement was seen as a tool to further the alleged sinister motives of the Communist Party of Great Britain (CPGB), whilst the British Union of Fascists (BUF) was perceived as a contradictory mixture of disillusioned right-wing patriotic Conservatives and revolutionary nationalists to whom Mosley inclined. The growth of civil unrest and what was perceived by the state as extremism in the interwar period, led to political surveillance of the CPGB and the BUF, by the secret agencies of government. The function of the police and the security authorities was to maintain public order and to investigate presumed linkages with foreign powers, particularly with regard to financing political activity, the dissemination of propaganda and the organisation of espionage and subversion. British security after 1921 was particularly concerned that the CPGB was controlled and directed by the Comintern, the Communist International, with its stated objective of organising the revolutionary overthrow of the British Empire and furthering the interests of the Soviet Union. With the approach of the Second World War, similar concern was felt that the links between the BUF, Italian fascism and German Nazism needed further investigation.

The formation and outlook of the Security Service

The Intelligence Committee formed the Security Service in 1931, as part of the attempted resolution of a complex turf war.[1] For reasons of efficiency, the need to cut public expenditure as a response to the deflationary impact of the economic crisis and the abandonment of the Gold Standard, British security underwent a further reorganisation. Although the existing division between the intelligence and security functions of the Secret State was maintained, the changes were intended to make clear the role of MI5 as the lead organisation in defending the security of the realm against foreign powers. In particular MI5 replaced Special Branch as the prime mover in investigating communism, the Comintern and the CPGB. Special Branch retained its political surveillance role of investigating both the open and the secret activities of the CPGB; however the analysis of this material was now made the responsibility of MI5. Some increased friction resulted as Special Branch were not pleased at losing some of its functions, but MI5 was to benefit from the transfer of Guy Liddell, who was to prove one of the most talented counter-intelligence officers. These changes made MI5 responsible for civilian security, as well as its existing duties of counter-espionage and resisting subversion in the armed forces. As part of the re-organisation, the four-strong liaison circulating section (originally SS1 of Special Branch) was transferred from the Secret Intelligence Service (SIS) to MI5. SS1 had already caused friction between SIS and Special Branch over its operational direction. From this developed the agent running section of MI5, B5b, organised by Maxwell Knight, who was also transferred from SIS to MI5 in 1931.[2] In addition the three-strong Special Branch research group (SS2) investigating communism at Scotland House, under Guy Liddell, was moved to MI5. Special Branch was to retain its responsibility for the political surveillance of anarchism and the IRA, as well as to act as the police arm of MI5. The existing duties of Counter-Intelligence were confirmed, with MI5 responsible for the security of the United Kingdom and the British Empire, and SIS for British interests outside the three-mile limit. Section V of SIS retained its role as a Counter-Intelligence circulating section with direct links to MI5.

During the 1930s there was close collaboration between the two organisations with regard to the political surveillance of Comintern and CPGB activities, even if there was continuing friction elsewhere. Section V of SIS (Counter-Intelligence) was to become increasingly reliant on the Registry of MI5 for its background files, and MI5 on the material SIS provided on Comintern and on some CPGB activities. Millicent Bagot, the MI5 expert on the Comintern, provided a cross-referenced source of information on the activities of international communism in the 1930s, which proved much more useful than the SIS files to the British security community.[3] This was particularly true after 1935, when MI5 concentrated on the leadership of the CPGB and Soviet agents, rather than the previous attempted blanket surveillance coverage of CPGB activities.[4] Poor pay, economic cuts and the old school tie recruiting network of both MI5 and SIS was to place both organisations at a disadvantage with regard to the main adversary, Soviet Intelligence. However the lack of imagination of its practitioners was partly compensated by the geographical advantages of Britain's security defences. Soviet Agents had a great deal of difficulty organising extended visits to the United Kingdom, which would pass the scrutiny of the Immigration Service and the Anti-Aliens legislation.

The 'Opening of the Books'

The sources for the study of the Security Service, the CPGB and the BUF expanded significantly, mainly during the 1990s, as a result of the 'opening of the books'. This represented both an international ripple effect of Soviet 'glasnost' and the perceived benefits for the stage-managed partial release of some information about some of Britain's secret intelligence and security organisations, like MI5. Whereas the Archive of SIS was to remain closed, some of the other important secret agencies of the British State began releasing a surprisingly large amount of hitherto secret files. These included MI5 (1909–54), the surviving files of the Special Operations Executive (1940–46), the Government Code and Cypher School from the interwar period, and the Joint Intelligence Committee (1936–68).[5]

Today researchers can consult as well the CPGB Archive at the Museum of Labour History in Manchester, and the Mosley and Robert Saunders papers at the Universities of Birmingham and Sheffield, for significant material on the BUF. At the National Archives (the renamed Public Record Office) MI5 (KV 1-6), Home Office (HO 45, 144 and 283) and Cabinet Office (CAB 23, 24, 65, 66, 129, 130) files provide material relating to state attitudes to political extremism and the surveillance of the CPGB and British fascism. Other private depositories, such as the Archive of the Board of Deputies of British Jews, have significant Intelligence information about anti-Semitic and fascist groups. There is also important material, not available in Britain in Moscow, relating to the CPGB, and in the National Archives in the United States about the exchange of Intelligence information relating to CPGB and fascist activity from the 1930s. It must, however, be emphasised that all these sources have to be considered carefully. All have been doctored, or censored to varying degrees. The content of released British government files, for example, is subject to several reviews over the years. This is partly a matter of routine; up to 98 per cent of the product of government bureaucracy is routinely shredded. There is nothing particularly sinister about this, although there is no input on what is retained by historians. 'Weeding', mainly by retired civil servants, is a process designed to relate the preservation of important historical documents to the space available.[6]

As frustrating to the historian is the operation of the Public Record Act of 1958, and its amendment in 1967. This gives the power, under sections 3.4 and 5.1 for Departments of State to retain material. Under this legislation the Departments of State are allowed to declassify material, depending on their sensitivity, usually in terms of a 30-, 50- or 100-year rule. There are important exceptions to what can be released. Thus censorship is justified in terms of 'national security', 'national interest' or releasing information which would divulge the identity of agents or sources. These criteria, however, are periodically reviewed, given resource limitations. Since the Waldegrave (later Open Government) Initiative in 1993, the public have been given the opportunity to request a review of closed documents, which has led to the opening of files relevant to our theme. Indeed, the success of the opening of Home Office material relating to British fascism between 1983 and 1986 acted as a precursor to 'liberalisation'. Most significant for our purposes have been the two releases a year of MI5 files covering the period 1909–54, since 1997. To date nearly 2000 files have been declassified. The majority of these documents relate to the Second World War, but there have been a significant number of personal files relating to CPGB and BUF members, and to Soviet Agents in Britain. Some general files have also been opened but this has been more in evidence with regard to BUF rather than CPGB material. Also it must be borne in mind that the CPGB files were the ones most affected by bomb damage in Wormwood Scrubs in the autumn of 1940; evidence of this can be seen in the charred edges of photocopied documents in several remaining personal files.

As well as censorship and bomb damage, other limitations need to be taken into account. MI5, like the rest of the intelligence and security community, suffered severe financial cuts during the interwar period. This had two consequences; both the quality and quantity of personnel were affected. Few highfliers were recruited (Dick White was the first graduate to be appointed in 1935).[7]

At the outbreak of the Second World War in 1939 there were seven officers involved in the assessment of the threat posed by the Soviet Union, Comintern and CPGB activities, and only one with relation to the political surveillance of the BUF.[8] It was therefore perhaps not surprising that the information available relating to British fascism, on what was later perceived as the most likely source of a fifth column threat, proved so lamentable. Recruitment, what there was, had been through personal recommendation. Officers were expected to have a private income, or pension from the armed forces or from the Indian police. This enabled low salaries to be paid. It also reinforced the existing prejudices towards radicalism and 'beastly Bolsheviks', and the mindset of MI5.

The state had mixed feelings about MI5. Although seen as a necessary security watchdog, it was given no executive authority. The Labour Party and the wider labour movement viewed the intelligence and security community with a particularly jaundiced view, holding it responsible for the 'Zinoviev letter' debacle in 1924, which many saw as being responsible for the defeat of the Labour Party in the general election of that year. Apart from Diehards, many in the Conservative and Liberal parties had little time for 'secret' or 'political' policeman, and were worried about the activities of MI5 as a potential menace to civil liberties. MI5 saw itself as a small research bureau, which advised the Departments of State on Counter-Intelligence and security matters. It was even dependent on Special Branch for the detention of suspects. In short MI5 was viewed as a necessary, but generally disregarded and under funded appendage of the State security apparatus, except during periods of perceived national crisis. This accounts for why its first chief, Sir Vernon Kell, was allowed to hold the record for the longest serving head of any government department or agency in the twentieth century. He remained as head from the creation of the Home Department of the Secret Service Bureau in 1910 until Churchill sacked him as Director of MI5 on 10 June 1940.

The Red menace

Kell's jaundiced views about communism provided the mindset for the organisation of the British security apparatus against the 'Red Menace' in the aftermath of the First World War. With the destruction of Imperial Germany, the impact of the Bolshevik Revolution and its domestic and international repercussions could be portrayed as the new 'main adversary', thus justifying the continued existence of MI5 in peacetime.

MI5 New Year cards in the aftermath of the First World War, depicting Britannia in various poses saving the Empire from the hydra-headed monster of Bolshevism, set the tone for how British Counter-Intelligence and Counter-Subversion Agencies viewed Soviet Russia and the CPGB.[9] This tendency towards ossification and stereotypical views towards 'political extremism', 'subversion' and the Bolshevik 'menace' underwent some modification during the Second World War. The catalyst for change was the widening of recruitment to include better educated, less right wing, more sophisticated and intelligent personnel than had been available under the traditional methods of entry, and the appointment as Director-General of Sir David Petrie in 1941.[10] Although rapid expansion caused administrative turmoil in 1939–40, the eventual appointment of Petrie led to a reorganisation of MI5 that enabled it to operate far more effectively. As a self-confessed 'dug out', the retired ex-head of the Indian police and the author of a published report, *Communism in India 1924–34*, Petrie held more sophisticated views on how to manage the communist challenge.

Under the managerial direction of Petrie devolved powers were given to the heads of sections, who made full use of the influx of talent and a few exceptional career officers. While, on Churchill's orders, he banned spying on allies after the Nazi invasion of the Soviet Union in 1941, the CPGB was kept under close political surveillance to monitor the domestic fallout from basking in the reflected glory of the exploits of the Red Army. This resulted in a more analytical approach, both in terms of the technology of surveillance and the interpretation of the evidence. While CPGB super patriotism after 1941 was viewed with grave suspicion, and the party became the 'enemy within' during the early Cold War, the reaction against the development of a 'British Gestapo' and the appointment of a relatively liberal, if undistinguished policeman, Sir John Sillitoe, in 1946, led to a more protracted debate on how to interpret the activities of the CPGB.

Yet for much of this period the dominant view of the CPGB in MI5 was that it was the domestic mouthpiece and paid agent of the Soviet Union.[11] Andrew Thorpe, in his recent work on the CPGB, has argued that the historiography of the party can be analysed using the same concepts as the debates on Cold War history, that is, traditionalist, revisionist and post-revisionist.[12] Within such a framework, the view of the CPGB from MI5 can be categorised for the most part as super-traditionalist. The core MI5 view, or prejudice, about the CPGB was formed in the 1920s, as a gut reaction of Diehards and military 'brass hats' to the Bolshevik revolution. These feelings were projected onto the 'evidence' derived from a variety of domestic sources. This included information from Special Branch political surveillance of the CPGB and political unrest (labour disputes 1919–21, the General and Miners strike 1926–27). Some insight was gained from the successful decoding of Soviet intercepts by the Government Code and Cypher School between 1920 and 1927 and the material taken from headquarters in 1925 when the leaders of the CPGB, the 'Communist twelve' were arrested (now available in KV 3/18-33). Other material was gleaned from the supposed evidence (or rather lack of it) from the Arcos Raid in 1927 and from SIS a mixture of real Soviet and White Russian forged documents. However it was not just the 'evidence' which was important, but also the way in which such material, both real and imaginary, was interpreted. MI5 viewed Bolshevism with a peculiar horror. It interpreted its strategic and tactical behaviour in terms of a tunnel vision mentality. Whatever the propaganda pitch of the CPGB to the electorate or British workers, its real policy remained the same according to MI5; the revolutionary overthrow and destruction of the British State and the British Empire.

There were a number of factors, which accounted for this overestimation of the threat posed by the CPGB. In the 1920s MI5 was not responsible for civilian security. This was the preserve of Special Branch until 1931, after the sacking and winding up of the Directorate of Intelligence under the flamboyant Sir Basil Thompson in 1921. MI5's brief was to fight Soviet espionage and attempts to subvert the armed forces. Hence its obsession with combating 'revolution', no matter how unreal the likelihood of an armed Bolshevik uprising on the Soviet model was in Britain during the interwar period. It was as surprised as the CPGB with the naval unrest following pay cuts during the 'Invergordon Mutiny' in 1931. Although a cool analysis followed this incident the 'threat' posed by the CPGB remained over exaggerated and MI5 increased pressure to outlaw communist propaganda aimed at the services. This was so, no matter how often the CPGB changed its tactical position, nor was it affected by the fluctuations in its membership during this period. There were a bewildering number of changes of line. After the 'third period' isolation of the late 1920s the Party adopted the 'United Front' with the Independent Labour Party in 1932. This was expanded to include other working and middle class radicals with the creation of the 'Peoples' or Popular Front after 1934. This was followed by the 'War on Two Fronts' in September 1939 against both Hitler and the Chamberlain government. Then new instructions from Moscow led to the notorious 'About Turn' and the 'revolutionary defeatism' of 'The Imperialist War' period from 1939–41. Hitler's invasion of the Soviet Union suddenly made the

CPGB ardent supporters of the war and the Party was transformed into the patriotic fervour of the 'United Nations' phase between 1941 and 1945. The coming of the Cold War led to the retreat from national unity after 1945. In spite of this failure of CPGB intellectual consistency, the dominant message from MI5 remained the same. The 'real' policy of the CPGB was unchanged whatever its tactical position.[13] It was the faithful tool of Moscow, which attempted to undermine democratic institutions and foment revolutionary uprising in Britain, and the British Empire. MI5 viewed the particular attempts to undermine the armed forces with grave concern. MI5 portrayed itself as the real champions of democracy, guarding traditional liberties against the 'totalitarian' threats of Bolshevism; the CPGB was only a supporter of liberty of its own freedom of expression, not those who were critical of its viewpoint.

Another Pavlovian reflex of MI5 psychology was an obsession with funding. 'He who pays the piper calls the tune', represented one of the fundamental maxims of MI5. The complex investigations into the sources of funding of both the CPGB and the BUF in this period 'proved' beyond reasonable doubt that the former was the 'slave' of Moscow, and the latter of Fascist Italy and Nazi Germany. This was so even if there was some difficulty in establishing the financial links between Mosley and Hitler. It must also be remembered that there was not much in the way of development of such views in MI5 between 1920 and 1939. Such an obsessive viewpoint, however, became less monolithic as a result of the war and developments in the early Cold War period, when the need to encourage communist dissidents demanded a more flexible attitude.[14]

If the CPGB was seen by MI5 as the British arm of the Comintern, with the Soviet Union as both its paymaster and its patriotic fount of allegiance, how did this square with the evidence collected and interpreted by the Security Service? Although some of the evidence of the techniques of political surveillance is retained under section 3.4 of the Public Records Act, much is revealed in the personal files, and the identity of some of the 'most secret' and 'delicate' sources can be plausibly suggested.[15]

There are important gaps in the release of personal files from this period, Rajani Palme Dutt, Willie Gallagher and Douglas 'Dave' Springhall for example. The file, however, on Dutt's wife, Salme Murrik, points to his significance from MI5's perspective. He was regarded through Murrik's close links with Otto Kuusinen and the leadership of the Comintern, as Moscow's successful minder of the potentially troublesome British brethren in the CPGB.[16] There are, despite considerable weeding and lost material, some fairly interesting files on such luminaries as Harry Pollitt, John Ross Campbell, Bill Rust, Robby Robson, Bob Stewart, Peter Kerrigan, James Klugmann and Percy Glading.[17]

There are also a reasonable number of files on middle rank functionaries. These included those in the secret apparatus, fellow travellers, and 'subversives'. With the exception of the section F3 history (KV 4/56) in the Second World War, the release of relevant general files relating to the CPGB has been disappointing. There has been little that has been declassified apart from the ex-Scotland House material on the King Street raid and the imprisonment of the leaders in 1925, and the Arcos Raid in the 1920s. The material on the Zinoviev letter still remains classified, although it has been seen by Gillian Shepherd in ' "A most extraordinary mysterious business": The Zinoviev Letter of 1924' (History Notes 14, Foreign and Commonwealth Office, February 1999). The files relating to fellow travellers in the 1930s, although relatively few in number at the moment, suggest that MI5 was aware of the sophistication of Soviet propaganda. They were aware of the development of a communist 'Solar System' to infiltrate, permeate and influence a much wider radical constituency than that provided by the CPGB, which never had more than 17,500 members throughout the interwar period. This is suggested in the personal files of such individuals like Dennis Nowell Pritt, John Strachey and Stafford Cripps, although more detailed analysis will be available once the relevant Organization Files are released in KV/5. MI5 assumed that the middle classes and public school educated youth were immune to the communist virus.

Analysis of the material gives a reasonable view of the nature of the secret sources available to MI5, and how they were interpreted. The evidence suggests that the interception of the mail of leading communists, through Home Office Warrants, was widespread. Leading figures in the Party had their telephone conversations monitored by primitive bugging devices and recording of messages at a special unit at Dollis Hill, which became an important form of political surveillance during the 1930s and the Second World War. So was the presence of Special Branch scribes at public meetings, and in secret cubbyholes to record meetings of the CPGB central and political committees. The B6 'watchers' were normally operated against Soviet embassy staff, but were also used in special surveillance operations involving members of the CPGB. Both Harry Pollitt and Wal Hannington tell amusing stories about Special Branch intrusion in their autobiographies; the former was tailed on his honeymoon. M section also infiltrated agents into the Communist Party. These included Olga Gray, who acted as Harry Pollitt's personal secretary between February and July 1935, and was instrumental as

'Miss X', as the agent who exposed Percy Glading and the Woolwich Arsenal Spy ring in March 1938.[18] They also included 'M3' (Tom Driberg) and 'M7' a member of the *Daily Worker* editorial board. In the Second World War a microphone was installed in the King Street headquarters. MI5 also borrowed and co-operated with other Intelligence and Security Organisations where outside knowledge or expertise was needed. Thus Inspector Kenworthy of Y service, involved in the detection of illicit radio communications, and the GCCS radio expert, Leslie Lambert, alias A. J. Allen, the 1930s BBC 'radio personality', were used in 1934 to locate the secret CPGB radio transmitter which communicated with Moscow from Wimbledon.[19] Similarly as Jack Curry, himself often scathingly critical of SIS, nevertheless acknowledged in his in-house history of MI5, that they had been extremely helpful in supplying secret Comintern material. This relates to the information provided by the Agent 'Jonny X', Johann Heinrich de Graff, which was instrumental in achieving eventual success for MI5's long run campaign aimed at the CPGB, to pass the Incitement to Disaffection Act in 1934.[20]

From this catalogue of secret sources, as well as the detailed research of open CPGB printed material, MI5 had reasonably detailed knowledge of CPGB activities both political and clandestine. Yet its blinkered, ideological perspective on the CPGB led to serious misinterpretation of its nature. The 'slaves of Moscow' tunnel vision masked the obvious discrepancy with some of the more important evidence which MI5 interpreted. This showed the mixture of both genuine admiration for the Soviet Union, the various factions within the CPGB, the long discussions about the relevant party line and the disagreements voiced by significant individuals about the decisions of the CPSU, the Comintern and the party. The most notorious were the heated discussions in October 1939 with regard to the 'About Turn' with regard to the Second World War. Whereas MI5 used the retraction of the opposition to the changed 'Imperialist war' theses by Harry Pollitt and J. R. Campbell as proof of Soviet and Comintern control of the CPGB, they failed to note the abstention, and subsequent behaviour of that 'Incorrigible Rebel', Arthur Horner. He ignored the change of line as he felt it disagreed with the economic and anti-fascist political interests of South Wales Miners.[21] Similarly the obsession with the revolutionary perspective, put MI5 out on a limb when other Government departments disregarded warnings about employing communists, now adopting an equally patriotic and anti-Nazi line as Winston Churchill, after 22 June 1941.

MI5's complacency about its political surveillance of the CPGB, not only led to the misreading of the tealeaves, but was also the victim of

Soviet deception. Although MI5 discovered, and was able to sack, a secretary who could have been a CPGB mole in the Security Service during the war, they were oblivious to the fact that a Soviet spy sat right in the heart of B division, the operational centre of MI5. Not only was Anthony Blunt a Soviet secret agent, but also some of the documents he passed to his controllers have been published from Moscow archives. These included 'MI5's Report on Russian Espionage' and details of the Glading Case in March 1938.[22] It is quite clear that Blunt passed to the Soviet Union details of MI5 surveillance methods and interpretation of the CPGB. This places the 'evidence' from the 'most delicate and secret source' of the Control Commission at King Street in a new light. The 'old lags', Bob Stewart, Bill Shiels and Robert Robson were spinning a yarn of harmless gossip for the benefit of the hidden microphones. Similarly, although the prosecution of the Glading case in March 1938, was a success for MI5, it also reinforced misleading preconceptions about the role of the CPGB and the nature of Soviet espionage. It assumed that members of the CPGB were the willing agents of Soviet espionage. MI5 surmised that Soviet 'illegal' agents managed spying, and that members left the party to become involved in Soviet espionage. MI5 also knew that Bob Stewart was the CPGB functionary in charge of secret activities and that Robson managed CPGB members in the armed forces. MI5 assumed that only working class or relatively junior functionaries, such as clerks, foremen or minor bureaucrats could become involved in espionage. These perceptions seemed to be confirmed by *Rex v Glading* (March 1938) and *Rex v John Herbert King* (October 1939). There was no conception of the recruitment of bright young university graduates, by Arnold Deutsch and Theodore Maly, like the 'Magnificent Five' at Cambridge, who were not directly linked to the CPGB or its activities, but who acted as future 'sleepers' or 'moles' at the heart of the British establishment. In that sense the CPGB acted as a clever deception spoof, by focusing MI5 attention on a relatively minor function of Soviet espionage in Britain.

Yet the discovery of Soviet espionage activity just before the Second World War had alerted British security to the continued sophistication of Soviet Intelligence and to revamp counter-espionage precautions. Although neither the Glading nor King cases were complete vindication of MI5 operational methods, there were positive features to both incidents. Maxwell Knight's operation of the penetration Agent 'Miss X' (Olga Gray) was a model of sophisticated management in the Glading case. It showed that Soviet Intelligence did not have a monopoly of 'sleepers' or 'moles' infiltrating targets. The later discovery that the ring had been run by the Soviet 'Great Illegal' Theodore Maly, and the later identification of his role in the King case, also, in retrospect made some in MI5 more aware of the threat posed by Soviet espionage. Whereas the Glading case represented active counter-espionage tradecraft, the King case was uncovered more by accident. The MI5 role in discovering King's espionage was of a secondary nature. Valentine Vivian, the head of Section V of SIS, carried out the investigation, into the leaky sieve of the Foreign Office Communications Department. Following on from his previous investigation of the (lack of) embassy security in Rome in 1937, it painted a grim picture of Foreign Office precautions.[23] The uncovering of King's espionage depended on three sources; the Soviet defector, Walter Krivitsky, the business partner of the Soviet Agent, Henri Christiaan Pieck, Conrad Parlanti, and the ex-SIS and wartime MI5 Agent, X (probably W. J. Hooper), whose testimony SIS tried to discredit.[24] The MI5 role was to collaborate in a successful joint investigation with SIS of the incident in September 1939. Krivitsky's information about King, and his claim that there were two other Soviet Agents operating in the Foreign Office and as a journalist in the Spanish Civil War, whose task was to kill Franco, we now know were accurate references to Donald Maclean and Kim Philby.[25] In January 1940 Krivitsky was interviewed by Jane Archer of MI5 in London, although the illuminating report was soon pigeonholed as a result of more pressing priorities during the Second World War.[26] Although Knight and Miss Bagot warned about the threat posed by Soviet espionage, the political directive that there was to be no political surveillance of allies after 1941, meant precautions were reduced to a minimum. Interestingly, after the war, MI5 interrogated the Soviet Agent Henri Christiaan Pieck in London, and because of his co-operation, allowed him to return to Holland without charge, despite his role in organising and managing Soviet espionage in the King case.[27]

MI5 and British fascism

From 1934, MI5 also became the lead organisation in the political surveillance of British fascism. In November 1933, after a conference at the Home Office it was decided that MI5 should produce periodic reports on the development of British fascism, using the surveillance material provided by Special Branch and information collated from the link between the Security Service and Chief Constables.[28] This arose originally, not from security concerns, but from a perceived threat to public order caused by increased political violence between fascists and communists and other anti-fascists during 1933. A sign of the times, was that Kell only agreed to accept this role for MI5 in six-months time, as there were insufficient funds to finance this development until the new financial year. Thus eight reports, of which seven have been released in Home Office files, were produced between June 1934 and the passing of the Public Order Act in December 1936.[29] The success, from MI5's perspective, of the Public Order Act, ended MI5's concern about the 'threat' from the BUF. This altered when the collapse of rump Czechoslovakia in March 1939, suddenly placed the BUF on a par with the CPGB as a perceived domestic fifth column. The problem then became acute, as the relative neglect of political surveillance of the organisation since its heyday in 1934 led to a lack of reliable information with regard to the security threat presented by the BUF. The lack of personal files relating to the members of the BUF was to prove a factor in the crisis in the Registry, which led to the near collapse of MI5 in the spring of 1940. It also added to the argument that an immediate change in leadership was needed in the organisation, and helped account for the scepticism with which the Advisory Committee on Internment viewed the evidence presented on individual members of the BUF.

The material presented in the MI5 reports between 1934 and 1936 is interesting, despite the overall vagueness of its conclusions. The reports show that MI5 were mainly concerned about the size and the nature of BUF membership, the sources of its finances, and the links with Fascist Italy and Nazi Germany. Of subsidiary interest to MI5 were fascist and anti-fascist political violence, the development of anti-Semitism, the internal feuding and the development of political factions within the organisation. MI5 interpreted the BUF as a hybrid organisation, which attracted a contradictory mix of disillusioned Tories with the National Government, and a more radical wing, to which Mosley inclined. This advocated the rebirth of the British Empire under the Fascist Revolution and the 'new man'. The MI5 view was a fairly perceptive and sensible summary of what was known about the membership of the BUF, although it was based as much on hearsay as reliable evidence. The appendices on membership from Chief Constables in the latter reports suggest that the movement be on the verge of collapse in some parts of the country.

MI5 portrayed itself as the guardian of democracy against totalitarian threats. The detailed appendices show that some Chief Constables had better sources of information on the BUF in their area than others, that some information was based on guesswork and other was based on detailed knowledge. There was much circumstantial evidence that

Fascist Italy, and possibly Nazi Germany, provided considerable funding for the BUF in the 1930s. The BUF went into political decline soon after the Olympia debacle in June, and the ridiculing of Mosley at the Hyde Park demonstration in September 1934. The MI5 view of the BUF appears to have derived mainly from second-hand sources. In the 1930s, from what has been released so far, they appear to have based their interpretation of the organisation on the views of Chief Constables or Special Branch. There was little in terms of smoking gun evidence of much illegal behaviour, beyond petty larceny, minor misdemeanours, some immoral conduct and the activities of conmen. It is quite clear that MI5 did not see the BUF as a significant threat or as a danger to national security before the Second World War. Its activities were viewed with disdain or ridicule. It was a public order nuisance, which gave the communists the excuse to mount street demonstrations and foment disorder. Although there had been links between state, private intelligence agencies and British fascism there is no evidence of collusion. Indeed MI5 viewed Mosley with particular distaste as an arrogant demagogue of wayward intelligence. MI5 saw itself, with its police allies, as maintaining the peace and protecting the maximum degree of civil liberties against both extremists of left and right in the 1930s.

The ongoing declassification of files relating to MI5 and the political surveillance of British fascism has increased scepticism about how seriously the 'menace' of British fascism was taken by the security authorities before the spring of 1940. It is now clear what accurate knowledge there was of British fascism before the war owed little to MI5 penetration agents. Indeed, the two individuals most suspected of being security 'moles', James Mcguirk Hughes (known as Captain P. G. Taylor in the BUF) and W. E. D. Allen do not appear to have been employed by MI5.[30] The former was regarded of dubious reliability by MI5, but probably acted as a source for Special Branch information on the leadership of the BUF. Allen, whose file has been released, (KV 2/879 and 880) did provide interesting information on the 'Mussolini monies' for the BUF, and Mosley's muscling in on his commercial radio scheme in 1938–39, but only in 1942. It is quite clear from the tone of the interrogation that he was not regarded as a professional MI5 or SIS agent, or as a friendly source. More accurate information probably became available to the authorities when the Defence Secretary of British Jews sent his Intelligence material to the Home Office in the spring of 1939.

The transformation in perception of the BUF from a discredited, failed political movement to a dangerous fifth column can be traced to the deterioration of relations with the fascist powers and the development of the military crisis between 1938 and 1940. While the BUF continued to be seen as politically irrelevant, and whatever residual fascist–communist hostility had been reduced still further by the CPGB change of line in 1939, MI5 was becoming concerned about the anti-war propaganda of the BUF and the activities of a minority of its members. During the phoney war (1939–40) the most notorious ex-member of the BUF, William Joyce was recognised as the main voice of 'Lord Haw-Haw' broadcasting Nazi propaganda on Radio Hamburg from Germany.[31]

MI5 was at the forefront of those who wished to intern all aliens and perceived potential members of a British 'fifth column', of whom the BUF were, allegedly, the secret organisers. Since Munich the BUF had not criticised a single action of the fascist dictators, and their continuing appeasement policy was increasingly viewed as suspicious. MI5 orchestrated a campaign against the more liberal scepticism of the Home Office, who resisted the implementation of Defence Regulations which restricted traditional civil liberties in the autumn of 1939, and called for determined action against those who opposed the war, or who were, allegedly, a danger to Britain's security.

The military crisis of spring 1940, the 'fifth column' scares and the fall of the Chamberlain government led to a strengthening of MI5 arguments and an increase in its influence. Three separate sources confirmed meetings between most of the extreme right political fringe in the autumn and winter of 1939 and 1940, allegedly designed to co-ordinate the activities of fascist groups the organisation of a pro-Nazi coup d'etat and the 'achievement of a Fascist Revolution'.[32] These included an informant employed by Special Branch in the 'inner councils of the BU since its inception' (possibly 'P. G. Taylor'), an MI5 agent who had penetrated the BU since the beginning of the war, and the wife of an ex-MI5 agent who was in contact with one of the participants in these talks, Admiral Sir Barry Domvile. Three women agents from M section under the management of Maxwell Knight, Joan Miller, Marjorie Amor and Helene Louise de Munck had also penetrated the Right Club. They discovered a real breach of security, the Tyler Kent affair. This suggested that the secret Roosevelt–Churchill correspondence was being passed to the Italians and through them possibly Germany, by Anna Wolkoff.[33] Out of this Maxwell Knight and Aikin Sneath from MI5 were able to press a plausible conspiracy theory that up to 50 per cent of the British Union (BU) would support the Germans in an invasion of this country. MI5 saw the Tyler Kent Affair, given that Mosley and Maule Ramsay were 'in relations' through the secret meetings, as evidence that the fascist fringe should be closed down.[34] Mosley told Aikin Sneath of MI5 when he visited the BUF headquarters in January 1940, that he thought the Nazis would find the BUF a good cover for agents. He wanted immediate peace, to stop Britain being reduced to a 'dungheap'.[35] Interestingly, Maxwell Knight, had himself been the British fascists' Director of Intelligence in 1927.

With the rapidly worsening military situation it was decided at the second war Cabinet of 22 May 1940, that both Mosley and Ramsay should be detained and 33 leading members of the BU should be interned.[36] During May and June 1940 at least 747 individuals from the fascist fringe were interned, the vast majority of them from the BUF. The successful aim was to close down permanently, the BU. This was achieved by the detention of varying duration throughout the war, of the national, regional and local leadership of the BU, and the proscription of the movement on 10 July 1940. Although fascists were to regroup during the early Cold War period, MI5 was successful in destroying 'Old Fascism'. The eventual crawling out of the political woodwork of what was called 'new fascism', saw the emergence of various syntheses of racial populist, anti-Semitic, and Fascist and Nazi mimetic movements after 1945, heavily influenced by the regrouping of Blackshirt traditions in the internment camps.[37] MI5 played an important part in the funeral rites of interwar British fascism, of temporarily dousing the 'sacred flame'. Its leading role in internment and the political surveillance of released internees effectively monitored and controlled the possibility of a post-war resurgence of fascism. This, however, was never a relevant possibility anyway. Anti-fascism was a prime ingredient of the national consensus during the war. Mosley, whose political failure was obvious to all before the war, had now become a political pariah, possibly the most unpopular British politician of all time. It was ironic that so much time and energy was spent by MI5 in monitoring a phenomenon that had become as dead as the dodo in the immediate post-war years after 1945.[38]

It also, through its research activities, during the war, solved many of the mysteries of the funding of the BUF, particularly the part played by Mussolini. Through a highly complex network of bank accounts the BUF was substantially funded between 1933 and early 1937 by substantial donations (up to £5,000 a month in 1935) from Mussolini. This involved the laundering of foreign currency from banks in Switzerland and Paris to two accounts in Belfast held by W. E. D. Allen, and then transferred to a secret BU account in the Charing Cross branch of the Westminster Bank. The story of this was mainly pieced together from two interrogations of W. E. D. Allen in 1942, and involved

Ian Hope Dundas, Archibald Finlay, and Mosley's solicitor, C.C. Lewis, as well as Allen and his secretary, Major Tabor.[39] The final confirmation of this was found amongst the papers found on Mussolini when he was shot while trying to escape into Germany in 1945; a letter from Count Grandi expressing Mosley's gratitude for funding the BUF.[40] Allen also suggested that Mosley received £40,000 from the 'ransom' which Hitler received from the release of Louis de Rothschild in 1937, and gave details of Mosley's scheme to fund the BUF through commercial radio and an agreement negotiated by Diana Mosley with Hitler, to build a transmitter in Germany.

From 1919 until the end of the Cold War, 'Bolshevism' in all its forms, represented the 'ultimate enemy' for MI5. Yet MI5 treated its perceived representative in Britain, the CPGB with kid gloves for most of its existence. A delicate game of cat and mouse ensued with the smug MI5 cat thinking it had the CPGB mouse trapped, when important deceptions ensured that it often failed to drink the cream. With the BUF a sledgehammer was taken to crack a nut. Whilst, unlike the CPGB, it was correctly perceived as a political irrelevance, draconian action was taken to destroy it. This was successful, even if it drove the emotions, ideas and feelings that inspired it into the political underground, from which it emerged in new forms after 1945. The BUF was a sideshow for MI5, until the 'fifth column' scare elevated it to centre stage in the spring of 1940. While Vernon Kell had been able to run MI5 as a security and counter-espionage research department on a shoestring budget in the interwar period, the penalties of serious under funding came home to roost with the misinterpretation of the menace supposedly provided by the CPGB, and the lack of reliable information about British fascism in the dark days of 1940.

Notes

1. National Archives (NA): KV 4/126, Note on 'A brief outline of the development of MI5', 3 November 1936; KV 4/151, 'Report of Secret Service Committee', February 1919; 'Report of Sir Warren Fisher's Committee on Secret Service', February 1922; 'Secret Service Committee Report', 1 December 1925, in G. Bennett, 'A most extraordinary and mysterious business: the Zinoviev Letter of 1924', Annex E, pp. 105–14, History Notes 14, Foreign and Commonwealth Office, London, February 1999.
2. Richard M. Bennett, *Espionage, Spies and Secrets* (London: Virgin, 2003), p. 175. I am grateful for information about Knight from David Turner.
3. J. C. Curry, *The Security Service 1908–1945* (Kew: Public Record Office, 1999), p. 351.

4. NA: KV 4/125, 'MI5 Policy in Regard to the Communist Party of Great Britain', 15 October 1935.
5. NA: KV 1-6; HW 3; CAB 80, 81.
6. R. Thurlow, 'The Charm Offensive: The "Coming Out" of MI5', *Intelligence and National Security*, 15, 1, Spring 2000, pp. 183–90.
7. T. Bower, *The Perfect English Spy* (London: Heinemann, 1995), pp. 22–3.
8. J. C. Curry, *The Security Service*, pp. 102–44.
9. C. Andrew, *Secret Service* (London: Heinemann, 1985), pp. 224–45.
10. F. H. Hinsley and C. A. G. Simkins, *British Intelligence in the Second World War, Volume 4, Security and Counter Intelligence* (London: HMSO, 1990), pp. 68–75.
11. R. Thurlow, *The Secret State* (Oxford: Blackwell, 1994), pp. 107–72.
12. A. Thorpe, ' "Comintern Control" of the Communist Party of Great Britain 1920–1943', *English Historical Review*, June 1998, pp. 637–62.
13. NA: KV 2/508, Len Wincott, MI5 Note on Invergordon Mutiny, 31 March 1932; F. H. Hinsley and C. A. G. Simkins, *British Intelligence*, pp. 283–91.
14. NA: KV 2/813, Henri Christiaan Pieck, 'Memorandum from John Marriott to Roger Hollis re Pieck Papers, 21 November 1946.
15. NA: KV 2/1181, Bob Stewart, Excerpts from Y Box 2127, 5 August 1943, 9 December 1943 and 8 February 1944.
16. NA: KV 2/513, Salme Murrik (Palme Dutt), Note on Rajani Palme Dutt and secret communist activity, 3 April 1934.
17. NA: KV 2/791, Norman John (James) Klugmann; KV 2/1042-1044, Harry Pollitt; KV 2/1049, William Rust; KV 2/1186-1188, John Ross Campbell; KV 2/1080-1081, Bob Stewart; KV 2/1177, Robert Robson.
18. NA: KV 2/1002, Percy Gladding, Statement of 'Miss X'.
19. NA: HW 3/81, Inspector Kenworthy and Y Service; M. Smith, 'The Government Code and Cypher School and the First Cold War', in M. Smith and R. Erskine (eds), *Action This Day* (London: Bantam Press, 2001), pp. 15–40.
20. M. Smith, *Foley: The Spy Who Saved 10,000 Jews* (London: Hodder and Stoughton, 1999), pp. 51–62; M. Smith, *The Spying Game* (London: Politico's, 2003), pp. 83–4, 159–60.
21. R. Thurlow, ' "A Very Clever Capitalist Class". British Communism and State Surveillance 1939–45', *Intelligence and National Security*, 12, 2, April 1997, p. 5.
22. N. West and O. Tsarev, *The Crown Jewels* (London: Harper Collins, 1998), pp. 279–93.
23. NA: KV 2/816, John Herbert King, Valentine Vivian, 'Leakage in the Communications Department, Foreign Office'; FO 850/2 Y775, 'Security of Documents in H.M. Embassy, Rome', January 1937.
24. NA: KV 2/815, John Herbert King, Interview with Mr. (X), 6 October 1939; KV 2/816, John Herbert King, Valentine Vivian, loc. cit., pp. 1–4.
25. NA: KV 2/804, Walter Krivitsky, 'Note on Imperial Council Source'; KV 2/805, Walter Krivitsky, 'OGPU Agents in the British Foreign Office and Diplomatic Service', pp. 46–9.
26. NA: KV 2/804, Walter Krivitsky, 'Interviews with Walter Krivitsky by Mrs. Jane Archer', January–February 1940; KV 2/805, Walter Krivitsky, 'Information Obtained from General Krivitsky During his Visit to this Country'.

27. NA: KV 2/814, Henri Christiaan Pieck, 'Report on the Interrogation of Henri Christiaan Pieck', 12–16 April 1950.

28. NA: HO 45/25386/54-59, Note of Conference at Home Office, November 1933.

29. The 'Reports of the Fascist Movement in the United Kingdom excluding Northern Ireland' are to be found at NA: HO 144/20141/293-322, HO 144/20142/108-122, HO 144/20142/215-235, HO 144/20144/262-274, HO 144/20144/123-131, HO 45/25385/38-49, HO 144/20160/53-56.

30. J. Hope, 'Fascism, the Security Service and the Curious Careers of Maxwell Knight and James Mcguirk Hughes', *Lobster* 22; J. Hope, 'Fascism and the State in Britain: The Case of the British Fascisti 1923–31', *Australian Journal of Politics and History*, 39, 3, 1993, pp. 367–80.

31. P. Martland, *Lord Haw-Haw: The English Voice of Nazi Germany* (Kew: National Archives, 2003), pp. 33–70.

32. NA: KV 2/835/35a, Sir Barry Domvile, 'Note with regard to our allegation'.

33. NA: KV 2/840, Anna Wolkoff, 'Case of Anna Wolkoff, Tyler Kent and Others'.

34. NA: KV 2/880, W. E. D. Allen, MI5 Interviews with W. E. D. Allen, 1942; KV 2/881, Ian Hope Dundas; KV 3/53, Evidence of British Union Subsidies from Abroad.

35. NA: KV 2/884, Oswald Mosley, Visit to British Union Headquarters in Great Smith Street.

36. NA: CAB 65/13; WM 133 (40), War Cabinet Minutes, 22 May 1940.

37. R. Thurlow, *Fascism in Britain: From Oswald Mosley's Blackshirts to the National Front second edition* (London: I.B. Tauris, 1998).

38. R. Thurlow, 'The Guardian of the "Sacred Flame": The Failed Political Resurrection of Sir Oswald Mosley after 1945', *Journal of Contemporary History*, 33, 2, April 1998, pp. 241–54.

39. See Note 34 for references.

40. NA: KV 3/54, Letter from Count Grandi to Mussolini, 30 January 1934; KV 3/55, Letter from Sir Orme Sargent, Foreign Office, to Sir Alexander Maxwell, Home Office, 8 May 1946.

3
'A plague on both their houses': Fascism, Anti-fascism and the Police in the 1940s

Graham Macklin

The issue of British fascism and the police is again in the news. In November 2003 the *Daily Express* exposed the 'Scandal of Nazi Police', detailing how approximately a dozen serving police officers in the West Midlands were members of the fascist British National Party (BNP).[1] These revelations were universally condemned by the Association of Chief Police Officers (ACPO), backed by the Home Secretary, David Blunkett, who stated categorically that any police officers who joined the BNP would 'render themselves subject of a misconduct investigation and their behaviour treated with the utmost seriousness.'[2] Whilst the furore quickly dissipated, a handful of observers may perhaps have drawn a historical parallel with the experiences of another Labour government half a century earlier.

After 1945 British fascism sought to reconstitute itself as a political force, a process which culminated during the late 1940s with the League of Ex-Servicemen. The league was a small fascist organisation which sought to pave the way for Sir Oswald Mosley's return to active politics, an event heralded by his formation of the Union Movement (UM) in February 1948. These developments did not go unopposed. Violent clashes between fascists and anti-fascists became a regular event in and around Ridley Road, Dalston, during 1947. Sanguinely observing this 'insignificant and disunited revival', MI5 believed that British fascism gave 'serious disquiet' only because its importance, 'has been magnified out of all measure by the organised opposition of Jews and communists, which has resulted in an enormous increase in the audience (mainly opponents and sightseers) and scenes of disorder resulting in prosecutions and inordinate press publicity'.[3] However, whilst opposition to British fascism inevitably drew 'sightseers' this is rather different from the inference that anti-fascism was the root cause of fascism. Instead this hostility to anti-fascism should be understood within the context of the desire by various institutions of the British State to manage and control the public order implications of this situation whilst upholding the principle of free speech.

It has recently been claimed that, despite their protestations to the contrary, the police, in managing these demonstrations, displayed partiality towards the fascists and in fact 'colluded' with them against left-wing opponents.[4] This interpretation was not merely the product of an intrinsic left-wing bias but a powerful corrective to earlier misconceived arguments that defined the police as neutral observers rather than active participants in a conflict in which British fascists were the innocent victims of anti-fascist violence.[5] Contrary to this, this chapter will argue that such a position represents an oversimplification of the role played by the police during the 1940s. It will argue instead for a more nuanced understanding of the attitudes and actions of the Metropolitan Police, demonstrating through several case studies, that the Metropolitan Police, though guided by a pronounced anti-left-wing bias, were ultimately pro-police rather than pro-fascist.

When Sir Philip Game retired as Commissioner of the Metropolitan Police in 1945 he was replaced not by another 'brass hat' like his predecessor Lord Trenchard but by a senior civil servant, Sir Harold Scott.[6] This symbolic change aside, the advent of the Labour government in 1945 failed to mark any radical departure from the established principles of public order, which had been followed since the 1930s. Indeed the continuity in policy is clearly observable in the findings of the Cabinet Committee on Fascism which was convened on 17 November 1945 by Prime Minister Clement Attlee, 'to review the available evidence as to the re-emergence of a fascist movement in this country and to consider amending the existing law with a view to checking the growth of such a movement'.[7] Having received a full report from MI5, the Committee, which reported on 5 April 1946, concluded that, unlike British communism, far from imperilling national security, British fascism could now be safely regarded as little more than a fly in the political ointment and therefore unable to justify the acquisition of greater legal powers to combat it. Adhering to the traditional liberal line an outright ban on its activities was never seriously considered.[8] For the Home Office British fascism remained an issue of 'free speech', even if, as Cabinet discussions surrounding the allocation of paper supplies to fascist newspapers were to show, this fine rhetoric was often little more than an ideological gloss.[9]

James Chuter Ede, the newly appointed Labour Home Secretary, perhaps eager to prove his 'tough' law and order credentials, embraced pre-existing Home Office policy. As a result Ede was notably in thrall to his senior civil servant, Sir Alexander Maxwell, Permanent Under-Secretary of State, who had implemented Home Office policy since 1938 and who, like his successor, Sir Frank Aubrey Newsam, was an effusive champion of the police force.[10] D. N. Pritt, the left-wing barrister and Labour MP observed the result of Ede's dependency first hand. 'One of his practices', noted Pritt, 'was to have a civil servant come quietly into the room and sit behind any MP visiting him to signal to him what answer to give; I had several interviews before I realised that the man was even in the room'.[11] These civil servants, whom Ede trusted implicitly, themselves implicitly trusted the police, dismissing without question any evidence presented to them to the contrary. As one civil servant observed, without irony from the detached confines of his Whitehall office, opponents of fascism, 'derive a wrong impression from what they saw, if they were present, or what they were told or what they read, on the morning after'.[12]

Ideally what is needed, and which unfortunately is beyond the scope of this chapter, is a study of the interaction between the police, the Home Office, their legal advisors and the judiciary itself in order to build a clearer picture of how the state reacted to fascism. Indeed on closer scrutiny, those who accuse the police of partiality in a particular case will often find that whilst the police pressed hard for a prosecution the other agencies of the state advised them to drop the case because a conviction was unlikely. Indeed this way of thinking was foremost in the minds of the Home Office mandarins for whom an unsuccessful prosecution was even worse than no prosecution at all because they believed it would send out completely the wrong message both to the fascists and the public regarding the permissible limits of dissent. In interpreting criminal prosecutions, or perhaps the lack of them, it is worth bearing this in mind.

Police partiality

Observing the welter of claims and counter-claims about the partiality of his police force during the 1940s Sir Harold Scott stated that:

> The position of the police was an unenviable one, for the Fascists complained that the police failed to protect them in the exercise of their right to free speech, while the Jews and Communists complained that the Fascists were being protected by the police while they organised grossly provocative and insulting meetings in areas

where they were calculated to be most resented. These contradictory complaints were good evidence to me that the police were maintaining an impartial attitude.[13]

The police it would appear regarded themselves as the guardians of free speech against 'local people [who] seem to want to ban it'.[14] What is notable in this attitude is any understanding that the police were not passively upholding free speech but actively imposing it upon local communities who did not wish for deliberately provocative fascist marches to be routed through their locality in the knowledge that they were only viable through an inordinately disproportionate police presence or, as was the case with the 1948 May Day rally, through a ban on *all* political processions to the detriment of the peaceful law abiding majority.

The resurrection of fascism quickly ran into opposition from militant direct action anti-fascists, particularly associated with the 43 Group, who deliberately sought to 'out violence' the fascists. As anti-fascists knew well, such a strategy guaranteed they would be regularly arrested and perhaps face more covert harassment from the Security Services. David Renton has clearly demonstrated that the police were three times more likely to arrest anti-fascists than fascists.[15] This of course is perfectly true. However, in and of itself, this does not indicate either police partiality towards fascism or collusion. As most anti-fascists would accept, by attacking fascist meetings they *were* committing a criminal offence and therefore the police were duty bound to arrest them. A distinction should be made, however, between direct action anti-fascism and other forms of anti-fascism such as heckling, though those engaged in such activities were not immune from police harassment or arrest.[16]

Once arrested the treatment received at the hands of the police could vary markedly. The memoirs of leading 43 Group member, Morris Beckman highlight incidences of anti-fascists being taken from the cells and beaten by police officers. Often ignored, however, are his reminiscences of sympathy and solidarity between the police and anti-fascists. Many constables confided to anti-fascists that they did not like being assigned to guard fascist meetings but felt they had to obey orders. Others found that they could find common cause with their arresting officer, particularly the younger ones who had served in the armed forces and were not unaware of the irony that they were guarding the proponents of an ideology, which until recently they had fought and died, to destroy. On such occasions individual officers would turn a blind eye to the activities of anti-fascists.[17] Such complex individual responses make it particularly difficult to gainsay general patterns of behaviour. It should also be noted at this juncture, however, that compared to the treatment meted out to anti-fascists, fascists often appeared to attack anti-fascist meetings with impunity. On 3 August 1947 for example, a 'considerable number' of fascists attacked an anti-fascist meeting amidst cries of 'Let's string up the Yids.' Despite a noted police presence no arrests were made.[18]

Given the level of violence directed at it by anti-fascists, the UM was painfully aware of its dependency upon the police for preserving its physical well-being. Mosley in particular offered effusive support for the police.[19] However, the occasional complaints by fascists that the police were not doing enough to protect them from anti-fascist violence were scoffed at by policemen who considered that, 'These people have had more than their share of protection, considerably in excess of that to which any normal citizen is entitled, or would indeed require.'[20] Aware of this the UM kept the Metropolitan Police well informed of its future meetings so that adequate arrangements could be made.

The mainstay for managing extremism since 1937 was the rather blunt instrument of banning processions in the capital. This practice was resurrected to counter the UM's attempt to hold a May Day march through the capital in 1948, a move which was resented within the wider labour movement whose activities were thus equated with those of a handful of fascist activists. This order was periodically renewed, often at the insistence of the Labour Home Secretary rather than the Metropolitan Police, until 1951. In 1948, however, the Metropolitan Police, apprehending serious disorder, requested and received the power to ban the march.[21] Seeking to defy the ban, the UM organised another march outside the prohibited area thus forcing the police to stage a significant operation involving over 800 police officers to protect them from attack.[22] The enduring impression created by such heavy-handed policing, however, was of a police rather than fascist procession. *Sunday Pictorial* journalist Frederic Mullally recorded the scene thus:

> Three police motorcyclists, followed by two police vans and wireless truck, led the procession. After them came nine mounted police preceding Mosley's drum band. Then came the main body of the parade, with two vans crammed with uniformed police and another batch of mounted police bringing up the rear.[23]

Such developments were understandably interpreted by anti-fascists like Mullally as evidence that the police were protecting the fascists. Had the police, 'been under the direct orders of Mosley himself', asserted the *Daily Worker*, 'they could not have made a better job of breaking the opposition to him'.[24] More soberly Major Lionel Rose of the Association of Jewish Ex-Servicemen (AJEX) asserted that 'there would have been no meeting and no march had there not been massive police protection for the Union Movement,' which of course was perfectly true.[25] Throughout the late 1940s Mullally was one of the staunchest critics of this policy though upon reflection he observed that, 'because of the intensity of the feeling at the time, as young men we questioned their function'. Given sufficient distance from such passions he now concedes, however, that the police 'were doing their job'.[26]

Of course the police did not always operate to protect fascist meetings. In Liverpool and Brighton, to the horror of the Home Office, the police stood aside allowing an 'ugly brawl' to develop intervening only to bring proceedings to a close, by which time many fascists had received 'broken heads'.[27]

The salient fact driving police hostility to fascist or anti-fascist demonstrators was their desire to protect their position as the guardians of public order. 'The police acted swiftly against fascists who challenged their monopoly on either uniformed stewardship or sought to develop their own 'quasi-military or police formations' to provide security.[28] More importantly the Commissioner of the Metropolitan Police was fiercely opposed to direct action anti-fascism on the ideological grounds that it was not for 'communists' to dictate who should and who should not be allowed to hold meetings. Indeed in the wake of 'a great deal of disorder and hooliganism' following a fascist meeting in John Campbell Street, Hackney, in August 1947, the Commissioner summoned his District Commanders to decide upon the best course of action to reassert police authority and re-establish public order. To a man his District Commanders recommended a tougher line, including the deployment of mounted policemen against demonstrators because, 'If we did not take this line now', argued one, 'we should have to do so later on' by which time circumstances could have deteriorated. The ACC agreed, 'and said he thought the more arrests the better'. Such heavy-handed policing was of course indiscriminate and those present conceded that inevitably 'a lot of innocent people' would be arrested so arrangements were made to expedite their quick release. Scott wholeheartedly agreed with his District Commanders, though reminded them that in the interests of impartiality, 'if possible arrests should cover both parties'.[29] From the police's point of view the preparations were a success. When anti-fascists arrived to disrupt the meeting mounted police cleared the area and closed the meeting (which also constituted a success for anti-fascism). The deployment of mounted police clearly had the desired pacifying effect. As one Deputy Commander explained to the Commissioner, 'the people appeared to be impressed by the presence of horses and were nothing like so aggressive as on previous occasions'. Thus the police settled on a hard-line pro-police policy towards anti-fascist opponents who attempted to disrupt fascist meetings.[30]

Their hostility to left-wing demonstrators was reflected in the attitude of the police to the presence of anti-fascist observers AJEX, refusing to accept the veracity of their information, particularly if it did not tally with the official police record of events. When the Home Office entered into correspondence with Sidney Salomon, the Board of Deputies press officer on the subject, Sir Frank Newsam privately vented his cynical belief that Salomon might be 'deliberately trying to make as much mischief as possible with the support of the Communist element in the Board of Deputies'.[31] This was untrue. Similar hostility was exhibited in responses to anti-fascists who complained *in situ* about police conduct at fascist meetings.[32] For many police officers policing fascist demonstrations involved, extra hours, cancelled leave, not to mention thankless, potentially dangerous duties. As one officer rather tellingly complained: 'If it wasn't for you I would be off duty.'[33] Attitudes towards anti-fascism, in so far as they can be reconstructed, do indicate that many Metropolitan Police officers blamed anti-fascists for inflaming the situation, a view articulated by one officer who grumbled to an AJEX observer that, 'if you ignored him [Mosley] and didn't hang around, no one would take any notice of him'.[34] Such was the view of the Home Secretary who, after a particularly violent confrontation in Tottenham in 1949, admonished anti-fascists for fuelling interest in fascism, without which it would 'soon die a natural death'.[35] Other constables, however, whilst sharing this attitude, 'hoped that, if it came down, it would turn out nastier for the fascists'.[36] Although anti-fascism was clearly blamed by both local police constables as well as the Home Office for giving fascism the oxygen of publicity, Harold Scott diffidently maintained that the police, 'thoroughly fed up with the whole business ... called down a plague on both Fascist and Communist houses'.[37]

If one takes Scott's remarks at face value then they lend considerable credence to the interpretation of the role of the Metropolitan Police as a neutral barrier between left and right; one which, as Gerald D. Anderson has noted, saw fascism and communism as 'reciprocating polarities'.[38] This was an interpretation spread contemporaneously by *Evening Standard* columnist Rebecca West who herself was close to Leonard Burt, the head of Special Branch who had assisted her with her study of William Joyce, *The Meaning of Treason*.[39] Locally this interpretation was disseminated by the right-wing *Hackney Gazette*, which, siding firmly with the police against either political extreme, likewise pronouncing 'a plague on both their houses'.[40]

In opposition to this interpretation of the police and British fascism D. S. Lewis has noted that the Public Order Act, 1936, was used more against the left than the right, thus demonstrating that the police operated according to an 'institutionalised anti-left bias'.[41] There is much to be said for such an interpretation which was shared contemporaneously by the anti-fascist journalist Frederic Mullally who noted that 'the British police were, and to a certain extent still are, imbued with a conventional antagonism towards left-wing elements'.[42] The Metropolitan Police itself was permeated root and branch by a right-wing subculture, remembered by one former constable to extend to the fact that left-wing or progressive newspapers like the *Daily Herald* were 'not among the newspapers bought for police station mess-rooms and recreation rooms' during the 1930s.[43]

Whilst the gripes articulated by individual Metropolitan Police officers regarding the knock-on effects that anti-fascist opposition had on 'bread and butter' issues like leave, further up the chain of command opposition to anti-fascism coalesced into a hostility towards left-wing politics, and more specifically communism to which it was inextricably linked in the eyes of senior police officers. Perhaps incapable of differentiating the subtle nuances of left-wing politics from the diktats of Stalinist orthodoxy to which the Communist Party of Great Britain (CPGB) was grimly subservient, Sir Harold Scott viewed the left wing but nominally non-political 43 Group as, 'a body of young Jewish Communists'.[44] The 43 Group, which because it contained some individual communists within its number, thus became, in the eyes of the authorities, part of a much wider subversive conspiracy aiming to undermine the *status quo*. The implications of this can be garnered from the memoirs Commander Leonard Burt, head of Special Branch, who recorded that, for him at least, the essential difference between fascism and communism was their propensity for overt and covert activity which made communism an 'active menace' to national security. Furthermore, in a rather telling passage of his memoirs, Burt states that he and his fellow officers were 'particularly conscious' of the fact that, as far as they were concerned, the fascists had 'patriotic motives' whilst the communists did not. 'All my experience in the police', asserted Burt, 'leads me to believe that it is impossible to be a loyal Briton and a Communist at the same time. If you are a Communist you cannot swear an oath of allegiance to Britain. You cannot be loyal to Her Majesty the Queen.'[45] Whilst it would take a considerable leap beyond the available evidence to conclude from this that the police were 'pro-fascist' it does demonstrate that both the Commissioner of the Metropolitan Police and the Commander of Special Branch viewed anti-fascism as synonymous with communism and therefore a part of a revolutionary conspiracy aiming to subvert and destroy the established order.

Mosley and the UM understood these prejudices, though they sought in vain to capitalise upon them. On 29 July 1950 the UM launched an attack on the Soviet embassy in Kensington Palace Gardens, hurling rocks at the building and breaking windows. The perpetrators, to the indignation of the police, were only bound over to keep the peace or else received nominal fines rather than being prosecuted for the more serious offences of 'unlawful assembly' or 'breach of the peace' due to a legal technicality, enshrined in Section 9 of the Public Order Act, 1936, which decreed that the embassy garden did not constitute a 'public place' within the meaning of the Act. The police, who initially favoured challenging the decision in the High Court until they were dissuaded by legal advice, were acutely sensitive to the disparity between this case and that of several left-wing protesters who, since they did not enjoy the protection of a legal loophole, received six weeks' imprisonment for chaining themselves to the railings of the American embassy in Grosvenor Square.[46] The incident was, however, instrumental in ensuring that the ban on political processions, due to have expired at midnight on 2 August, was renewed for a further three months.[47]

Although the magistrate's decision had been correct as a 'plain finding of fact', the perceived leniency fuelled fascists to shed their inhibitions. As Cold War ignited into hot war in Korea, the UM continued to disseminate increasingly virulent anti-Semitic and anti-communist propaganda.[48] Seeking to place itself in the vanguard of the anti-communist struggle, the UM orchestrated a series of attacks of CPGB sponsored 'Peace' meetings and marches in Dalston, in the hope that it would receive 'toleration' if not 'recognition' for these acts.[49] Far from colluding with the fascists the police sternly dealt with these attacks, leading to a jail sentence for one fascist. All told, all the UM achieved was to reinforce the general public's view that it was 'a party of lay-abouts lacking any political argument'.[50]

Harold Pinter

Although the UM was unable to benefit from the anti-communism of either the police or the security services, one revealing case hints that it may have prejudiced at least one anti-fascist seeking justice as a result of fascist violence. During early 1949 the UM, frustrated with its lack of progress, reverted to a campaign of anti-Semitic violence. In March 1949 a gang of fascists attacked two young Jews in Dalston. One of them, Harold Pinter, arguably Britain's most famous living playwright, often ran into 'trouble' with fascists, though he later remembered that 'this was the only time I ever reported it to the police'.[51] However, rather than fully investigate the case, the police belittled Pinter's version of events. Inspector Satterthwaite vehemently denied that anti-Semitic 'gangs' were prevalent in the area, though he contradicted himself by stating that he was 'fully aware' of the potential for trouble. He remained adamant, however, that because Pinter and his friend refused to pursue the matter further, 'it is clear that no serious assault in fact occurred in this instance'.[52]

However, when Pinter's case and those of other young Jews was taken up by the National Council for Civil Liberties (NCCL), and the file was thus passed upwards for Home Office perusal, the police did everything they could to discredit his story, checking with the Criminal Record Office to see if they could obtain anything 'detrimental to the characters' of the victims of fascist violence.[53] The police were particularly hostile to the intervention of the NCCL whom they felt harboured 'a perennial desire to find fault with the actions of constituted authority'.[54] Likewise, the Home Office regarded the NCCL as a 'Communist-inspired body',[55] a view hardly tempered by a hostile MI5 report which claimed in 1951 that, 'the number of Communists and Communist sympathisers serving as officers of the NCCL (including their Executive Committee) has increased since 1935 and today approaches 100%'.[56]

Following the attack on Pinter, two more Jewish youths were viciously assaulted with knuckle-dusters.[57] Again the police denied that the attacks on Jewish citizens in Dalston were organised 'by Fascists or any other group'.[58] This fallacy was undermined the following month when a gang of fascists attacked two more Jewish teenagers, leaving one with a fractured skull and the other 'seriously injured'. This time, however, the culprits were apprehended and a local fascist, whom the judge conceded was the leader of a 'Dalston strong arm squad', was sentenced to one-year imprisonment.[59] This failure of policing, and in the case of Pinter, the active attempt to discredit his case rather than investigate it, caused considerable anxiety amongst the Jewish community.[60] This was hardly surprising given that between 9 October 1948 and 8 October 1949, a period which mirrored an increase in anti-Semitic radicalisation within the UM itself, the Metropolitan Police recorded that of 800 assaults reported, 55 were anti-Semitic of which 14 were explicitly 'political' in nature.[61]

It would be wrong to infer, however, that the police did nothing in the face of developments. As a result of this increase in fascist violence the East End was flooded with plainclothes police officers, prosecutions of fascist speakers increased and a 'high police official' approached the local AJEX branch requesting to be informed 'direct' of any matter relating to fascism which warranted investigation.[62]

The Hadlow affair

At this juncture it would perhaps be wise to examine two specific instances involving allegations of police partiality and the government's attempts to manage public perceptions of the police. On 24 September 1949 the *New Statesman* ran a story by 'John Hadlow' (a pseudonym for *Daily Express* journalist Richard Martin), which claimed to be an account of a meeting in the East End during the course of which the police had stood by and watched a man being attacked by fascists, intervening only after the assault to manhandle the victim whilst subjecting him to anti-Semitic abuse. Such incidents, stated 'Hadlow', contributed to a climate of fear in which Jews were scared to go out.[63] The article caused a furore. Aware of the damaging perception such newspaper reports created, Scott, who had assiduously cultivated the media upon assuming office, wrote to Kingsley Martin, editor of the *New Statesman*, urging him to persuade 'Hadlow' to come forward and substantiate these 'very grave allegations'. Scott gave his personal assurance that 'Hadlow's' press card would not be jeopardised, provided of course that he had acted in 'good faith'.[64] Having been persuaded of 'Hadlow's' *bona fides* during the course of a personal interview prior to the publication of the story, Martin repeatedly insisted that 'Hadlow' had indeed acted in 'good faith' and on this basis steadfastly guarded his reporter's anonymity.[65] The Home Secretary took 'so serious a view of the matter' that he promised Martin that, if 'Hadlow' came forward, he would institute a full and independent judicial review. The review would, however, be necessarily limited to investigating 'Hadlow's' specific allegations rather than police partiality in the round.[66] Even so, Martin felt a 'real satisfaction' with this offer and scheduled a meeting with 'Hadlow' to discuss their options.[67]

In the meantime, however, the news editor of the *Daily Express*, in whom 'Hadlow' had confided, warned him to back out 'at once' or he would be unable to save him from dismissal. Unwilling to jeopardise his career, 'Hadlow' backed away from the startling concession that he and his story had wrung from the government.[68] Martin sought to salvage the situation but 'Hadlow' declined to meet him.[69] In the event 'Hadlow' was dismissed from the *Daily Express* anyway on the rather thin pretext that, by printing his story in the *New Statesman* he had implied that the *Daily Express*, 'would have been indifferent to your representations'.[70] In the House of Commons John Platts-Mills, Labour MP for Finsbury claimed that the police had visited the offices of the *Daily Express* and secured his dismissal, a charge, which was emphatically denied by the police.[71] Platts-Mills himself later admitted this allegation was based on incorrect evidence, though the incident continues to be recycled by contemporary historians as evidence of police perfidy.[72]

Having stood resolutely by both his story and his reporter, Martin received a devastating blow when he was approached by an unimpeachable anti-fascist source, Sidney Salomon, press officer for the Board of Deputies of British Jews (BDBJ) who presented him with evidence that seriously disputed 'Hadlow's' version of events. Furthermore Salomon confided to Martin that 'Hadlow' was regarded on Fleet Street as 'a somewhat excitable and unreliable writer' who had previously been dismissed from his post 'because he could not bring convincing proof to support the statements made by him'.[73]

'Hadlow's' consistent refusal to publicly substantiate his claims earned him widespread condemnation from not only the police but also from his Fleet Street colleagues. It also forced Martin into a humiliating climb down.[74] Thereafter the Home Secretary could confidently issue a statement in the House of Commons categorically denying the allegations once and for all, thus giving the Metropolitan Police a clean bill of health.[75] Commissioner Scott effusively thanked the Home Secretary for his wholehearted support and had his statement to the House of Commons reprinted in 'Police Orders' as a boost to police morale.[76]

Phil Piratin MP

Coinciding with the 'Hadlow affair' was another instance involving allegations of police partiality, albeit one against an individual police officer. In his oral interviews with local anti-fascists David Renton revealed that Inspector Charles Frederick Satterthwaite, head of G Division, which included Finsbury, Stepney, Hackney and Bethnal

Green was remembered and reviled as both pro-fascist and anti-Semitic.[77] However, vocalising such sentiments publicly and without any explicit evidence could be a costly affair as Phil Piratin, the Communist MP for Mile End found out. During the course of a meeting in Stepney on 4 October 1949 called to commemorate the 'Battle of Cable Street' Piratin, who had a wealth of experience fighting fascism, claimed the police protected fascists and only took action against them when forced to do so by public opinion. More specifically, he accused Satterthwaite of being 'detested by his men', and of being, 'one of the worst enemies of the working class' who 'should have been kicked out of the police force years ago'. The following day Piratin made further disparaging remarks about Satterthwaite, accusing him of being a 'friend to Fascists', revealing to his audience that he had written to the Home Secretary in an attempt to have him removed from his post.[78] Approaching retirement and feeling his reputation to have been impugned, Satterthwaite, who had always enjoyed the full confidence of Sir Harold Scott, sued for slander. Piratin lost and was forced to pay Satterthwaite £1500 in damages, which forced him into bankruptcy and destroyed his political career.[79]

As both the Hadlow affair and Phil Piratin's libel case demonstrate, rashly asserting that the police colluded with fascism could be an embarrassing not to mention costly affair which ultimately undermined the credibility of the case for probing more deeply into the complicated individual and corporate attitudes of the Metropolitan Police. This is not to dismiss concerns about the partiality of the Metropolitan Police as fiction. Indeed as this chapter has demonstrated, there were eminently justifiable reasons for alarm.

Anti-Semitism

Anti-fascists, both then and now, argue that their actions are justified by the provocative and hateful nature of fascist speeches. Surprisingly, whilst not condoning the illegal methods anti-fascists used to shut down fascist meetings, many senior policemen concurred with the view that fascists deliberately and strategically provoked the violence from the platform whilst just staying within the margins of the law. Mosley, observed Sir Ronald Howe, head of Scotland Yard's Criminal Investigations Department (CID) disparagingly:

> Never permitted his followers to strike the first blow, it was his technique so to infuriate the opponents in his audience with verbal

jibes and sneers, that finally those opponents were liable to take the law into their own hands. On almost every occasion when there was a prosecution following disturbances at one of Mosley's meetings, he was able to show that it was not his supporters who had started the fight. Smugly, they would plead self-defence. The matter was extremely frustrating for the police. It seemed impossible to proceed in a prosecution against Mosley, yet we knew perfectly well that if he and his party had not existed, the disturbances which troubled us would not have taken place. Speeches which bordered on the seditious, but were never quite inflammatory enough to enable us to prosecute.[80]

This strategy of violence and incitement was quite deliberate intending to incite opponents and generate publicity, which cast them as the respectable injured party and therefore induce further support. Aware that the source of the trouble was the presence of Jeffrey Hamm, the police and the Home Office were equally keen to prosecute him, which they did in 1947, though Hamm only received a derisory sentence because the magistrate, seemingly impressed by the honesty of his anti-communism, though rather less so by his anti-Semitism, ignored police protests that he was already bound over and so merited a custodial sentence.[81] Similarly, when the police brought a prosecution against Duke Pile for a virulently anti-Semitic speech, the Magistrate, Blake Odgers, disregarded police evidence of incitement, and to their horror, interpreted his speech as 'fair and reasonable discussion', declining to do more than bind him over.[82]

Indeed, these cases hint at a definite bias can be inferred during the sentencing phase of fascist and anti-fascist trials. Whilst there has been no sustained research into this area, the impressionistic evidence suggests that anti-fascists faced greater hostility from sentencing magistrates. The case of Herbert Malone is instructive. Sentencing one anti-fascist, Malone the magistrate derided the man's war record and sentenced him to six months, though on learning he had had a distinguished career in the RAF reduced his sentence to a fine.[83] In another case the Jewish defendants were admonished by Odgers for their 'un-British' behaviour, thus disenfranchising them at a stroke.[84] However, other magistrates like Daniel Hopkin took a more balanced view. Having admonishing the defendants for taking the law into their own hands, he lamented the police failure to arrest the fascist speaker for a 'highly provocative' speech.[85]

The raw material such cases were often built on was the evidence of conspicuously placed shorthand note takers of Special Branch whose presence, 'invariably led to a moderation in the tone and content of platform speeches'.[86] Indeed, there is evidence that the presence of shorthand note takers did have a salutary effect on fascist speakers. As one told his audience, although he had a 'solution' to the 'Jewish problem' they would have to wait until, 'we don't have the shorthand taker from Scotland Yard here'.[87] However, there is also a considerable volume of evidence to suggest that this crucial source of evidence was frequently unavailable or worse, was manipulated and misused.

In Brighton, for instance, where fascists staged meetings at The Level, an observer noted that 'There were two constables and one sergeant on duty at the meeting and I noticed they often shared the anti-Jewish amusement of the crowd. I particularly *searched* for a plain clothes man taking notes, but did not see one at all.'[88] Even when a note taker was present there was no guarantee that action would be taken. Watching the conduct of the note takers one observer noted with astonishment that, 'during one particularly violent anti-Semitic outburst on the part of the orators, they were *not* taking any notes'.[89] Perhaps even more damning than this omission is evidence that, on at least one occasion, police officers whether by design or default, misused their shorthand notes to undermine the defence of anti-fascists who claimed that the fascist speaker had provoked them to action by his anti-Semitism. Under questioning Inspector Innes stated:

Q: What was the worst provocation you heard from the platform?
A: I did not hear any particular provocation; the speaker was speaking in most general terms on the subject of Palestine.
Q: Meetings are frequently held in that part which is a strong Jewish area.
A: Yes.
Q: The reason why meetings are held is to provoke the Jewish people.
A: I have no knowledge of that.
Q: Did you hear the words 'PJ' shouted from the platform?
A: I did not hear those words shouted from the platform but I heard someone in the crowd shout them.
Q: Did you not hear the speaker drink a glass of water and give the toast 'PJ'.
A: No.[90]

In this case Inspector Innes testimony was at marked variance with the original shorthand notes, withheld from the defence, which confirmed that speaker did indeed shout 'People's Justice', a seemingly innocuous phrase invoked to disguise its real meaning: 'Perish Judah'.[91]

Independent 'observer's reports' commissioned by the BDBJ also indicated that many police officers shared the anti-Semitism of the fascist speakers they were supposed to be monitoring. At Ridley Road it was noted that the police note taker 'giggled at sallies made by the speaker' and afterwards remained to talk to his supporters accepting a cigarette from them.[92] On another occasion an observer noted that when 'humorous remarks', were made about the Jews by fascist speakers 'several of the police had filthy grins on their faces and were apparently enjoying the meeting'.[93]

Observing the increasing number of complaints levelled against the Metropolitan Police Force for anti-Semitism, Sir Harold Scott, in conference with his District Commanders, noted frostily that there was a 'pro-Jewish element' that sought any opportunity to make 'capital' out of any remark or action that might impute bias. If this impression of partiality was allowed to take hold, Scott cautioned his District Commanders, then the ability of his force to police political demonstrations would be severely compromised. It would therefore, 'be most unfortunate, both for the individual officers and for the Force as a whole, if either side found ground for complaint in some incautious remark or expression of view in public'.[94] Scott's concerns were timely. Between 1946 and 1947 complaints against the police for incivility, improper attitude and remarks as well as bad language had tripled.[95]

But whilst Scott cautioned his force against injudicious outbursts, police report after report routinely presumed anti-fascists to be 'Jews,' of 'Jewish descent', or 'of Jewish appearance' an exercise in racial stereotyping, which continued well into the late 1960s.[96] Needless to say, however, many senior police officers remained grossly insensitive to the effects of anti-Semitism. Upon receiving a report of a fascist speech which claimed that Belsen and Buchenwald were 'Jewish lies' whilst paradoxically lauding Hitler because, 'he knew how to handle the Jews', the Chief Constable of Bath reported that there was nothing to which exception could be taken 'except by persons of the Jewish faith'.[97] Nor was the Home Office averse to turning a blind eye to visceral fascist rhetoric, concluding on more than one occasion that, whilst a speech was 'technically seditious' it was, 'not worth a prosecution when addressed to only 25 people with no violent consequences', as if the implementation of the law was a numbers game.[98]

Such an attitude is hardly surprising given that some Home Office officials clearly lacked the intellectual vigour to understand even the most basic tenets of fascist anti-Semitism, causing one official to note incredulously, 'the speakers tend to *mix up* Communism with what they call

"Judaism" ', when of course the conflation was quite deliberate.[99] On numerous occasions fascist speakers escaped prosecution for the most virulent anti-Semitic speeches, the flavour of which can be surmised from the following offering, which was by no means unique:

> The Jews are filthy, parasitic vermin feeding off the political body of this country and the sooner we get rid of the lot the better. Hitler closed the doors of his gas chambers too soon, and that if he [the speaker] had his way he would send all Jews to Palestine with a one-way ticket and then supply the Arabs with atom bombs.[100]

The failure to prosecute such speeches, whether by design or default, was to contribute to a climate of legitimisation and licence whereby fascist speakers drew succour from what they mistook for tacit approval and were thus prompted to ever greater excesses. The consequence of this failure to invoke the full weight of the law against fascist activists was increasingly apparent against the backdrop of the deteriorating situation in Palestine. Seeking to broaden their appeal the UM equated the struggle in Palestine against the 'dirty Jewish murderers' with its own campaign against the Jews in the East End.[101] In such a climate anti-fascist speakers found, much to their discomfort, that when they accused their hecklers of being fascist 'some members of the crowd objected on the grounds that one could be anti-Jewish without being a fascist'.[102] Similarly the Board of Deputies lamented the decision of local authorities to allow the UM access to school halls cordoned off by the police because of the atmosphere of 'adventure' it conveyed to local school children who were thereafter often inclined to anti-Semitism.[103]

At this juncture it is perhaps worth considering the issue of the Metropolitan Police's decision to recruit a number of officers from the notoriously anti-Semitic Palestine Police Force (PPF).[104] Indeed, its reputation was such that the novelist Arthur Koestler was moved to characterise the PPF as 'one of the most despicable organisations in the British Commonwealth' and 'riddled' with former Black and Tans and BUF members. Many of these BUF members, claimed Koestler, were involved in a clandestine terrorist bombing campaign against Jewish targets including the Jewish Agency's Press Office on 16 March 1946.[105]

Given the climate of escalating violence and anti-Semitism the Director of Public Prosecutions acknowledged that, if the situation deteriorated further, 'the fascists might look forward to a steady stream of recruits amongst the British Forces returning home from Palestine'.[106] Indeed the presence of former members of the Palestine forces who spoke at a fascist meeting in Ridley Road in May 1948 'caused quiet a stir and sensation'.[107] However, the recruitment of PPF officers should not be exaggerated. Upon the demobilisation of the PPF the Metropolitan Police recruited just 168 officers of which only 27 were posted to police stations in the East End.[108] Nevertheless, those who were recruited could be vehemently anti-Semitic, more so perhaps than any fascist speaker.[109] Other demobilised PPF officers were involved in more violent demonstrations of anti-Semitism.[110] However, it should not automatically be assumed that service in Palestine was *a priori* a psychologically disfiguring experience. Many of PPF officers returned from Palestine well disposed towards the East End's Jewish population.[111]

Despite these observations regarding police anti-Semitism there is scant evidence to suggest an overt fascist presence within the police force. The only evidence of extremist police officers to so far emerge is an internal survey conducted in 1962, which found that there were only 16 officers who held extreme political associations and a further 45 who were in contact with them due to family or friends, a situation monitored by Special Branch.[112]

Conclusion

In Italy where it has been claimed that most policemen were 'conservative nationalists' the police regarded the rise of Mussolini, who alone could control his *squadristi* thugs leaving them free to concentrate on the revolutionary left, as, 'the only acceptable alternative to anarchy'.[113] If one views fascism as a form of 'crisis politics' then clearly the economic, social and political conditions in Britain after 1945 are not even remotely comparable to that of the revolutionary turmoil which engulfed Italy after 1918. Indeed there is not much of a comparison to be made between the vigour of the early Italian fascist movement in 1919 with the disillusioned and envenomed residue of a fascist party already crushed by the power of the British State in May 1940. The Metropolitan Police of the late 1940s unlike the various institutions of the Italian police during the 1920s and 1930s were very far from operating as the vanguard of incipient proto-fascism.

What this chapter has sought to demonstrate is that whilst hard-line policing of fascist demonstrations aimed to neutralise disturbances at fascist meetings and preserve public order, this approach inevitably prejudiced anti-fascist activists. In this sense it would perhaps be fairer to categorise the ideological forces at work within the Metropolitan Police force not merely as pro-police but as representing an institutionalised anti-anti-fascist bias. Indeed whilst there is little evidence of sustained, active *collusion* between the police and the fascists both harboured a set of shared attitudes, assumptions and prejudices, particularly with regards to anti-communism and, to a lesser extent anti-Semitism that sit ill at ease with the dominant liberal interpretation of the Metropolitan police as an impartial barrier keeping an 'unbiased watch' between the political extremes. Without indulging too far in the realms of counter-factual history such observations are at least suggestive that, given a different set of socio-economic and political circumstances, these shared prejudices, might well have intersected to create an 'anti-anti-fascist' consensus in which British fascism could have found the necessary 'political space' to ascend from the political ghetto in which it languished for the remainder of the century.

Notes

1. *Daily Express*, 3 November 2003.
2. http://www.acpo.police.uk/news/2003/q4/BNP [Accessed 7 November 2004].
3. TNA HO 45/25399/865252/329.
4. David Renton, *Fascism, Anti-Fascism and Britain in the 1940s* (London: Macmillan, 2000), pp. 101–29 and David Renton, 'An Unbiased Watch? The Police and Fascist/Anti-fascist Street Conflict in Britain, 1945–1951', *Lobster*, Summer, 1998, pp. 12–19.
5. Stephen Cullen, 'Political Violence: The Case of the British Union of Fascists', *Journal of Contemporary History*, 28, 2, 1993, pp. 245–68. Cullen also wrote two articles for *Comrade*, journal of the Friends of Oswald Mosley (FOM).
6. Herbert Morrison to Sir Alan Lascelles, 16 April 1945 in TNA HO 45/25697. Sir Arthur 'Bomber' Harris, former chief of RAF Bomber Command, had initially been favoured for the post.
7. TNA CAB CM (45) 63rd Conclusions, minute 3, 17 November 1945.
8. TNA PREM 8/1410.
9. Norman Brook to Clement Attlee, 20 March 1948 in TNA PREM 8/1410.
10. *The Times*, 27 April 1964.
11. D. N. Pritt, *The Autobiography of D. N. Pritt: Part Two, Brasshats and Bureaucrats* (London: Lawrence and Wishart, 1965), p. 52.
12. S. H. E. Burnley, minute, 16 October 1947 in TNA HO 45/24470.
13. Sir Harold Scott, *Scotland Yard* (London: Mayflower, 1970), p. 143.
14. L. Quincey, note, 28 September 1949 in TNA MEPO 3/3095.
15. David Renton, *Fascism, Anti-Fascism*, pp. 101–29.
16. For more on varieties of anti-fascism see David Renton, *Fascism, Anti-Fascism*, pp. 71–100 and Nigel Copsey, *Anti-Fascism in Britain* (London: Macmillan, 2000), pp. 81–115.
17. Morris Beckman, *The 43 Group* (London: Centreprise, 1992), pp. 32 and 95.
18. AJEX Meeting, Buckfast Street, Bethnal Green, 3 August 1947 in BDBJ C6/5/2/1.
19. *News Chronicle*, 28 November 1947.

20. TNA MEPO 3/3092.
21. TNA CAB CM (48) 30th Conclusions, minute 6, 29 April 1948 in TNA PREM 8/1410.
22. *Hansard*, Vol. 450, HC Debs., 5s., col. 1430–4, 6 May 1948.
23. *Sunday Pictorial*, 2 May 1948.
24. *Daily Worker*, 3 May 1948.
25. Major Lionel Rose, 'Mosley Rally and March, 1 May 1948' in BDBJ C6/1/1/3.
26. Frederic Mullally interview with the author, 19 July 2003.
27. Fascist Activities: May–June 1948 in TNA KV 3/51.
28. Inspector Satterthwaite to A2, undated minute, in TNA MEPO 2/8895.
29. District Commander's Conference, minute, 2 September 1947 in TNA MEPO 2/10417.
30. District Commander's Conference, minute, 9 September 1947 in TNA MEPO 2/10417.
31. Sir Frank Newsam, minute, 3–6 January 1950 in TNA MEPO 3/3095.
32. Special Branch, report, 'Meeting', 14 September 1947 in TNA HO 45/24470.
33. Observers report, Ridley Road, 7 February 1948 in BDBJ C6/9/1/12; C. H. Rolph, *Living Twice* (London: Victor Gollancz, 1974), p. 91.
34. Observers report, Ridley Road, 7 February 1948 in BDBJ C6/9/1/12.
35. *Hansard*, Vol. 463, HC Debs., 5s., col. 38–41, 21 March 1949.
36. C. H. Rolph, *Living Twice*, pp. 91–2.
37. Sir Harold Scott, *Scotland Yard* (London: Mayflower, 1970), p. 143.
38. Gerald D. Anderson, *Fascists, Communists and the National Government: Civil Liberties in Great Britain, 1931–1937* (Columbia: Missouri University Press, 1983), p. 203 and Richard Thurlow, *Fascism in Britain: A History* (Oxford: Blackwell, 1987), pp. 114–15.
39. In her *Evening Standard* columns whilst West attacked fascist anti-Semitism she also accused the Communists of cynically fomenting street fights with the fascists in order to further their own propaganda and gain the Jewish vote. According to her biographer her unpopularity on both sides of the ideological divide was boundless and, extremely unlikely as it sounds, 'at the mention of her name the Fascists and the Communists would stop fighting and boo and hiss her.' See, Carl Rollyson, *Rebecca West* (London: Hodder and Stoughton, 1995), pp. 221–2 and Professor Hyman Levy, *An Open Letter from Professor Hyman Levy: Rebecca West and the Resurgence of Fascism* (London: Our Time Publications, 1947).
40. *Hackney Gazette*, 31 March 1948.
41. D. S. Lewis, *Illusions of Grandeur: Mosley, Fascism and British Society, 1931–1981* (Manchester: Manchester University Press, 1987), pp. 116–17.
42. Frederic Mullally, *Fascism Inside England* (London: Claude Morris, 1946), p. 51.
43. C. H. Rolph, *Living Twice*, p. 91.
44. Sir Harold Scott, *Scotland Yard*, p. 143.
45. Leonard Burt, *Commander Burt of Scotland Yard* (London: Pan Books, 1959), pp. 109–10.
46. TNA MEPO 2/8896.
47. James Chuter Ede to Clement Attlee, 2 August 1950 in TNA PREM 8/1410.
48. *Russia Threatens War: Korea Today – Britain Tomorrow* (UM handbill) and *Can You Guess?* (UM handbill).
49. Union Movement, *Political Commentary*, No. 14, September 1950.

50. John Bean, *Many Shades of Black: Inside Britain's Far Right* (London: New Millennium, 1999), pp. 69–77.
51. *The Observer*, 6 January 2003.
52. Inspector Charles Satterthwaite to A1, 11 April 1949 in TNA HO 45/25465.
53. Special Branch, report, 26 March 1949 in TNA HO 45/25465.
54. [Illegible signature] to Sir Harold Scott, 15 June 1945 in TNA MEPO 3/1894.
55. Mrs Nunn, Home Office minute, 24 May 1945 in TNA HO 45/25465. This view informed the decision of novelist E. M. Foster, first President of the NCCL to resign in 1948; see Mark Lilly, *The National Council for Civil Liberties: The First Fifty Years* (London: Macmillan, 1984), p. 73.
56. K. Morton Evans to Miss E. H. Harting, 4 July 1951 in TNA HO 45/25465.
57. *Jewish Chronicle*, 8 April 1949.
58. Detective Inspector H. Sparkes to Division Inspector, G. Division, 11 April 1949 in TNA HO 45/25465.
59. *Jewish Chronicle*, 6 May 1949.
60. *Civil Liberty*, Vol. 10, No. 3, April 1950.
61. *Hansard*, Vol. 468 HC Debs., 5s., col. 744, 20 October 1949.
62. BDBJ C6/1/1/3; BDBJ C6/2/1/5; BDBJ C6/3/1c/9 and BDBJ C6/9/1/12.
63. John Hadlow, 'Fascists and Police', *New Statesman and Nation*, 24 September 1949.
64. Sir Harold Scott to Kingsley Martin, 7 October 1949 in 11/1, New Statesman archive, University of Sussex (hereafter NS archive).
65. Kingsley Martin to Sir Harold Scott, 13 October 1949 and Kingsley Martin to James Chuter Ede, 25 October 1949 in 11/1, NS archive.
66. James Chuter Ede to Kingsley Martin, 18 October 1949 and 9 November 1949 in 11/1, NS archive.
67. Kingsley Martin to James Chuter Ede, 19 October 1949 in 11/1, NS archive.
68. Richard Martin to Kingsley Martin, 20 October 1949 in 11/1, NS archive.
69. *New Statesman and Nation* Manager to Richard Martin, 21 October 1949 and Kingsley Martin to Richard Martin, 24 October 1949 in 11/1, NS archive.
70. *Daily Express* to Richard Martin, 1 November 1949 in 11/1, NS archive.
71. Sir Harold Scott to Miss J. J. Nunn, 8 November 1949 in TNA MEPO 3/3095.
72. David Renton, *Fascism, Anti-Fascism*, p. 116.
73. Sidney Salomon to Kingsley Martin, 14 November 1949 and 15 November 1949 in 11/1, NS archive.
74. Richard Martin to Kingsley Martin, 21 November 1949 in 11/1, NS archive.
75. James Chuter Ede to Kingsley Martin, 18 November 1949 in 11/1, NS archive.
76. Commander's Conference, minutes, 1 November 1949 in TNA MEPO 2/10419 and Sir Harold Scott to James Chuter Ede, 28 November 1949 in TNA MEPO 3/3095.
77. David Renton, *Fascism, Anti-Fascism*, p. 104.
78. *The Times*, 7 June 1950; 8 June 1950 and 9 June 1950.
79. TNA B 9/1447. Piratin remained a Communist, working first as a 'political organizer' and then 'circulation manager' for the *Daily Worker*, but 'was never a public figure again'. He later became 'the director of a merchant bank in the City'. See Henry Felix Srebrnik, *London Jews and British Communism, 1935–1945* (London: Valentine Mitchell, 1995), p. 217.
80. Sir Ronald Howe, *The Pursuit of Crime* (London: Arthur Baker, 1961), p. 40.
81. *Daily Express*, 22 September 1947.

82. WCS, minute, 27 July 1948 in TNA MEPO 2/8659.
83. *Hackney Gazette and North London Advertiser*, 14 September 1949.
84. Special Branch report, 19 January 1947 in TNA HO 45/24469.
85. Lionel Rose, *Survey of Open-Air Meetings held by pro-Fascist Organisations, April–October 1947* (Factual Survey 2: February 1948).
86. Nigel West (Rupert Allason), *The Branch: A History of the Metropolitan Police Special Branch, 1883–1983* (London: Secker and Warburg, 1983), pp. 117–18.
87. Special Branch report, 22 August 1947 in TNA HO 45/24469/9621717/341-400.
88. Observers report, The Level, Brighton, 15 June 1947 in BDBJ C6/4/2/6
89. Morris Franks to Mr. Roston, 21 September 1947 in BDBJ C6/3/2/13.
90. Special Branch, 'Court Proceedings', 16 June 1947 in TNA HO 45/24469/383.
91. Special Branch, 'Meeting', 1 June 1947 in TNA HO 45/24469/367. For more on this contrast see Dave Renton, *Fascism, Anti-Fascism*, pp. 111–12.
92. Observers report, Ridley Road, 20 April 1947 in BDBJ C6/9/1/3.
93. Observers report, Ridley Road, 8 June 1947 in BDBJ C6/9/1/3.
94. District Commander's Conference, minutes, 22 August 1947 in TNA MEPO 2/10417.
95. District Commander's Conference, minutes, 13 May 1947 in TNA MEPO 2/10417.
96. *Jewish Gazette*, 18 February 1966.
97. Chief Constable Hind to the Home Office, 23 July 1949 in TNA HO 45/24968.
98. Home Office, minute, 1 January 1947, in TNA HO 45/24469.
99. Home Office, minute, 2 September 1947 in TNA HO 45/24470.
100. Jewish Defence Committee, Meeting report, 5 December 1948 in BDBJ C6/1/1/3.
101. *Union*, No. 25, 31 July 1948.
102. AJEX Meeting, Buckfast Street, Bethnal Green, 3 August 1947 in BDBJ C6/5/2/1.
103. BDBJ deputation to South London LCC, 9 March 1948 in BDBJ C6/3/2/13.
104. For evidence of the everyday anti-Semitism of PPF officers see Colin Imray, *Policeman in Palestine: Memories of the Early Years* (Devon: Edward Gaskell, 1995) and Michael Lang (ed.), *One Man in his Time: The Diary of a Palestine Policeman, 1946–1948* (Sussex: The Book Guild, 1997).
105. Arthur Koestler, *Promise and Fulfilment: Palestine, 1917–1949* (London: Macmillan, 1983), pp. 15 and 148.
106. F. S., Home Office, minute, 25 November 1947 in TNA HO 45/25129.
107. Meeting report, Ridley Road, Dalston, April/May 1948 in BDBJ C/10/4/2.
108. *Hansard*, Vol. 466, HC Debs., 5s., col. 2320, 7 July 1949.
109. Morris Beckman, *The 43 Group*, p. 95.
110. *West Lancashire Evening Gazette*, 11 June 1948.
111. Henry Morris interview with the author, 4 September 1998.
112. Commander's Conference, minutes, 4 December 1962 in TNA MEPO 2/10431.
113. Richard O. Collin, 'Italy: A Tale of Two Police Forces', *History Today*, September 1999, pp. 27–33.

4
Feminism and Anti-fascism in Britain: Militancy Revived?

Julie V. Gottlieb

British resistance to fascism at home and abroad gained the support of the vast majority of politicised women, perhaps like no other cause since suffrage. Women's opposition to fascism had the *potential* to transcend party political sectionalism, heal the rift between 'Old' and 'New' Feminism, and revitalise the women's movement in staunch opposition to the male supremacy, misogyny and terror characteristic of fascist regimes and movements. The rise of fascism posed the greatest challenge yet imaginable to the political and social gains achieved by women after the First World War. Certainly the continuity between women's suffrage militancy and anti-fascist mobilisation was not lost on contemporaries. Ethel Mannin explained how 'all that the long-drawn-out fight of the Suffrage Movement achieved for women, all that the Great War made possible for them, at its own bitter price, will be swept away in a few months if Fascism comes to this country, and women will have no say in the matter, and be allowed no protest'.[1] In November 1936 the *Morning Post* reported as follows: 'About 30 Fascist interrupters were ejected by the police last night at Bow Baths, where Mr. George Lansbury and Mr. Herbert Morrison were addressing a meeting ... One woman who was incensed at the attacks on Mr. Lansbury by a youth swung her bag and hit him across the face, shouting: "You would have been thrown out long before this in the old Suffragette days." '[2] As this report suggests, the construction of women's resistance to fascism was in many respects distinct from the construction of men's. Thus this chapter is concerned with the ways in which British women responded to Mosley's British Union of Fascists (BUF) and to the rise of fascism in Europe more generally, offering a gendered reading of the ultimately successful but also largely disorganised and splintered British anti-fascism movement of the 1930s.[3]

As Nigel Copsey has convincingly demonstrated, British anti-fascism was politically 'reactive' and needs to be understood as a 'thought, an attitude or feeling of hostility towards fascist ideology and its propagators which may or may not be acted upon'. Anti-fascist sentiment and action manifested itself as a 'mosaic', and was a 'variegated phenomenon'.[4] By definition, then, Britain's anti-fascist movement was prone to organisational fragmentation and ideological crossing of wires. One of the schisms within Britain's anti-fascist movement that has not as yet received much scholarly attention is that between men and women. This chapter will explore crucial differentials according to sex with regard to contemporary interpretations of fascism;[5] female-led and female-dominated campaigns of fascist resistance; the gendering of anti-fascist violence both in actual experience and in media representations; and the importance for women of reasserting their feminist credentials to frame and to fortify their anti-fascist positions. Indeed, by tracing the evolution of all of the above, a more or less coherent feminist anti-fascist ideology and discourse can be discerned and defined. However, it must also be noted from the outset that it is very difficult to present a linear narrative of women's progressive mobilisation and organisation for the anti-fascist front. Johanna Alberti has rightly observed that 'Feminists in the 1930s belonged to a number of organizations, including different political parties, and there was no one central focus of thought and activity. Neither was there any one single Fascist view of women.'[6] Regardless of the vast opportunities presented by the spectre of fascism for bringing British women of the left, centre and the right together, the disunity and political fissures of the British anti-fascist movement (and the United Front campaign) likewise precluded women's unity or the co-ordination of motivations and tactics in female acts of resistance to fascism.

The debate about Labour and Communist Party collaboration in the fight against fascism illustrates these points. When in June 1934 the Conference of Labour Women debated an amendment on 'Fascism and Democracy', delegates reflected the same differences of opinion and conflicting plans for actions as did the men's section of the party.

[Miss Dorothy Elliott (National Union of General and Municipal Workers)] wanted to say one word on why they were not able to accept the amendment which was down in the name of the Scarborough Labour Party. It was very tempting, and particularly was it so in local organisations, to want to work in a United Front against Fascism and Democracy. It was only when it came to working it out in practice that it was evident that it was very difficult to achieve.

This amendment could not be accepted, because there was a fundamental difference between the philosophy of the Socialist Party and of the Communist Party. It was impossible to work hand in hand when two conflicting philosophies were in question.

In contrast to Elliott's misgivings, Miss Carry (Scarborough) supported the amendment: 'She said her party felt strongly that all working-class organizations should combine. There ought to be mass action of all the workers acting in unity to stop the menace of Fascism before it gained further strength. Unless the working classes did organise together they would not be able to resist and abolish Fascism. They must not allow Fascism to gain ground and force down the position of the workers.' In the event, however, it is important to note that, on this occasion, 'the amendment was overwhelmingly defeated',[7] as Labour women fell in line with their party's policy of non-collaboration with the Communist Party of Great Britain (CPGB).[8]

More strikingly, when Labour women did try to bridge the ideological and tactical gulf between Labour and CPGB anti-fascist efforts, their sex offered little protection against political character assassination, and only opened them to puerile and sexist attacks. Ellen Wilkinson's sex was no shield against either fascist attacks or even attacks from her far-left-sometime-allies. The *Daily Worker* had reviewed her co-authored book, *Why Fascism?* (1934) in a particularly poisonous way, going as far as labelling her a fascist. Indeed, from the CPGB's point of view, any attempt to consider fascism's appeal to the working class was considered a betrayal of class war. When she responded with a letter to the CPGB's organ, which they printed, Willie Gallagher took a further opportunity to mock and goad her. Wilkinson wrote:

The *Daily Worker* and the 'Communist Review' have denounced me as a Fascist because in our book ... [we] insisted that in order to understand the growth of Fascism in the working class one must realise the amount of Socialist appeal that both the Nazis and the Italian Fascist incorporated into their programme; that in fact the 'socialism' of National Socialism provided them with the mass basis that the old capitalist parties had not been able to attract.

Gallagher replied in the most condescending and offensive language:

At this point I feel like saying almost unprintable things about Miss Wilkinson, but with commendable restraint (which I hope she will appreciate) I hold myself in check. I will speak to her as to a child, an erring child. My dear Miss Wilkinson, pray give me your attention ... My dear Miss Wilkinson, please do me two big favours. One, drop Conze, he's not worth holding on to. Two, don't bother me with your foolishness any more.[9]

That such journalistic mud-slinging was both politically counter-productive and ideologically myopic is obvious. Its wrong-headedness is further evidenced by Wilkinson's reputation in Nazi circles, and there can be no doubt that Wilkinson represented a formidable anti-fascist force. 'Sir Nevile Henderson, the British Ambassador in Berlin, told Hugh Dalton in 1937 that when he had suggested to Goering that he should visit England, Goering had replied: "If I came to London all your Ellen Wilkinsons would throw carrots at me." '[10]

Historiography

While it is clear that there was a distinctively feminine response to fascism in Britain, conditioned both by the voicing of woman-specific concerns and by the structural subordination of women in anti-fascist political organisations, it is still the case that there has been little research on and scholarly engagement with the topic. We need to ponder why historians have tended to neglect women's contributions to British anti-fascism, beyond the occasional mentions of leading figures such as Ellen Wilkinson, Sylvia Pankhurst, Isobel Brown, Leah Manning, Eleanor Rathbone and a roster of literary women who used their journalism and their fiction as a platform or vehicle for their fight against fascism,[11] and beyond somewhat dismissive claims that 'there were ... soon to be small stirrings over political developments in Italy and, later, in Germany. As with welfare work on the Continent, campaigning against fascism remained the active concern of middle-class women; it never turned into a mass mobilisation of support.'[12] Promisingly, Nigel Todd has noted that 'women were often evident in the anti-fascist crowd scenes as well, and their comprehensive presence in the struggle has been invariably overlooked'.[13] However, his treatment of women's contribution to anti-fascist activism is explored in a chapter titled 'The Female Touch', as he falls into the trap of recounting the activities of a small number of women 'worthies', and celebrating the bravery and heroism of women with *bona fide* socialist credentials.

Why is there a gap in the historiography? First, in the wider context, Susan Pedersen has observed that for all the historical attention conferred upon British political history and British women's history separately, the two sub-fields have rarely been merged, with the result that the history of women and British politics is one of the most neglected fields of study in twentieth-century British historiography.[14] Second, and with more specific reference to the study of political marginality and popular politics in interwar Britain, historians of the far left and the extreme right have tended to neglect the insights of women's and gender history, with the result that the field has been dominated by male perspectives, and the stories told are those of men's actions, political reactions and male perpetration or heroism. Women are included in these studies as incidental, and historians have yet to ask how gender identities conditioned and informed activists' temperamental, intellectual and active responses to the spectre of Mosley at home and to Mussolini and Hitler abroad. Third, it is important to bear in mind that British fascism has received far more scholarly attention than anti-fascism, indeed, one could well argue that the BUF has received attention well out of proportion with its significance in interwar politics. Again, it is Copsey's recent study that breaks new ground here as he has 'made the first attempt to write a broad history of British anti-fascism as a continuous phenomenon from the 1920s'.[15] Further, only more recently has this gender imbalance been redressed, although it is still the case that studies of women's support for fascism have led the way here.[16] The obverse side of British women's support for fascism, namely the story of feminist anti-fascism, remains largely to be excavated, explored and analysed. Finally, another factor that might explain this blind spot in the historiography is that, as already alluded to, the history of women's resistance to fascism belies easy conceptualisation and neat narrative recounting, presenting a challenge to the historian seeking to record women's resistance as a clear and identifiable political phenomenon.

This paucity in the secondary literature can also be partially accounted for by the reality of the virtual silencing of women's voices in the critique of fascism during the 1930s, a state of affairs that Virginia Woolf described in her diary. Woolf noted the uphill struggle faced by British feminists to integrate sex-specific concerns into anti-fascist campaigns:

> A teasing letter (the other night) from Elizabeth Bibesco. 'I am afraid that it had not occurred to me that in matters of ultimate importance even feminists cd. wish to segregate and label the sexes. It wd. seem to be a pity that sex alone should be able to bring them together' – to which I replied, What about Hitler? This is because, when she

asked me to join the Cttee of the anti-Fascist Exn. [an anti-fascist exhibition initiated by the Cambridge anti-war Council], I asked why the woman question was ignored. So we go on, sparring and biting. I shouldn't mind giving that woman a toss in the air.[17]

While it is clear that those women who prioritised their feminist identity rightly felt that women's issues were demoted in anti-fascist mobilisation, I would nonetheless argue that we need to modify the perception of a feminist retreat. It will be seen that political women from all points on the political spectrum were fully awake to the need for a woman's perspective on European affairs, and, quick on the heels of that awareness, the urgent necessity for women *qua* women to arm as ideological combatants against the fascist menace. It is by taking a closer look at women's political writing in the period, their constructions of the European women living under dictatorship, the forms and influence of women-dominated internationalist organisations, as well as the more personal responses to European politics that a definable position of feminist anti-fascism can be identified and mapped, even as this position was acutely sensitive to the unprecedented acceleration of the political crisis leading to the outbreak of war.

The ideological precepts of feminist anti-fascism

While the female response to fascism shared some basic premises with men's interpretation of domestic and world events, there were also some important differences informed by sex. The marriage of feminism and anti-fascism was virtually instinctive for the majority of women. British political women came to realise that feminism could only function within a democratic framework, and as Storm Jameson put it: 'only under Western democracy is it still possible for a feminist movement to exist'.[18] Women on the left were attuned early on to the threat posed to them both as a sex and as class warriors. Already in 1932, the National Conference of Labour Women discerned that 'what fascism means to women' is 'a menace which especially endangers the political emancipation of women ... Fascism exalts all those human qualities which react most strongly against the welfare of women in family, social, industrial and professional life'.[19] Similarly, the secretary of the General Council on Fascism, W. M. Citrine, 'expressed profound abhorrence of the suppression of freedom and democracy, the nationalists and military tendencies, and the racial intolerance and degradation of the status of women which were characteristic of fascism'.[20]

The CPGB also gained mileage from the conflation of fascist tyranny and fascist misogyny, with blasting headlines declaring 'Fascism degrades women',[21] prefacing statements by disillusioned German women under Hitler's regime. In February 1934 the Oxford Union debated the resolution 'that Fascism is a menace to world peace', and N. MacDonald, the student who proposed the motion, argued that 'Fascism is not only a menace to international peace, but to the peace between the sexes and the peace between the classes. I believe ... humanity should live without discrimination of sex and nationality.'[22]

Pondering what women could do to prevent the spread of British fascism, Oliver Baldwin was under the impression that women, in their essentialist feminine roles, were best placed to deflate its homo-social and aesthetic appeal, arguing that

> women can do so much more than men to stop tyranny, as they can do to stop wars. Instead of 'How nice you look in your uniform' or 'Blackshirt', I suggest, 'You look a bigger idiot than ever', or 'Bring in the cat; he'll have a laugh at any rate' ... A non-cooperation movement of mothers and sweethearts will prevent their sons from finding an early grave and their lovers from being maimed, for such is bound to be the result if doctrines of Nationalism become the order of the day.[23]

As Robert Brooks prescribed in 1935: 'Feminists of democratic countries may find something to admire in Soviet Russia, on the other hand Fascist dictatorships must represent to them rapid descent into the abyss of black reaction.'[24] In 1936 Ray Strachey prophesised that 'if fascism, or some form of military dictatorship, is established, women will probably lose every scrap of freedom they have won'.[25] As the latter statements suggest, women had a particular stake in the defeat of fascism.

From the First World War, British feminists became well versed in international issues, and, into the 1930s, only by confronting fascism did they come to terms with the essential marriage between women's rights and democratic government. Certainly the International Alliance of Women (IAW) – in which British women played prominent roles – identified this logical progression of concerns along this historical trajectory. Outlining their goals, the IAW explained:

> The work and programme have gradually evolved from the single aim of suffrage, to work for other forms of sex equality, moral, legal and economic. Now something even wider is necessary: how can women

really participate in government and in world affairs. What form of national state and of international co-operation best accords with their needs? Already in 1939, the need for a wider view was felt when the Copenhagen Congress declared: 'There can be no freedom for women when freedom is no longer a recognized right of every individual. There can be no justice nor economic freedom for women, when all justice depends on the will of an oligarchy.'[26]

While sometimes ambiguous in its stand on fascism, employing a number of euphemisms for fascism in its pre-1939 literature (e.g. authoritarian, autocracy, dictatorship, non-democratic),[27] and mindful not to abandon its affiliates in non-democratic countries to their fate, the IAW did perform a number of symbolic gestures in order to make its anti-fascist stand patent. At the 1935 Istanbul Congress they refused to accept the delegate of Mussolini.[28] Also at the Istanbul Congress it was described how 'a thrilling session was held to consider women under different forms of Government. The resolution gives no ideas of the passions and feeling for democracy expressed in the speeches.' Ironically, these speeches were followed by a reception held for the delegates by none other than Ataturk, who 'impressed us all as a man of great personality and drive'.[29] The IAW's German association dissolved rather than take orders from the Nazi Party. And 'at Copenhagen in 1939 our Congress showed its full awareness of the imminent dangers to democracy and the need for women to fight against the totalitarian idea'.[30]

A British feminist critique of fascism emerges from an examination of how writers, journalists and political commentators imagined and portrayed their female counterparts living under repressive regimes. The gendered responses of British political women shared a number of features and observations about the rise of fascism in interwar Europe, and the specific impact of dictatorships on their female populations. First, with different emphases, they all noted the plight of the women of Italy, Germany, Austria and Spain in the face of fascist misogyny, resurgent patriarchy, racism and the oppression of liberal intellectuals. Indeed, it was an almost unanimous view that these regimes represented the return to patriarchal paradigms of the state, and as Naomi Mitchison put it: 'In the re-constituted Teutonic home, the patriarch is again supreme. The state has solidified itself out of the Hegelian abstract into the concrete father god, Wotan, the most sworded and hairy-bellied and prolific of them all.'[31] The most frequently cited evidence of retrogressive measures in these states included the dismissal of women from the professions, the blatant sexism of marriage loan schemes, the forced return of women to the three Ks (Kitchen, Children and Church), drives to increase the birth rate which confined women once again to the sphere of home and family, and the persecution of the Jews and intellectuals – each of which resonated with British women as they reflected on the precarious expansion of women's rights in their own country, and where similar solutions to socio-economic crises were being advocated by more reactionary politicians in their midst. Winifred Holtby was particularly attuned to these resonances. Holtby noted: 'When in the autumn of 1933 the British industrialist, Sir Herbert Austin, acknowledged his desire to turn all women out of his employment and replace them with men, he quoted the example of Herr Hitler.'[32] Comparing and contrasting the backlash against feminism in Germany and Britain, Holtby was also one of the few feminist political critics who gave thought to the threat posed by British fascism and by Mosley's sexist policies to the already precarious position of women in notionally liberal-democratic Britain. She warned: 'Since what has happened in Germany is not unique, it may be worthwhile to consider the attitude of our most conspicuous English candidate for the dictatorship',[33] and she went on to analyse Sir Oswald Mosley's pronouncements on gender roles. Similarly, in a letter to the editor of *Time and Tide*, Betty Archdale noted that there were disturbing similarities between the condition of women in Britain and that of women in Germany before the Nazis seized power. The only difference, she felt, was that 'in England it is generally conceded that women should advance towards equality, whereas Fascism believes in putting the clock back'.[34] Ellen Wilkinson also warned that 'signs are not wanting that indicate the development of Fascism in this country. One way we can help to resist such happenings is to give unstinted support to the victims of the terror in Germany.'[35]

As the last statement suggests, as a second *leitmotif*, anti-fascist women frequently referred to the more tangible evidence of the imprisonment and the torture of women, thus emphasising the inherent contradiction between the fascist exaltation of maternalism and acts of inhumanity against the 'fairer sex'. The 1934 pamphlet *Fascist War on Women: Facts from Italian Gaols* noted that 'such barbarity to political prisoners – to women prisoners in particular – is an outrage upon every standard of decency and humanity … The British public must be made aware of this terrible situation of these horrors and persecutions directed against the very honour of women.'[36] Ellen Wilkinson took up the cause of persecuted women in Nazi Germany, just as Sylvia Pankhurst had earlier embarked on relief work on behalf of individual women victims – she had organised the campaign to free Mrs Matteotti from house arrest, under the auspices of the International Women's Matteotti Committee. Wilkinson spoke of

> the ruined refugee women who have had to leave their homes and their useful work and flee for life itself, the large number of suicides of women once prominent in their various spheres, of which Frau Hanna is a conspicuous example, give only a slight idea of the ruin and misery among women workers that Nazi action has caused ... While it is true that male victims of Nazi ill-treatment far outnumber the women who have suffered, the signed statements we have, either from the women themselves or from their friends, show that their sex has not protected them from the most ferocious brutality.[37]

To stress the point, Wilkinson's pamphlet included a graphic photograph of Mrs Maria Jankowski, the district social director in Berlin, after a beating by Brown shirts, ill-treatment and torture that led to her death. Further, Monica Whatley wrote a pamphlet published by the Six Point Group in 1935 entitled *Women Behind Iron Bars*, drawing attention to women opponents to fascism. In June 1938 Rathbone, Wilkinson, Rhondda and Lady Violet Bonham-Carter co-operated in trying to get a reprieve for Liselotte Hermann who was beheaded in June 1938 after she had tried to publicise abroad evidence of Hitler's rearmament of Germany.

Significantly, reports of the torture of women had a different charge when they came from male commentators. John Strachey, Mosley's former ally in the New Party, worked to establish the Committee for Co-ordinated Anti-Fascist Activity, and among the tactics he used to arouse public anti-fascist indignation was the emphasis on the fascist abuse of women. The menace of fascism and Nazism included the victimisation of women, and he related episodes that had been reported in *The Times* where women were 'stripped and beaten', or 'immediately shot'[38] for disobedience. However, the use of these images revealed a certain opportunism on the part of male writers, as women became objectified once again by standing as symbols to arouse male protective instincts.

A third common thread in British women's conceptions of European fascism was an appreciation of national historical and cultural differences (often explored through an anthropological approach or a comparative sociological one) that were seen to account for both the uneven development of women's liberation across Europe, and for the rise of authoritarian regimes themselves. Holtby could see how the distinct national tradition in the sexual division of labour in Germany meant that, with only some exceptions, 'German women submit. They have always followed fashions and this is a fashion. They have always accepted discipline, and this is the order of authority. They have always been seduced by theory and this has able apologists to rationalise it.'[39] Ethel Mannin also offered a comparative gender history of Italy and Germany to highlight the much greater tragedy of misogynist policies in Nazi Germany. Mannin noted that in Nazi Germany 'all that progressive women have worked for years has been lost', all the more catastrophic in Germany than in Italy because 'the Roman Catholic hold had kept back the feminist movement, so that Italian women had less to lose by Fascism than had the German women, and the anti-feminism of Italian Fascism is therefore less apparent than the German brand'.[40]

Fourth, many women drew on more personal and private experiences – most often gained through travel to the countries concerned, and thus first-hand, if subjective, experiences – that gave them insight into the regrettable counter-revolutions in sexual politics. For instance, Ellen Wilkinson's critique of fascism in the aforementioned pamphlet was based on more than casual observation or the reading of British newspapers, and she had been in Germany in July 1932 as a guest of the Social Democrats just before the autumn Reichstag elections. She was a member of the Committee on Delegated Legislation (set up by the Lord Chancellor to study the effects of the growing power of the Executive over the House of Commons, inspired by events in Germany), along with other anti-fascist women including Isobel Brown (Secretary) and Dorothy Woodman, she sat on the Committee for the Relief of German Victims of German fascism. It was at her flat that 'British anti-fascists from all parties formed a body known as the Reichstag Trial Defence and German Delegation Committee';[41] and she went to Berlin again in 1934 with John Strachey where a People's Court was to try yet more political prisoners. While her interest and activities may have been gender-neutral, one of her biographers notes that it was not only 'the destructive cruelty of Fascism which incensed Ellen. Her feminism was revolted by policies perpetrated by the Nazis against women as women, excluding them from the universities and the professions, from public service and from politics.'[42]

Fifth, British women tended to categorise European women, collectively, as unqualified victims of authoritarian patriarchal states, while evoking their examples to despatch their own warnings about reactionary policies and retrogressive trends in gender relations within British itself. What is clear is that these women were by no means unaware of or undaunted by the mounting political crisis. They imagined, narrated and constructed (and perhaps unwittingly constricted) the history of European women living under authoritarian regimes, and they used these stories of victimisation to reinforce their own claims for inclusive citizenship.

Indeed, it was not until during the Second World War itself that the tone of these contemporary studies of women under fascism shifted, by this point acknowledging the culpability and the agency of Nazi women for Hitler's regime. One of the first texts published in Britain in which women's responsibility for Nazism was acknowledged was Katherine Thomas' *Women in Nazi Germany* (1943). Thomas was not a detached observer of the condition of women in Germany: she was herself a German feminist (and attended the 1929 Congress of the IAW in Berlin where she much admired Mrs M. Corbett Ashby), the widow of a German First World War officer, the mother of one son, a practicing journalist when Hitler came to power, and, at the time of writing, a refugee in Britain from Nazism. Part wartime propaganda, part reflection on personal experience at the very heart of women's politics in Germany, and part journalistic witness, her text begins to represent German women as responsible for the regime and for the war, rather than its hapless victims.

> From my newspaper office I myself noticed the growing number of 'Letters to the Editor', advocating more and more bluntly the need of German youth for some sort of militaristic education ... It seemed astonishing that women with the tragedy of the last and lost war still fresh in their memories, should think of 'goose-stepping' as an educational ideal. I was so disturbed that I took the trouble to enquire into their social backgrounds. It was not difficult to find out that many of them belonged to the former military class that had been dismissed by the Republican Government in accordance with the Treaty of Versailles ... But there were others who had not even this excuse – they were just fascinated by uniforms, the poison of militarism was raging in their blood, the 'revanche' idea did not frighten them, though it obviously meant leading directly into a new war.[43]

At the one and only Hitler meeting she attended in October 1932, she was surprised by the large proportion of women, and also observed how

Hitler made an appeal to them. 'At the meetings of the German Women's Movement we had never managed to secure audiences wither of this number or – still more important – of this sort. These here were the housewives of the lower middle class – predominating among others of all classes.'[44] Thomas also acknowledged that half of the votes cast for the National Socialists were by women. She admitted that women could be dedicated Nazis, and even more callous and ruthless than their male counterparts, regardless of the sexism of the regime: 'How many genuine Nazi fanatics there are among the women (women fanatics who in some respect appear to be capable of a greater degree of dehumanisation than the men) is not known; but in any case it is certain they are not the majority.'[45] Her study concluded with a note of hope and forward planning, hope that women could be awakened to their errors, and plans to target German women with Allied propaganda, and to de-Nazify German womanhood at the point of victory. 'Up to now, however, women have been given only little separate attention; and I suggest, as one long familiar with German women both individually and in the mass, that it is in the highest interest of the Allied war and peace effort that the oversight should be remedied in the future.'[46] While Thomas was breaking new ground by acknowledging women's agency, she was perhaps less aware of an already important library of British feminist anti-fascist literature.

In fact, during the 1930s, the texts in which a brand of feminist anti-fascism became most finely articulated and theorised include Winifred Holtby's *Woman and a Changing Civilization* (1934), Naomi Mitchson's *The Home and a Changing Civilization* (1934), Hilda Browning's *Women and Fascism and Communism* (1935), Hiliary Newitt's *Women Must Choose: The Position of Women in Europe To-day* (1937), Ethel Mannin's *Women and the Revolution* (1938), and, of course, Virginia Woolf's seminal feminist anti-fascist essay *Three Guineas* (1938). One can thus refer to a feminist anti-fascist genre, which extended to the fiction of Katherine Burdekin (*Swastika Night*, 1937), Margaret Storm Jameson (*In the Second Year*, 1936) and Phyllis Bottome (*The Mortal Storm*, 1938), among others. Nor did women writers confine their rage to literary efforts, and Margaret Storm Jameson became president of the P.E.N. Club, the international writers' organisation responsible for helping European refugee intellectuals. Further, women's gendered readings of fascism can be discerned through varied journalism, contributions to the publications of the political parties and a close reading of a range of travel literature that had a more implicit political purpose and impact.[47]

Perhaps the neglect of these texts by historians and Thomas's likely ignorance of this significant body of literature has to do with the fact that the self-contained field of what we would now call 'women's history' or 'women's studies' was in its infancy. It should be noted that the very practice of women writing the history of European women was at an early stage of development, especially when it came to the adoption of methodologies that were political rather than merely social, and broader in their spacial parameters than the confines of the constricted interior of the family. As Winifred Holtby explained: 'The historians of women take it for granted that she is primarily concerned, not with geography, but with biology, not with philosophy, but with personal morality and ideal character.'[48] Permeating these sexist boundaries, the above-mentioned texts each entered male-defined intellectual spaces of journalistic interest and academic study, and are themselves products of feminist achievement, as well as documents that could only be produced outside the fascist context. It is therefore important not to neglect women's contribution to the intellectual history of British anti-fascism, even as there were stringent limits to the ways in which concerned women could give political form and potency to their discerning observations and to their profound fears of both Continental and domestic fascism.

Feminist anti-fascists and British anti-feminism

What accounts for the relative failures of a feminist anti-fascist movement in Britain? It would be too convenient to place the blame on the women themselves, based on an optimistic and idealised vision of the interwar British gender order, especially as British gender relations and the legislative gains women had made since the granting of the suffrage in 1918 contrasted so starkly with the profound sexism and misogyny of fascist regimes. However, we cannot ignore the fact that while a peculiarly woman-centred response to fascism emerges to view upon the closer scrutiny of women's texts, these women were writing against the backdrop of feminist backlash in Britain, and more specifically in the context of an anti-feminist reaction within each political party more specifically. As a result, even when the speech-maker or the author of an anti-fascist pamphlet, article or monograph was female, there was a tendency to downplay gender differences, in order to imply that women did not by necessity have to adopt a female point of view in making a claim for their intellectual and active inclusion in anti-fascist politics. Thus Labour women adopted the language of a class war against fascism with greater facility than a language of a feminist struggle against fascist tyranny; Liberal women towed their party's line by regarding fascism as the greatest threat to liberal democracy, to disarmament and to world peace; and, perhaps predictably, Conservative women tended to place party above sex in their support for or their opposition to appeasement. On the eve of war, even Eleanor Rathbone, Independent MP for the United Universities and president of the 'New' Feminist NUSEC (National Union of Societies for Equal Citizenship) told journalist Rom Landau: 'We must make people at home realise more fully what our democracy and our sense of freedom really mean. Only thus can we strengthen our civilization and fortify our people to stand up for what is best in our own traditions. At present many of them are still ignorant of real conditions in totalitarian countries and are tempted by these doctrines.' This seemingly gender-neutral response to the intensifying world crisis led Landau to judge that Rathbone had identified herself so completely with collective security and a universal perspective that she had shown 'disregard of the less tangible, purely feminine issues'.[49] Similarly, Stephen Spender's harsh judgement of Virginia Woolf – whose *Three Guineas* has since been acknowledged as the most theoretically sophisticated feminist critique of fascism to have emerged in the 1930s – illustrated well the sense that women could do no right in the eyes of their male colleagues. In his autobiography, Spender chose to remember that 'critics like Virginia Woolf, who reproached our generation for writing too directly out of a sense of public duty, failed to see that public events had swamped our personal lives and usurped personal experience'.[50] Spender neglected to mention Woolf's contribution to either the anti-fascist or the feminist cause, constructing her instead as the unengaged, art for art's sake, Bloomsbury intellectual *par excellence.*[51] H. G. Wells had also expressed such a dismissive and myopic view when he chose to note that 'there has been no perceptible women's movement to resist the practical obliteration of their freedom by Fascists and Nazis', a charge that was less a reflection of fact and far more an illustration of fascist-like sexism in Britain itself.[52]

Women's internationalist organisation

Were there grounds for H. G. Wells' accusation? Indeed no greater proof for the inaccuracy of this charge can be provided than a catalogue of British women's organised opposition to fascism at home and abroad, and it is to the activities of British women that I now turn. In a related context, Carol Miller has argued that 'historians of the interwar women's movement in Britain have interpreted feminists' preoccupation with pacifist and internationalist work as one cause for the decline of domestic feminism ... Such interpretation fails to consider the feminist dimension of women's international work' at the League of Nations.[53] Women mounted a number of female-led campaigns against fascism, both in its Continental and British variants. The proliferation of women-led pacifist and anti-fascist groups was a notable feature of the interwar years, and this certainly put to rest any presumption that women should be denied citizenship because they could not think beyond their limited domestic sphere. These women-led organisations included the Women's International League for Peace and Freedom (founded in 1915); the Women's Peace Crusade (founded 1916); the Women's International Alliance (Mrs Margery Corbett Ashby served as president); the Women's Peace Pilgrimage; the Women's Advisory Committee to the Labour and Socialist International; and the Women Against War and Fascism (established in 1934 as the British branch of the Women's World Committee Against War and Fascism). The latter was backed by communist women as well as by Charlotte Despard, Sylvia Pankhurst, Ellen Wilkinson, Vera Brittain, Margaret Storm Jameson, Dame Evelyn Sharpe and Sybil Thorndike. Although the name of this organisation would imply that it was the organised embodiment of feminist anti-fascist ideology, its demands included not only the repeal of the Anomalies Act and the Means Test, and rent exemption for the unemployed, but also the right of married women to work, free maternity hospitals, birth control to be available at local clinics, legislation of abortion and – most daringly – release of all women imprisoned for abortion. 'Only the final section of the charter demanded the disbandment of all fascist organizations, support for Russia's demand for total disarmament, and the conversion of all armament production to production for social use.'[54] Indeed, one could argue that it was a yet another expression of the feminist pacifist line, rather than of the more sophisticated feminist anti-fascist critique that was emerging in women's polemical literature.

The records of the Women's Section of the Labour Party also reveal how central disarmament, foreign policy, and later rearmament were for the women of the party, leaving little doubt that international affairs defined the priorities and anxieties in women's politics in the period. For example, during the inter-war years the Standing Joint Committee of Industrial Women's Organisations lent its members support to the Women's Socialist International, the No More War Movement, the National Council for the Prevention of War, the Peacemakers'

Pilgrimage, the League of Nations Union, the British-American Women's Crusade, the Women's Peace Crusade, and the Women's International League, and in October 1936 set up a 'Women's Committee in Aid of Spanish Workers' (in association with the International Solidarity Fund and the Medical Aid Committee). Women were also involved in the Co-ordinating Committee Against War and Fascism, of which Leah Manning (Labour candidate for Sunderland) became a joint secretary.

With more specific concentration on anti-fascism as such, women also mounted a number of campaigns and organised a number of meetings that focused on the question of women's relationship to fascism. Ellen Wilkinson arranged an anti-fascist conference at Jarrow in April 1934, attracting 600 delegates and addressed by the German Socialist refugee, Edward Conze – leading to their co-authorship of the 1934 book *Why Fascism?* 'The Socialist League's anti-fascism [also] highlighted the place of women in opposing Fascism. The League operated a women's group in 1933–34 and, from the end of 1933, League members presented a series of meetings designed to unite anti-fascists on the Left. Ellen Wilkinson addressed a large public meeting at the Westfield Hall on 'Workers and Women under Fascism' in December 1933, and Constance Barrett, a former Suffragette and Labour parliamentary candidate, delivered a Socialist League lecture on the evils of Fascism at the People's Theatre in Newcastle in March 1934.'[55] In March 1935 Mrs J. L. Adamson, vice-president of the National Labour Party and prospective candidate for Stockport, spoke on the 'Menace of Fascism' at the Stockport Central Hall.[56] While, at face value, the list of organisations and campaigns speaks for the mature politicisation of women in their engagement with foreign affairs and in their reaction to fascism, what is also striking is the absence of a unified movement that would bring together these like-minded women: the debilitating ideological schisms and the failure to mount a popular or united front in democratic countries against fascism was just as characteristic of women's politics as the weakness of interwar political radicalism and 'reactive' politics more generally.

Gender roles in anti-fascist campaigns

It is also interesting to note that grassroots anti-fascist campaigns tended to be framed within the parameters of women's domestic roles, and particularly their role as consumers. Women's groups and the women's sections of political parties initiated a number of boycotts of goods produced in fascist countries. For example, in 1934 the Labour

Party's Committee of Industrial Women's Organisations supported a scheme to purchase toys made by German refugees: 'the Secretary reported on the efforts made with a view of establishing a market in England for toys made by German Socialist refugees in Paris'.[57] In 1937

> a hundred women shoppers from all parts of London met at the Grosvenor Gardens Club, Victoria ... to discuss a boycott of the aggressor nations. Miss Monica Whately, who presided, said: 'We are at a turning point today when democracies must stand together in friendship as the Fascist nations do, and where a boycott of the Fascist nations is the only alternative to the destruction of democracy.' The Duchess of Atholl declared that Franco since April had stamped himself with the chief hall-mark of Fascism – he had obliged all parties to join in one of which he was the chief.[58]

The CPGB also placed emphasis on what women could do as consumers to fight fascism. The Holborn City Council of Action sent out the following appeal: 'Here is what YOU can do now. 1. When you buy goods ask your shopkeeper "Are they German?" If so, refuse. 2. Support shopkeepers who display notice "No German Goods Sold Here." ... Money for German goods means more arms for Hitler not more food for the German people. Play your part for peace.'[59] Across the parties, women also built on a long tradition of female philanthropy by sending aid to the victims of the Spanish Civil War; the Women's Section of the Labour Party set up the 'Women's Committee in Aid of Spanish Workers' (in association with the International Solidarity Fund and the Spanish Medical Aid Committee);[60] and women were at the forefront of a range of organisations set up to help refugees. All this suggests a sexual division of labour in anti-fascist politics. Women also built on a long tradition of women's petitioning by sending countless resolutions to the National Government on the armaments industry, the international crisis, the worsening situations in Spain, China, Abyssinia and so on. However, it might well be argued that the high volume of petitioning was a fair indicator not only of women's concerns and intense engagement in international affairs, but also of their ultimate powerlessness and continued exclusion from the centres of parliamentary power.

Women and violence

However, less tied to essentialist notions of women's social functions, women were also conspicuously present as demonstrators and hecklers at BUF meetings, ready to counter the violence of male and female Blackshirts.[61] In this context I am interested not only at the remarkably high level of female participation and the inclusion of women in popular politics, but also in the way that they were represented by the media. In fact, newspapers rarely missed the opportunity to note the sex of those arrested at anti-fascist demonstrations, and in their descriptions of women's violence, reporters evoked both the memory of the Suffragettes as well as occasionally repeating the condescension and even shock once reserved for Suffragette militancy. Further, it is difficult not to acknowledge that the spectre of woman-on-woman violence excited the male gaze.[62] Whenever possible 'women' were put in the headline, even when upon reading the article it became clear that women had actually played only a minor part in the disorder and violence – this was familiar stomping ground for the tabloid press in particular, reflecting the notion that any form of transgressive behaviour on the part of women sold newspapers. On the one hand, women in street-level combat jarred with cultural constructions of female domesticity and peaceability, and women's political violence evoked once again fears of sex war and gender anarchy. On the other hand, however, it cannot be denied that some pride was expressed at the resistance mounted by women to fascism, in recognition of the particular threat posed to their sex by fascism.

Certainly the BUF press led the charge against its women opponents, constantly questioning the masculinity of its 'Red' and 'Pink' enemies for sending women to the front lines to do their work for them – these were the so-called 'sub-women' of the BUF's racist and misogynist fantasy. And there can be little doubt that being a woman facilitated entry into BUF meetings. For example, in 1936 at a BUF meeting in the Albert Hall: 'ten women anti-Fascists had barricaded themselves in a box. During Sir Oswald's speech they dropped down banners bearing the slogan, "London says NO to Mosley," "Down with Fascism and War." "When the banners were dropped a number of Blackshirts jumped into the box and flung us outside," said one of them. 'One girl was flung out of the building, and a Blackshirt, pointing to an ambulance man, said to her "You'll be in good hands". I was kicked.'[63] Thus women did develop anti-fascist tactics that were specific to their sex.

However, as the press noted, each time with undiminished surprise and disgust, being a woman was no protection from Blackshirt violence. The *Daily Telegraph* reported in 1935: 'Several times Sir Oswald warned hecklers that questions could be taken only at the close of his address, and that if the uproar continued offenders would be forcibly ejected.

Three other persons, including a woman, were later ejected. The police did not interfere, except to release a woman who was surrounded by women Fascists.'[64] Indeed, the violence of fascist/anti-fascist political clashes seemed almost unprecedented, even from the point of view of those women who had fought in the vanguard of the militant Women's Social and Political Union (WSPU) before the war. When speaking at a meeting of the Ex-Servicemen's Movement Against Fascism in Victoria Park, London, in August 1936, 'Miss Sylvia Pankhurst, who was hit in the face by a stone, said she had spoken in Victoria Park many times before, but this was the first time that she had been struck. She did not think the missile was deliberately aimed at her, and it did not do much damage.'[65]

We have already explored the ways in which British women constructed and imagined the women living under fascist regimes in Europe. While there was a general consensus among British feminists that European women were the unwitting and hapless victims of Italian Fascist and Nazi policies of pronatalism, and that the feminist project was completely undermined by the dictators, readings of BUF women were more ambiguous. How did British feminists understand the figure of the Blackshirt woman in Britain? Indeed, the figure of the Blackshirt woman – proud, active, militarised, as well as somewhat heroic in her ability to stand up in the face of anti-fascist jeers and attacks – posed something of a conceptual problem for British feminists intrigued by her presence. In short, it was difficult for even the most committed feminist anti-fascist to deny that Blackshirt women were exercising their political free will and their agency, even to the point of hijacking the image and legacy of the Suffragette. In Irene Clephane's view 'among the oddest spectacles of the day is that of the young woman dressed in black shirts, standing on the pavement edges offering for sale the literature of the fascists, one of whose aims is to deprive women of the very freedom which makes it possible to stand unmolested as they do'.[66] But for Cicely Hamilton the case of Blackshirt women evoked other memories of Suffragette experience, leading her to feel almost protective towards BUF women who were in the line of anti-fascist fire.

> I noticed, by the by, that the crowd's idea of insult had altered little since the early days of the century; when the women's contingent passed us by, the jibes to which it was subjected by certain of my neighbours were the same as the jibes with which we who fought the battle for the suffrage were familiar in the days long ago ... Spite attainment of the vote and all the vote implies; spite freedom

claimed by the younger generation; the tradition that woman's place is in the home and nowhere else, is evidently one that dies hard.[67]

If nothing else, Hamilton's analysis emphasised that feelings of feminist solidarity could sometimes transcend opposition to fascism.

From this exploration of the gender dimension of British anti-fascism, the inevitable conclusion to be reached is that the nature of women's contributions to the anti-fascist campaign was just as individual, just as spontaneous and just as amorphous in collective terms as male-directed anti-fascism. But there was one key difference between male and female anti-fascism, a divergence of experience that male-centrist approaches have been wont to ignore or overlook. Writing in *Time and Tide* in 1934, Betty Archdale noted:

> Our power is very slight, partly because of our subordinate position [as women], and partly because we are in the very weak position of being anti-Fascist without being pro anything else. To prevent Fascism spreading it is essential to have an alternative. The obvious alternative is Socialism. But it is difficult for a convinced feminist (or a convinced Socialist for that matter) to join the Labour Party. One would almost feel safer with the Fascists than with many Trade Unionists ... The working-class women can join the Communist Party (though even the *Daily Worker* has a Woman's Page), but for middle and upper class women, not convinced of the necessity of class war and revolution, the path is not so easy.[68]

The ideological and organisational challenges faced by British anti-fascist women thus cut to the heart of the tensions and the disappointments in women's politicisation and in their inclusion in post-enfranchisement interwar politics. As has been demonstrated, feminist anti-fascism was a definable creed, yet it was also a creed that could find no viable political vessel in the still male-supremacist world of British party and popular politics of the 1930s. Women anti-fascists were trapped within a double helix of exclusion, and their continued exclusion from the historiography only reinforces the truth of this observation.

Notes

1. Ethel Mannin, *Women and the Revolution* (London: Secker & Warburg, 1938), pp. 201–2.
2. 'Fascists Thrown Out', *Morning Post*, 9 November 1936.

3. British Communist historiography has certainly long emphasised the discord and lack of co-ordination of anti-fascism.

> The anti-fascist struggle was many sided and in spite of its small size and ideological isolation, the Communist Party was able to make a major contribution to initiating and sustaining the fight of those sections of the British people, who for many and various reasons opposed fascism and war. ... The anti-fascist and anti-war movements recorded many successes and engaged many and various people in action, but these movements tended to remain informal with the leading body of the labour movement refusing to take part officially. (Mike Power, 'The Struggle Against Fascism and War in Britain 1931–39', *Our History*, Pamphlet 70.)

4. Nigel Copsey, *Anti-Fascism in Britain* (Basingstoke: Macmillan, 2000), p. 4.
5. See also Dan Stone, *Responses to Nazism in Britain, 1933–1939* (Basingstoke: Palgrave, 2003).
6. J. Alberti, 'British Feminists and Anti-Fascism in the 1930s', in Sybil Oldfield (ed.), *This Working-Day World: Women's Lives and Culture(s) in Britain 1914–1945* (London: Taylor & Francis, 1994), pp. 111–22. Alberti also suggests that 'generational difference may in subtle ways have undermined the resistance that feminists undoubtedly offered to Fascism'.
7. 'Fascism and Democracy', *Report of the Fifteenth National Conference of Labour Women*, Town Hall, Cheltenham, 20, 21 and 22 June 1934.
8. For women in the Labour Party, 'economic depression, reactionary governments and the spread of fascism threatened the very survival of their class and the party, appealing to their deepest political instincts to protect the down-trodden and pushing their struggle for rights as party women into the background'. From the perspective of feminist history this may have been unfortunate. However, Labour women were apt to hold the sentiment that the 1930s were the apex of their political careers and consciousness, and felt satisfied that 'in these years, Labour men and women marched together against the hated Means Test; they joined arms to make barriers against Mosley's blackshirts; they raised money for Spanish republicans and collected signatures for the Peace Ballot.' (Pamela Graves, *Labour Women: Women in British Working Class Politics 1918–1939* (Cambridge: Cambridge University Press, 1994), pp. 181–2.)
9. 'Miss Wilkinson is Puzzled: Fascism and Socialism', *Daily Worker*, 7 June 1935.
10. Pamela Brookes, *Women at Westminster* (London: Peter Davies, 1967), p. 118.
11. Organised opposition to a Mosley Rally at Albert Hall on 22 March 1936:

> 'the campaign for a counter-demonstration to the Mosley Rally is going ahead with increasing speed. No less than 23 prominent personalities have given their names in support of the appeal made by John Strachey for organising all the anti-Fascist forces in London against Mosley's poisonous propaganda. These names represent people of different shades of political opinion, including:- ... Victor Gollancz, Sylvia Pankhurst, Ethel Mannin, Storm Jameson. ...'

'Mosley Causes Tide of Protest: Strong Opposition by Well-Known People', (*Daily Worker*, 11 March 1938). There are a number of studies in literary criticism/literary history that deal with British women writers and fascism. See Phyllis Lassner, *British Women Writers of World War II: Battlegrounds of their own* (London: Macmillan, 1998); Marlou Joannou, *'Ladies Please Don't Smash These Windows': Women's Writing, Feminist Consciousness and Social Change 1918–38* (Oxford: Berg, 1998); Daphne Patai, *The Orwell Mystique: A Study in Male Ideology* (Amherst: University of Massachusetts Press, 1984). For women's literary response and resistance to fascism on the Continent, see R. Pickering-Iazzi (ed.), *Mothers of Invention: Women, Italian Fascism and Culture* (Minneapolis: Minnesota University Press, 1995).

12. Helen Jones, *Women in British Public Life* (Harlow: Longman, 2000), p. 113. While Jones provides enlightening evidence about the range of women's anti-fascist activities, I do not feel that she has gone far enough in her evidentiary base, thus leading to what I feel is an unfair conclusion about the nature and the scope of women's anti-fascist activities.

13. Nigel Todd, *In Excited Times* (Whitley Bay: Bewick Press, 1995), p. 42.

14. Susan Pedersen, 'The Future of Feminist History', *Perspectives: American Historical Association Newsletter*, 38, 7, October 2000, pp. 1, 20–5.

15. Nigel Copsey, *Anti-Fascism in Britain*, p. 1.

16. See Martin Durham, *Women and Fascism* (London: Routledge, 1998); Julie V. Gottlieb, *Feminine Fascism: Women in Britain's Fascist Movement, 1923–1945* (London: I.B. Tauris, 2000); Dave Renton, *This Rough Game: Fascism and Anti-Fascism* (Stroud: Sutton, 2001), pp. 38–50.

17. (Sunday, 6 January 1935) in Anne Oliver Bell (ed.), *The Diary of Virginia Woolf: Vol. IV: 1931–1935* (London: Hogarth Press, 1982), p. 273.

18. Ethel Mannin, *Women and the Revolution* (London: Secker & Warburg, 1938), pp. 201–2.

19. *Report of the National Conference of Labour Women*, Brighton, 14, 15 and 16 June 1932, p. 26.

20. *The Times*, 5 September 1934.

21. Anti-Fascist Special: Facts Against Fascist Fancies (n.d), CP/CENT/SUBJ/ 04/09. 'The younger generation of thinking women is already beginning to feel that it gave its support to a peculiar masculine madness when, acting on the basis of the highest national feeling, it elevated the active leaders of German liberation to the position of unqualified masters of its own fate.'

22. 'Fascism—Is it for Peace? Opposing Views at Oxford Discussion', *Oxford Mail*, 22 February 1934.

23. Oliver Baldwin, 'A Farewell to Liberty', *Daily Herald*, 14 June 1933.

24. Robert C. Brooks, *Deliver Us from Dictators* (Philadelphia: University of Pennsylvania Press, 1935), p. 114.

25. Ray Strachey, 'Changes in Employment', in Ray Strachey (ed.), *Our Freedom and its Results* (London: Hogarth Press, 1936), p. 153.

26. International Alliance of Women, Fourteenth Congress, Interlaken, 10–17 August 1946; M. I. Corbett Ashby papers, Box 483, International MICA/C.

27. 'On Tuesday a thrilling session was held to consider women under different forms of Government. The resolution gives no idea of the passion and feeling from democracy expressed in the speeches.' (M. I. Corbett Ashby, 'Twelfth Congress: Istanbul', *International Women's News: Jus Suffragii*, 29, 9, June 1935.)

28. Notwithstanding the IAW's snub of 1935, while Corbett Ashby was secretary of the International Women Suffrage Alliance, an association representing

progressive women of forty countries, the annual conference was opened in Rome in 1923 by Mussolini. 'Prominent Liberal Women: Mrs Corbett Ashby', *Liberal Women's News*, No.42, March 1925. The WNLF's Miss Garland told the story of her first fascist encounter, her impromptu meeting with Mussolini at the same 1923 conference. See 'Miss Garland and Mussolini', *Liberal Women's News*, May 1933.

29. M. I. Corbett Ashby, 'Twelfth Congress: Istanbul', *The International Women's News: Jus Suffragii*, 29, 9, June 1935.
30. Re: The International Democratic Federation of Women (n.d), Corbett Ashby Papers, Box 483: International MICA/C, Women's Library.
31. Naomi Mitchison, *Home and a Changing Civilization* (London: John Lane the Bodley Head, 1934), p. 104–5.
32. Winifred Holtby, *Women and a Changing Civilization* (London, 1934), p. 152.
33. Winifred Holtby, *Women and a Changing Civilization*, p.161.
34. 'Fascism', *Time and Tide*, 28 April 1934.
35. Ellen Wilkinson, *The Terror in Germany* (British Committee for the Relief of the Victims of German Fascism, 1934), p. 19.
36. *Fascist War on Women: Facts from Italian Gaols* (London, 1934), p. 30–1.
37. Ellen Wilkinson, *The Terror in Germany*, p. 12.
38. John Strachey, *The Menace of Fascism* (London: Gollancz, 1933), p. 9.
39. 'A sense of bitterness inflects many public utterances, speeches and article, made on the subject of women's position in the state. The economic slump has reopened the question of women's right to earn. The political doctrine of the corporative state in Italy and Germany had inspired new pronouncements upon the function of the woman citizen. Psychological fashions arouse old controversies about the capacity of the female individual. The problems which feminists of the 19th century thought to solve along the lines of rationalism, individualism, and democracy, present new difficulties in an age of mysticism, community and authority.' (Winifred Holtby, *Women and a Changing Civilization*, p. 7.) Holtby also adopted a comparative and relative perspective of women's historical progress across Europe: 'The explanation of the women's readiness to go [from employment] is largely historical. The post-war economic independence of women was not only more novel in Germany than it was in England, it was more disturbing. Far more deeply rooted in Germany than in English consciousness was the tradition that women's interests should be confined to "Kinder, Kuche, Kirche"' (p. 154). She could see how this distinct national tradition in the sexual division of labour in Germany meant that, with some exceptions, 'German women submit. They have always followed fashions and this is a fashion. They have always accepted discipline, and this is the order of authority. They have always been seduced by theory and this has able apologists to rationalise it' (p. 157). As such, Holtby acknowledges German women's complicity and responsibility for the regime under which they now live.
40. Ethel Mannin, *Women and the Revolution* (London: Secker & Warburg, 1938), p. 200.
41. Vera Brittain, *Testament of Experience: An Autobiographical Story of the Years 1925–1950* (London: Gollancz, 1957), p. 93.
42. Betty D. Vernon, *Ellen Wilkinson* (London: Croom Helm, 1982), p. 157.
43. Katherine Thomas, *Women and Nazi Germany* (London: Gollancz, 1943), pp. 11–12.

44. Katherine Thomas, *Women and Nazi Germany*, p. 24.
45. Katherine Thomas, *Women and Nazi Germany*, p. 65.
46. Katherine Thomas, *Women and Nazi Germany*, p. 99.
47. See, for example, Rosita Forbes, *Women of All Lands* (in 18 weekly parts, *c.*1939) – a politically ambivalent look at the condition of women in countries around the world, based on the observations of a world traveller with amateur anthropological interests; Cicely Hamilton, *Modern Italy: As Seen by an Englishwoman* (London: J.M. Dent, 1932) – while critical of Italian Fascism, somewhat less so than one would imagine; Muriel Currey, *A Woman at the Abyssinian War* (London: Hutchinson, 1936) – although she was pro-Fascist, her book still fits into this genre.
48. Winifred Holtby, *Women and a Changing Civilization*, p. 4.
49. 'Miss Rathbone was against Germany, against Italy and Japan, not because she disliked any of these countries – in fact, she confessed to having a weakness for most of them – but because she was convinced that their policies threatened Western civilization; and because she has learnt during her life that evil cannot be combated unless each in his private life and in his own small way acts upon his principles.' When I asked her what she considered the necessary long-view policies, she replied: "How can we think of such policies while all these horrors go on in Germany, China and Spain! We must first concentrate on helping the victims" ... Her entire work is overshadowed by the horror of modern barbarism. 'Landau argues that Rathbone has identified herself completely with collective security etc., and shown "disregard of the less tangible, purely feminine issues".' (Rom Landau, *Love for a Country: Contemplations and Conversations* (London: Nicolson & Watson, 1939), pp. 308–9)
50. Stephen Spender, *World Within: The Autobiography of Stephen Spender* (London: Hamish Hamilton, 1953), p. 164.
51. Spender's characterization is all the more incongruous when set beside the following entry in Woolf's diary: 'There are incessant conversations – Mussolini, Hitler, MacDonald. All these people incessantly arriving at Croydon, arriving at Berlin, Moscow, Rome; flying off again – while Stephen [Spender] and I think how to improve the world.' (Saturday, 20 April 1935), in Anne Oliver Bell (ed.), *The Diary of Virginia Woolf: Vol. IV: 1931–1935* (London: Hogarth Press, 1982), p. 303.
52. Quoted in Virigina Woolf, *Three Guineas* (London: Chatto & Windus, 1984), p. 155.
53. Carol Miller, ' "Geneva—the Key to Equality": Inter-war Feminists and the League of Nations', *Women's History Review*, 3, 2, 1994, pp. 219–45.
54. Jill Liddington, *The Life and Times of a Respectable Rebel: Selina Cooper, 1864–1946* (London: Virago, 1984), p. 411.
55. Nigel Todd, *In Excited Times*, p. 45.
56. Adamson said that

> in Italy when the Fascists seized power the first thing that happened was the entire suppression of the Socialist and Co-operative movements. She had met leading international Socialists who had told her that Fascism could not come to any country but Italy, but within a short period a Fascist dictatorship was set up in Germany. In this country Sir Oswald Mosley and his Blackshirts were flouting the law by the training of a private military

and air force, and Sir John Gilmour, the Home Secretary, had evaded the issue when he was challenged on the point. In addition, the Fascists were trying to worm their way into the trade unions and Labour and co-operative movements, and, at the other end of the scale, money was being found to finance the movements by leading industrialists.' ('The Growth of Fascism: A Spreading Evil', *Manchester Guardian*, 4 March 1935)

57. Minutes, 12 October 1933, Standing Joint Committee of Industrial Women's Organizations, General Purposes Committee, 1922–156, Box I, Labour History Museum.

58. 'Women's War on Fascism', *News Chronicle*, 17 December 1937. Whately felt compelled to disassociate herself from the CPGB, and emphasize that anti-fascist activism was not always the outgrowth of the opposite extreme.

> 'I desire to state: I am not and have never been a member of the Communist Party, nor could I have affiliation with the Party as long as they deny freedom to any to practice their religious beliefs. As a Catholic with full freedom to practice my religious beliefs in a Protestant country, I realize that only under a Democratic system can such religious freedom exist, and for that reason I am opposed to Dictatorships, Fascist or Communist.' (27 February 1937 (CP/CENT/SUBJ/04/04))

Of course women, like men, were opposed to fascism for a variety of reasons, fear of sexual repression and the denial of women once again of their citizenship rights were among the reasons. Female anti-fascist could be motivated by primary fealty to religion, class, or region, or fear for the status of the artist and the intellectual under fascism etc. However, it must be seen as more than incidental that they were also women, and inevitable their gender identity coloured their anti-fascism.

59. "To Save Peace and Save Britain Hitler must be Stopped', Issued by Holborn and City Council of Action, 84 Grays Inn Rd., WC1 (CP/CENT/SUBJ/04/04).

60. 'Help for Spain: The Secretary [Miss Sutherland] reported the interview she had with Senora de Palencia at Edinburgh, as a result of which she had sent an appeal to Women's Sections asking them to assist the Spanish workers by contributing wool or knitted garments, and a conversation with Miss Lawrence and Dr Somerville Hastings, who agreed that it would be desirable if a Committee were set up under the auspices of the SJC to deal with the matter.' (SJC minutes, Thursday, 15 October 1936.)

61. See, for example, 'Women Fight at Fascist Meeting', *Morning Post*, 23 October 1936; 'Cars Fired: Girl Hurled into Window', *Daily Mail*, 12 October 1936.

62. 'Hand-to-hand fighting broke out at Hampstead Town Hall last night during a Fascist meeting, and there was further disorder when the Fascists, at the close of the meeting, marched to their headquarters. They were surrounded by a crowd yelling "Down with the black rats." ... Mr Joyce was frequently heckled during his speech, and pandemonium broke out when the stewards were called upon to eject a woman interrupter. Chairs were overturned, men and women struggled on the floor and the rest of the audience shouted. Some women were involved in a scuffle and several of them were seen to be exchanging blows.' 'Women Fight at Fascist Meeting', *Morning Post*, 23 October 1936.

63. 'Baton Charge Against London Crowd', *Daily Herald*, 23 March 1936.

64. 'Six Arrests at Fascist Meeting', *Daily Telegraph*, 25 July 1935.
65. '18 people were arrested in London yesterday as a result of two political disturbances. At a demonstration in Victoria Park organized by the Ex-Servicemen's Movement against Fascism nine arrests were made, and nine people were also arrested in consequence of disturbances at a meeting in Parliament Fields, Hampstead, held by the BUF ... Miss Sylvia Pankhurst, who was hit in the face by a stone, said she had spoken in Victoria Park many times before, but this was the first time that she had been struck. She did not think the missile was deliberately aimed at her, and it did not do much damage.' ('Anti-Fascist Demonstrators Attacked', *Manchester Guardian*, 31 August, 1936.) The Ex-Servicemen's National Movement, headquartered at 102 Whitechapel Rd. East London, also consisted of a Women's Section headed by Mrs McKennie (see CP/CENT/SUBJ/04/07) Isobel Brown also spoke at Stoke Newington Town Hall under the auspices of the Ex-Servicemen's National Movement on the subject 'In Defence of Democracy: Against Fascist Intolerance and Persecution' (CP/CENT/SUBJ/04/07).
66. Irene Clephane, *Towards Sex Freedom* (London: John Lane the Bodley Head, 1935), p. 228.
67. Cicely Hamilton, *Modern England as seen by an Englishwoman* (London: J. M. Dent, 1938), pp. 73–4.
68. Betty Archdale, 'Fascism', *Time and Tide*, 28 March 1934.

5
'Left-Wing Fascism' in Theory and Practice[1]

Philip M. Coupland

Although there have been more nuanced interpretations available from the left, the conceptualisation of fascism within the labour movement has often more or less reflected the 1930s dogma that it was, or aspired to be: the 'terrorist dictatorship of capitalism in extreme decay'.[2] In recent years the theorisation of fascism has undergone a significant transformation with Roger Griffin and others arguing that fascist parties cannot be seen simply as an agency of a bourgeoisie, nor their ideology merely as a front for 'class interest'.[3] This so-called 'liberal' approach has in turn been criticised. For example, David Renton has argued against seeing 'fascism as being simply a set of ideas, observable in the discussion of intellectuals', instead stressing that 'fascism should be understood historically, through an examination of the relationship between its professed ideas and its actual practice, which involves looking at what it did at least as much at what it said'.[4] Although the work that Renton upbraids does not generally present fascism as a 'positive movement',[5] his emphasis on the need to examine both language and action is a valid one and, given the stress on the power of 'discourse' in contemporary historiography, perhaps timely.

Renton's critique also took in a number of studies of the British Union of Fascists (BUF), one of which he criticised for asserting that the BUF was 'left-wing'.[6] The article in question actually sought to suggest that the BUF included *some* blackshirts drawn to fascism for reasons which in other circumstances might have drawn them to socialism and that fascist discourse contained *elements* in common with left-wing parties.[7] As Renton has written on this topic: 'fascism could be a contradictory, even Janus-faced phenomenon, *both* a class ideology, acting in the strategic interests of at least some members of the capitalist class, *and* also a mass movement, made up of ordinary people'.[8]

As *Fascism: Theory and Practice* observes, fascist movements of the 1930s could seek support with 'socialist rhetoric' at the same time including 'social reactionaries' whose identity as class actors orientated them against the realisation of such rhetoric.[9] This chapter argues that an analysis of the evolving relationship between practice and discourse in relation to fascist promises to transcend class conflict sheds light on this apparently incongruous 'left-wing' aspect of a 'reactionary' movement. Specifically, it will focus on the relationship between, on the one hand, attempts by the BUF to speak on issues, and to constituencies, associated with the working-class movement and, on the other, the fortunes of working class and former socialist activists within the fascist movement.

In brief summary, 'socialism' in Britain during the 1930s implied two major projects. First, the betterment of the lives of working people by engendering full employment and through measures later spoken of collectively as a 'welfare state'; second, the fostering of a new relationship between persons by dissolving class conflicts and inequalities. The BUF pledged to achieve these objectives within their utopia, the 'corporate' state, promising full employment in a high-wage economy and enhanced facilities for health, education and so forth. Blackshirts also stressed that the 'Greater Britain' would be classless, achieved not by socialising private property but via the corporate state to harmonise contending economic interests and a 'spiritual revolution' by which class conflict would be transcended in the creation of a harmonious nation built around people's common identity as Britons. The practicality of these aims is not at issue here, our interest in them is as a body of rhetoric – the allure of which the Marxist intellectual John Strachey could not deny – spoken to persuade the working class.[10]

Turning from rhetoric towards action, the BUF – via the abortive New Party – emerged, as Rajani Palme Dutt wrote, 'from the heart of the Labour Party and the Independent Labour Party' (ILP).[11] Mosley had been a member of the ILP, a Labour minister and sat on the party's National Executive Committee. Aneurin Bevan helped to write the *National Policy* with which the New Party was launched and Mosley counted the miner's leader Arthur Cook and John Strachey among his collaborators.[12] H. G. Wells described him as having been 'a promising new convert to the Labour party, with communist leanings' and another well placed observer recorded that before his break with the party '[n]obody ... could have doubted the genuineness of Mosley's Socialism'.[13] A long-time collaborator with Mosley, George Catlin, similarly believed that 'the objects of Sir Oswald Mosley were – and about this I can venture to speak with some assurance – frankly socialistic'.[14]

A host of figures from the left followed Mosley into the BUF. Ellen Wilkinson and Edward Conze noted in 1934 that 'many of his followers and a surprising number of headquarters' staff of the Fascists were members of the Labour Party or the I.L.P.'[15] These included Robert Forgan and John Beckett, both former socialist MPs, George Sutton, previously chair of North St Pancras Labour Party, Wilfred Risdon, ex-divisional organiser of the ILP in the Midlands and the socialist and one-time suffragette Mary Richardson.[16] Other ex-ILP and Labour Party activists prominent in the BUF included John Scanlon, Thomas Moran, Marshall Diston, W. J. Leaper, Henry Gibbs, Leslie Cumings, Rex Tremlett and Alexander Miles.[17] Among ex-communists to join were Alexander Raven Thomson, the chief blackshirt ideologue and E. D. Randall, the author of the BUF's 'Marching Song'.[18] Many rank-and-file Blackshirts during this early period were also from the left.[19]

In his unpublished contemporary memoir 'After My Fashion', John Beckett wrote:

My speeches were practically the same as those I had made in the Independent Labour Party, because my change of organisation had no effect upon my Socialist convictions and policy. Indeed I found in the British Union of Fascists far more sincere and earnest Socialist conviction than I had ever seen in the Labour Party ... About twenty per cent of the membership were mainly conservative in outlook, but the great majority of the membership were either converted Socialists or young people who, ten years before, would certainly have found their way into the Socialist movement.[20]

Commenting on Mosley's debate against his erstwhile ILP comrade James Maxton at the Friend's Meeting House in early 1933, *The New Clarion* wrote that '[f]or the first twenty minutes Mosley talked Socialism, except that he referred to a corporate state instead of the co-operative commonwealth'.[21] A supporter of another fascist organisation dismissed 'the propaganda of the British Union of Fascists' as 'merely a Socialistic attack on capitalism under the name of Fascism'. Mosley had 'practically staffed the BUF' with ex-socialists who had 'brought their ILP propaganda with them'.[22]

The political background and ideological imperatives of the early BUF were also reflected in the creation of the Fascist Union of British Workers (FUBW). The FUBW was originally formed as a local initiative on the part of the BUF Battersea branch under J. P. D. Paton, in 1934 a Covent Garden porter and formerly a local leader of the National Unemployed

Workers Movement (NUWM) and Michael Goulding.[23] In February 1933 *Blackshirt* boasted that the FUBW had emerged from 'one of the staunchest strongholds of the Moscow men', the one-time constituency of the Communist MP Saklatvala.[24] In April that year Charles Bradford, a Welsh ex-communist steel erector, took charge and the FUBW was then integrated into the national organisation, moving to the newly opened 'Black House' headquarters in August 1933.[25] While subordinate to its 'parent body' the FUBW had a distinct identity with its own leadership structure, membership cards and insignia.[26] An internal BUF document suggested that the FUBW's role might be 'compared to that of the TUC in relation to the Labour Party'.[27] Although it recruited from amongst existing members of the BUF it was also possible to join the FUBW exclusively. It was presumably those who were solely members of the latter body who wore the brown shirt which was its official uniform.

Under the title 'What is the FUBW?' the organisation described itself as the 'forerunner of the one big administrative union which will represent the workers' interests under fascism'.[28] The FUBW saw itself as anticipating the 'Central Trades Union Administration' which one day would deal with matters like 'health, unemployment, and death benefits, workmen's compensation' for all workers in the corporate state, leaving individual unions to deal with the 'industrial side' of trade union work.[29] At the same time, fascists, 'in readiness for the Occupational Franchise', were commanded to campaign for single industry unions to replace bodies like the Transport and General Workers' Union (TGWU).[30] The FUBW, like the projected corporate state, was divided up into 'a special section for each industry'.[31] Groups established included coach drivers, civil servants, musicians, catering staff, actors, taxi drivers and tourism workers.[32]

Regarding the membership of the FUBW, one early report described 'the Brown Shirt Section' as recruiting 'unemployed manual workers of the navvy type as distinct from the younger and rather better educated men who make up the Black Shirts'.[33] A communist analysis of the BUF in Autumn 1933 admitted that 'the fascist movement attracts to itself ... certain sections of the proletariat. Disappointed by the policy of the Labour Party and its "labour governments"... some sections of the unemployed are caught by the grandiloquent slogans of fascism'.[34] Geographically the FUBW seems to have been strongest in London. Manchester, Newcastle, Stoke and Birmingham were also centres of activity and Luton, Longton, Oxford, Wolverhampton and Bath were mentioned as locations of FUBW branches.[35]

'[P]articular attention to the organisation of meetings in working class districts' was noted. As to the message articulated at these meetings

Communist International recorded that recruitment from the working classes was

> achieved by putting forward a slogan of struggle against the Means Test, demagogy 'against bankers and speculators – for the unemployed', demands of work for the unemployed, and so on. Against the Means Test the fascists put forward the slogan of a 'job test' and of work and decent wages. At the same time fascists are verbally against wage cuts and salary cuts.[36]

Alongside these policy pledges was criticism of the performance of the Trades Unions and Labour Party. In a case in Falmouth, recruits were sought with literature attacking both the TGWU and the Seaman's Union.[37] Typically, trades union officials were portrayed as cowardly placemen, interested only in lining their own pockets or as communists who put politics and the interests of 'foreigners' before British workers' interests. One circular to 'all lower trade union organisations' declared: 'fascism fights for you while the Labour organisation betrays you'.[38] Concerning the potential of rhetoric of this type Wal Hannington, leader of the NUWM, saw that its danger lay 'in its deceptiveness, because in the ears of so many workers it rings true'.[39]

In addition to street corner rhetoric, 'Fascist clubs for the unemployed' were established in, among other places, London and Manchester where it was reported that unemployed men were offered 'cigarettes, a plate of soup and sometimes even a few shillings'.[40] The FUBW, perhaps reflecting the ambitions of the 'Central Trade Unions Administration' to come, also provided services to unemployed workers, including a licensed employment bureau and the representation of workers before Public Assistance Committees.[41] Legal interventions conducted under the auspices of the FUBW included interventions in Court of Referees cases and it also advertised its concern for the 'sweated worker', citing the case of 'ten girls (one consumptive) working in a room barely five feet wide without a window, lit continually with gas' which it discovered and reported.[42]

Direct action was taken as well. This included preventing evictions, with, in one case, blackshirts defying bailiffs and the police.[43] Blackshirts also attempted to intervene in support of strikers at the Firestone factory in Brentford in 1933. An anti-fascist recorded that 'a few days after the beginning of the strike, fascists made their appearance and expressed their solidarity with the workers. They also offered their services as pickets, and brought tea and sandwiches for the workers.'

Despite being rebuffed, the blackshirts continued to court the strikers and attend their meetings, leaflets were distributed and at one such event a busman from the Turnham Green garage spoke in favour of accepting the fascists' help.[44] In another case, it was claimed that the FUBW had successfully intervened in a strike by acting as intermediaries in a wage dispute.[45] An unsuccessful attempt to intervene at a dispute at the Avon India Rubber Company and a case of fascists persuading members of the TGWU to strike (who later lost their jobs) were also recorded in spring 1934.[46]

Members of the FUBW were encouraged to join a wide range of workers' organisations in a bid to gain influence. An internal BUF circular directed that

> Fascists should be elected through the Trade Union Branch Committees ... Such Fascist members of the Trade Union committees will be able to stop grants of money which would otherwise go to the Labour Party ... Members of the FUBW should take part in the activities of all unemployed associations, mayors' funds, even [the] NUWM, pressing forward the policy of the FUBW and making efforts to be elected to committees of such associations.[47]

The communist White described the fascists as responsible for 'great activity among the workers' and reported that 'cases of workers coming to work in blackshirts ... occur more often'.[48] This was echoed by a confidential intelligence report obtained by the National Union of Railwaymen (NUR) in which the FUBW was described as having in 'three cases ... obtained a strong footing in Trade Unions'. The same report also mentioned a 'Fascist Club' set up in a non-unionised firm of 2,000 employees where 'some of the workers wear blackshirts in the factory'.[49] TUC General Secretary Walter Citrine was clearly aware of these tactics and their intention and named a possible source of inspiration for them:

> They were using the methods of the Communists. They were using every strike, every grievance, as a means of agitation. Their speakers were to be found outside the works where strikes took place, particularly unofficial strikes, where there was a chance of criticising the union officials or organisers. ... They were conducting their agitation among the unemployed. They were posing as representatives before Public Assistance Committees. In short, they were adopting all the means in their power to ingratiate themselves into the lives of the

working class in this country. They claimed to be a working class organisation.[50]

In view of the many blackshirts who had crossed over from the left these were tactics readily to hand.

Alexander Miles, whose contemporary account of his time in the BUF is in the TUC archives,[51] would have required no instruction on 'communist' technique. A seaman by occupation, Miles came from a working-class family of strong socialist convictions and joined the ILP in 1919. At one time Secretary of the Gateshead Branch of the National Unemployed Workers Committee, Miles cited the corruption and failure of the Labour councillors of Gateshead as being among his reasons for later joining the BUF. He also served as Honorary Chairman of the Newcastle Branch of the National Boilermen's and Firemen's Union and was Tyneside leader of the Seamen's Minority Movement, taking part in the 'Unofficial Seaman's Strike' of 1925. The failure of the 'Tyneside Leadership of the Communist Party, which virtually controlled the SMM' was cited by Miles as the reason for his abiding distrust of the CPGB. After that he withdrew from active politics until approached in 1933 by 'an old friend and associate' from his time in the ILP, Wilfred Risdon, who had become BUF Director of Propaganda.[52]

Miles' assessment of the early BUF matched that of Beckett. He wrote that

> Older members of the Socialist Movement, having experienced the fervour of the pioneer days, and others who remember the spirit of the Socialist and Labour Party membership in the years immediately after the war, may find it difficult to believe that in the Fascist Movement in 1933 there was a spirit of comradeship or brotherhood, equal to the best of the early days of the Socialist Crusade's youth and early maturity.

'[Y]outhful Fascists [who] had no previous political experience' were drawn in by Mosley's message of 'Patriotism plus Revolution' and 'Down with the Old Gang'. Even as a man with political experience to 'steady' him, Miles 'was swept up in this hot flood of feeling that here was a Leader who typified Youth and the revolt of Youth against "things as they are" '.

Posted to Liverpool in August 1933, Miles worked on a draft of the BUF's shipping policy and got 'some sympathy among seamen and dockers' in the area.[53] At this time Liverpool, along with London, were recorded by the TGWU as areas where fascist propaganda was 'particularly prevalent'.[54] To back up these efforts, plans were laid to expand the FUBW such that an Industrial Organiser was required and Miles put forward a Mr Davies, 'a docker, and civil servant, an ex-communist' for that role. Miles claimed that the FUBW 'was growing more rapidly than the parent body' at this point, but it was then that he 'ran up against' what he later would realise was 'Mosley's distrust of a working class wing of organised character' and no finance was forthcoming.

The BUF made particular efforts to recruit among transport workers. In London, fascists, including 'some holding official jobs on the [London Passenger Transport] Board' (LPTB), distributed a pamphlet promising busmen 'the moon' in October 1933.[55] Then, the following month, Bradford of the FUBW, in a 'craftily worded' letter to Bert Papworth, a communist and leading member of the London busmen's Rank and File movement, sought to show that fascist sympathies lay with the militant busmen against the leadership of the TGWU. Papworth wrote: 'They agree with R and F policy, which is out for better conditions for London Busmen.' They 'are not against Trade Unions, but against political graft of such as Peters and Bevin'.[56] Naturally, Papworth made clear that no help was needed from fascists. Nonetheless, blackshirts continued to try to exploit tensions between transport workers and the TGWU leadership. Like Papworth's movement, the BUF proposed a 'T.O.T' (Trains, Omnibuses, Trams) to unite transport workers against the combined employers of the LPTB.[57] *Blackshirt* also reported the FUBW's representation at a disciplinary board of a fascist called Hewitt who was also a member of the Rank and File movement.[58] The Labour Party received reports of fascist 'activities in [the] T & G Workers Union' in Gateshead and, in Newcastle, the 'attempt to form a Transport Union' which had 'about 50 members including Corporation busmen'.[59]

Moving to Sparkbrook in September 1933, Miles 'discovered that the Birmingham Corporation Municipal Bus Service was seething with discontent over the speeding-up of schedules and what the employees declared to be a secret understanding between the officials of the Corporation and the officials of the Transport and General Workers Union'. Some time earlier, in disgust at the reaction of a TGWU official to a pay cut, 200 workers at the Acock's Green bus garage had formed a break-away organisation, the Birmingham Municipal Busworkers Association. Miles, working with one of the drivers, Jesse Hill, set about taking the new union over. The *Daily Worker* recorded that the fascists were 'responsible for destroying the unity among the busmen ..., taking over 200 of the best fighters out of the T and G.W.U., under the slogan "Your leaders have sold you!" and [had] formed a new union'.[60] Evidence to bring an action against the Corporation for breaches of the Road Traffic Act was gathered but although the FUBW won the case, the drivers were fined as well, meaning that the result was, to say the least, mixed.[61] Despite this, in a leaflet addressed to 'Fellow Busmen' later circulated in a TGWU branch in East Ham, the BUF put itself forward as an alternative to both the Union and the Rank and File movement, and pointed to how in Birmingham it had 'proved ... infringements and enforced the law'.[62]

In any case, Miles' plans were much more ambitious. In view of the 'great discontent' among bus workers elsewhere, he hoped that success would 'capture the Municipal Busworkers Association for Mosley'. However, he was again foiled, being sent to Lancashire before the case came to court, leaving matters in less experienced hands so that the opportunity was lost.[63] Mosley, Miles recorded, explained that 'he did not propose to countenance anything in the way of a Trade Union rivalling the existing Trade Union machine' and forbade him from 'setting up Fascist Trade Unions'. Miles' belief was that 'the real explanation' was that Mosley 'feared the growth of the Fascist Union of British Workers and was determined to put a stop to its progress'.

Moving to Manchester in early 1934 Miles described the local branch as being 'mainly of working class origin' and as including James Tynan and Joseph Sawlor who were both ex-communists and officers of the FUBW, whose local membership had been recruited from the 'Municipal Lodging House, and the Labour Exchange queues'.[64] Miles was described as working with 'dockers and stevedores regarding their conditions of employment' and meetings 'at or near the Labour Exchanges' were also held. In addition a publication dealing 'with dock side problems ... called the "Siren" ' was published by Miles which was later joined by *Voice of the Workless,* another local publication.[65] The former was still extant the following year, described in a Home Office report as 'well established' in the Ferranti works.[66] Once again, Miles came into conflict with the leadership when he 'met and crossed swords with Commander Tillotson' who had been imposed by NHQ 'over the heads' of the local leadership. This episode also introduced Miles to 'Mosley's fondness for military and naval officers as Administrators'.

Recalled to London at the end of February 1934, Miles became embroiled that May in what he called 'London's Strangest Strike' at the Ham River Grit Company. Following a report of discontent among the firms' drivers and grievances against the TGWU for its performance in negotiations, Miles called a meeting at the BUF's Hammersmith branch 'attended by almost the whole of the drivers and several others employed in other capacities about the yard'. After discussions with Mosley and the BUF's legal officer, Miles received ' "carte blanche" to use the whole of the organisation in support of the strikers' and called the drivers out the following day. During the short strike that followed, fascists used 'pressure, threats and whatnot' including adding sugar to the petrol tanks of lorries and boarding moving vehicles to compel 'blackleg' drivers to abandon their vehicles. One of the company's major contracts was to supply material for work on the Bank of England and Miles claimed that he called for volunteers to stop the deliveries. At this point, 'Sir Oswald got cold feet' and would not promise to support the men's dependents if they were imprisoned and so Miles called off what he wrote of as 'the first, and I believe only Fascist strike England will ever see'. In a later brush with the TGWU Miles was contacted by G. W. Alexander, Chairman of the union at the Viscose Development Company's works, inviting him to put the BUF's case at the William Morris Hall in Bromley so that the strikers could decide whether or not to enlist the fascists on their side. In the end the meeting was cancelled when the TGWU threatened to withdraw its support of the strike.[67]

Miles recorded that a worker's insurance scheme for the membership of the FUBW – which he numbered at 5,000 – was also proposed by its Director, J. Barney who had been recruited by Robert Forgan, ex-Labour MP and the Deputy Leader of BUF, to act as 'technical adviser to the Movement in the industrial field'. Miles described Barney as 'an official in the Trade Union Friendly Society and an active worker in the National Union of Clerks' and Barney described himself as a Chairman in that union. He was almost certainly the same person who wrote anonymously as 'A T.U. Branch Chairman' on 'Fascism and Trade Unions' and 'The Tragedy of the Blackcoats'.[68] Although described by Miles as being of working-class background, Barney's membership of a union which lacked the solid allegiances and working-class solidarity of 'blue collar' organisations may have made it easier for him to contemplate combining fascism with trades unionism.[69] Certainly the BUF did specifically target such sections of the workforce, also issuing a leaflet addressing workers in the catering trade.[70] Barney laid plans for a 'national health insurance organisation' and in April *Blackshirt* mentioned that 'an announcement will shortly be made regarding the British Union Approved Society'.[71] But nothing more was heard and Miles believed that the insurance scheme, although popular with the 'rank and file' had been 'wet-blanketed' by the administrative officers. Once again, his conclusion was that 'no body having the faintest semblance of working-class character, has a place in Mosley's scheme of things'.

Such was the growth of the FUBW under Barney, Miles wrote, that 'the ground was being tested for the registration of it under the Friendly Society's Acts on a national basis'. Instead it was wound up as a separate organisation, being merged into the Industrial Section of the Propaganda Department, and the last mention of the FUBW in the BUF press was at the beginning of June 1934.[72] That summer Barney resigned, declaring to Miles,

> Our 'team' is smashed, as was the FUBW and, working as single units, we are heading for disaster, but our leader must see, ere a year has past, that his Administration is anti-industrialist. ... I am certain we are distrusted by those who control the Movement. Time will prove whether we of the working-class are wanted.

The reason that the efforts of Miles and other 'left-wing' fascists were frustrated at every turn is primarily traceable to a transformation in the BUF leadership occurring at the same time. The internal ructions of the BUF during this period have received some discussion, being interpreted as 'centred around the contentious issues of organization and finance and their links to ideological differences'.[73] This explanation is correct as far as it goes but ignores the major part that the politics of class identity played in this episode.

A report in *The Observer* in January 1934, a week into Lord Rothermere's support for the BUF in *The Daily Mail*, provides a snap shot of the organisation before this change. The paper noted how Mosley had 'stolen the thunder both of the Left and the Right' and that 'as with the Nazis there is a reactionary wing composed of violent anti-Socialists, and a revolutionary wing, recruited from the I.L.P. and the Communists'. Indicating a picture similar to that recalled by Beckett and Miles the paper commented

> the Left wing is considerably stronger than the Right, for when Mosley founded the movement he took over with him many discontented members of the Labour movement. Tremendous headway too has been made in the big industrial centres of the North, where many of the unemployed have become disillusioned both with the Labour Party and the Communists. This success in the areas that have remained unshakeably loyal to Labour for so many years is the most impressive fact about the Fascist movement. It is not surprising that

Mosley should be the uncrowned king of Brighton; it is surprising that he has been able to build up a strong organisation in Manchester and that to-day he should be holding a mass meeting in the Birmingham Bingley Hall, which holds 15,000 people.[74]

The BUF's existing 'reactionary wing', drawn most significantly from the ultra-conservative British Fascists, many of whom came together with the rump of the New Party to form the BUF in 1932, was now to be enormously boosted in influence.[75] Miles wrote of an 'influx of Generals, Admirals, big business men and so forth'. Kay Fredericks, one-time BUF photographer, in another contemporary memoir, blamed 'Lord Rothermere's patronage ... for the influx of all these ex-officers and titled people' and alleged that it was at this moment that the BUF 'rapidly lost all semblance to the true ideas of Fascism.'[76]

It is telling that whilst later writing of the absence of class distinction in the movement, Mosley at the same time stressed its military quality, thereby linking the BUF to an institution which, even in perhaps the most class conscious nation in Europe, was almost feudal in the exclusiveness of its officer corps and its division between commissioned and other ranks.[77] Furthermore, as Martin Petter has shown, the ex-officer, or 'temporary gentleman' of the Great War was frequently someone whose heightened sense of social status was all the more sensitive because of his often weak hold on the material and cultural resources to maintain that identity.[78]

Thus, whereas Mosley and others later spoke of the BUF as 'classless', at the time a state mole reported 'considerable unrest among the rank-and-file ..., which takes the form of grumbling about food, class-conscious officers, discipline, and the hours of work'.[79] Fredericks' account detailed the pervasive class culture amid the putative 'brotherhood of fascism'. In the Black House the 'men's canteen' catered for the rank and file, while the so-called 'Mixed-canteen' was known as the 'boss-class canteen'. Fredericks wrote that 'if a Blackshirt who was employed as a cleaner at H.Q. went into the mixed canteen, he would not be turned out, but would certainly be made to feel uncomfortable and ill at ease'. Those with money wore superior uniform shirts which 'immediately became known as "boss-class" shirts'. As elsewhere in society, 'titles, both civil and military' were 'a great help in the securing of rapid promotion'. Although the majority of the 'rank and file' were 'drawn from the working classes', Fredericks noted that 'when the Blackshirts throw a ball they do so at places ... where these men feel out of place and unwanted'.

In this way the BUF brought together 'ex-Socialists, Conservatives, Liberals, Communists, the officer class, the public school-boy, younger sons of the diplomatic and consular families'. Miles' judgement was that to 'control and unify such divergent types, without allowing the social and class prejudices they brought to the movement to disrupt its unity, was a task too big for Mosley'. The 'Policy and Propaganda side' which was controlled by Risdon and dominated by ex-socialists like Miles and had 'some idea of putting reality into the Socialist phrases in the Party's programmes' increasingly clashed with the organisational wing dominated by 'the great influx of the ex-officer caste' of the Rothermere period, for whom the 'BUF was an organ to strengthen their social privileges.' Beckett also wrote that 'a greater part of national headquarters' staff were either complete boobies, or unbelievably like the caricatures of Fascists published in the "Daily Worker" '.[80] Miles charted the struggle whereby the 'Conservative side' stripped Risdon of authority to enable thereby 'the Tory side to weed out any and every speaker who showed even the faintest tinge of "Red" '. In this way, Fredericks believed, the BUF, while previously having a 'slight division between the "right" and the "left" ' had been turned 'into a glorified branch of the Conservative Party'. Miles concluded that 'fascist unity is a farce, that the talk of wiping out class distinctions is on par with it and the Fascist movement is a class-instrument, and not a working class instrument either!'

Changes were also afoot at the highest level of the BUF leadership. Often underestimated in accounts of the BUF, Robert Forgan, as Director of Organisation was Mosley's 'right hand man' and was described by Miles as 'the biggest figure at headquarters at that time'. With Forgan as Deputy and Risdon as Director of Propaganda, the left wing of the BUF was in a strong position. By September 1934 Forgan, although still nominally Mosley's deputy, had been sent to inspect the Scottish branches 'in order to get him away from headquarters', leaving the ex-Conservative F. M. Box as 'the virtual deputy for Sir Oswald Mosley'. Among the charges against Forgan were that he 'had shown bad judgement in his choice of subordinate officers'.[81] In the 'official' history of the BUF this point has been linked to the recruitment of the feckless and criminal, but it may equally have related to his appointment of working-class socialists like Miles.[82]

Forgan was, Fredericks suggests, 'exceedingly popular with all members of the BUF "left" wing' and his resignation in October 1934, Miles wrote, caused a 'revolt that nearly split the Party in half'. Rumours spread through the BUF and there were 'murmurings of discontent, and the possibility of an outbreak'; 'almost a revolution in the movement' as the BUF's ' "left-wingers" ... plotted to take over the movement by force and oust those officers who had crawled in during the boosting period of the "Mail" '. At his later ' "court martial" ' it was alleged that Bradford, once head of the disbanded FUBW and leader of this revolt, had threatened to attack the 'Deputy Chief of Staff', Archibald Findlay, and had 'prepared a plot to seize the building and make demands to Sir Oswald Mosley that certain officers be dismissed'.[83] Mosley 'called the Headquarters staff together in the Club room' of Black House and there, protected by 'a dozen picked men', managed to damp down discontent. Being financially dependent on the BUF, the 'mutineers' were in a weak position and Mosley managed to convince them that Forgan 'had not left the ranks for ever but would return when [his] health permitted'.[84] Hence, in the BUF press the following week the notice of Forgan's resignation was amended to resignation from 'active participation' due to ill health.[85] Bradford's punishment was to be suspended for three months although it is doubtful that he ever returned. Fredericks recorded that two of the 'ring-leaders were expelled some few weeks later'. In any case, that December it was 'decided to purge the movement of undesirable elements' which consisted 'to a large extent of ex-members of the Communist Party and National Unemployed Workers Movement' whose presence, it was reported, hindered 'the recruiting of the better class of citizen.'[86] This was despite, as a fascist commented earlier that year, former socialists and communists providing the BUF's 'most valuable recruits'.[87]

At around the same time as this purge, Risdon too was reported to be 'organising some subversive plot' and to be nursing a 'grievance because some of the people who joined the movement after he did have been given prominent positions' and he was accused of plotting with other disenchanted Lancashire blackshirts to present 'an ultimatum to Sir Oswald Mosley, demanding ... the dismissal of certain officials at King's Road'.[88] For whatever reason, nothing came of this and, with Forgan's departure, the national leadership had fundamentally shifted from left to right. The victorious 'organisational side' was first headed by Box and then after his departure, by Neil Francis-Hawkins who came to dominate the BUF. Previously of the British Fascists – which Mosley had once alluded to as the 'white guard of reaction' – and a member of OMS during the General Strike, Francis-Hawkins' ascendancy eloquently illustrated the direction that the BUF had taken.[89] The background of other leading figures told the same story: Bryan Donovan, ex-Indian Army; General J.F.C. Fuller; Colonels Sharp and Crocker; Major Cleghorn;

Captains Atherley, Butler and Gordon-Canning; Eric Hamilton Piercy, who was also an Inspector of Special Constabulary; 'Dick' Plathen, ex-Consular Service and Ian Dundas, a former Royal Navy officer.[90] This domination by the ex-officer class was also apparent at the next level of leadership, the BUF's District Inspectors.[91] As one anti-fascist commented 'where we haven't a rank we have a double-barrelled name, always a good indication that the bearer is a loving friend of the workers'.[92]

As to the intentions of the BUF towards the working-class movement if it came into power, when Forgan met Neville Laski secretly in July 1934, among the reasons for his disenchantment was that he expected that a 'Fascist state in England ... would assume a different form to that adumbrated by Mosley in his speeches.'[93] The BUF always made clear that there would be no political parties in the corporate state but promised that trade unions would be strengthened. One voice from within the BUF was as sceptical as Miles on this point – indeed it probably was Miles.[94] George Chester, General Secretary of the National Union of Boot and Shoe Operatives (NUBSO), recalled a conversation with someone who had recently left the BUF and was now 'organising meetings in opposition to Fascism'. Chester reported

I invited his comment upon certain aspects of Fascism, particularly its relationship to the Trade Union Movement and the Labour Party, and he told me as a very definite statement that I could rely upon, that the Fascist Movement had already scheduled all the information they possibly could with relation to the Labour Party and the Trade Union Movement; that they had an organisation on paper which could step into the position of the Trade Union Movement on similar lines to that obtained in Germany at the present time, immediately they are in sufficient power to do so.

When ... I told him who I was ... he told me that the National Union of Boot and Shoe Operatives were pretty high up in the list of Organisations to be dealt with immediately the revolution of the Fascists has taken place.[95]

The appointment of ('Major') 'P.G. Taylor' – that is James McGuirk Hughes of MI5 – as the BUF's 'Industrial Advisor' to take over the role of the disbanded FUBW is eloquent of the fascists' true attitude to the working-class movement and 'socialism' national or otherwise.[96] In the established secret service practice of using radical-right groups as an auxiliary force against the 'red menace', at the same time as seeking to convince organised labour of the benign intentions of the blackshirts, Hughes was using 'the BUF as a cover for MI5's own covert operations against the left'.[97] That Mosley knew of Hughes' other employer from the outset and that the BUF paid for the agents he placed in left-wing bodies, including the CPGB, suggests that there was no conflict between the two organisations in this respect.[98] Mosley had made clear that the blackshirts would act as a counter-revolutionary force if needed and indeed, one ex-blackshirt has speculated that Hughes was placed within the BUF to be 'in a position which they thought might have been useful in the organisation of BU's well known fighting qualities should a "Red Revolution" erupt and threaten a take-over of the State'.[99]

Hughes' interests were also much wider than the CPGB. Years earlier he had worked to infiltrate and undermine socialist and trades union activity in Liverpool and Charles Dolan, another former communist in the BUF, which indicated the presence of fascist *agents provocateurs* within trades unions and other bodies.[100] Miles commented that 'if to be an Industrial advisor means that one controls a number of people who burrow into organisations such as Trade Unions ... so that the controller of these ferrets may "advise" his employers of their intentions and actions, then, of course Mr. Taylor was rightly described'. Given that 'Taylor' oversaw the shift in BUF policy from the creation of a separate body of fascist workers to the 'permeation' of the unions by blackshirts he was well positioned to so 'burrow'.[101]

Miles provides a telling comment on fascist rhetoric. Regarding a visit to the shipping magnate 'Sir Shadford Watts' [sic] to discuss BUF policy, he recorded that although Watts found reasons for rejecting anything 'favourable to seamen against owners' Miles left him feeling that he had managed to keep his side of the argument up.[102] Only later did it dawn on him that 'all this stuff on paper doesn't really matter'. Mosley was, he felt, 'too sensible ... to attempt to put anything into practice that will destroy the possibility of shipping profits and again, one can always have a word with him in private.'

Nonetheless, despite the rightward swing at the level of the national leadership, 'left-wing' fascism remained a prominent part of the BUF's propaganda. Indeed, the movement made an increased use of quasi-socialist and anti-capitalist rhetoric. Blackshirts called themselves 'National Socialists', explaining that if 'you love your country you are national, if you love its people you are socialist'. The *Blackshirt* became 'the patriotic workers' paper' and the BUF targeted campaigns at workers in mines, mills and transport. Rather than distancing itself from socialism, the Blackshirts presented themselves as the inheritors of a specifically British socialist tradition represented in fascist eyes by figures including William Morris and Robert Owen.

Furthermore, although the right wing of the BUF had triumphed at national leadership level this did not mean that an alliance of social fractions could not be sustained when rhetoric was not obviously contradicted by practice. Thus, in 1936 Charles Wegg-Prosser was able to write that the BUF could 'proudly claim to be a Revolutionary Worker's Movement, seeking to set up the only genuine Workers' State, which is the Corporate State'.[103] It was only when he moved from the isolation of the BUF's Hertford branch to take part in the East End campaign and come face to face with an organisation led by 'a small narrow-minded group of ex-Army officers' that this illusion was shattered.[104]

Consequently, while there were no further attempts to build up specifically working-class bodies, the BUF continued to have a heterogeneous membership, but crucially like wider society, it was a stratified one. The best available studies of BUF membership reflect this. W. F. Mandle's survey of the BUF's national leadership finds it safely in the hands of the middle and upper classes.[105] In contrast, Stephen Cullen's grass roots fascists were predominantly of the 'respectable' working class/lower middle class and the proportion of those from a family background on the 'left' actually increased among those who joined after 1934.[106] In the fascist stronghold in the East End, Fenner Brockway noted that 'Mosley had succeeded in securing the support of a considerable number of Irish and British workers', an evaluation supported by Thomas Linehan's impressive empirical evidence.[107] An indication of the occupational backgrounds of blackshirts in this later period was the presence at the BUF's mass rally at Earls Court in 1939 of banners representing trade union groups in transport, mining, clerical, textile, iron and steel, and agricultural sectors.[108]

The example of Northampton BUF illustrates this socio-cultural divide in microcosm.[109] The 'reactionary' credentials of the first prominent local fascist, Harry Frisby, were impeccable. Previously of the Junior Imperial League and the son of a substantial local manufacturer, Frisby joined the BUF during the Rothermere period. Writing to the local press he contrasted Lord Carson's defence of empire and 'time honoured institutions' with the activities of the 'so-called conservatives' of the National Government.[110] Reflecting his social status he became County Propaganda Officer and parliamentary candidate for Harrow. However, it was not Frisby who was the driving force of fascism in Northampton, but the District Leader, George Callow, who was on the local committee of the National Union of Railwaymen. Callow wrote of it being 'well known' at the NUR District Executive Committee that he was a black-shirt and of how his workmates, knowing of his politics, had still elected him as their delegate.[111] For him, blackshirt rhetoric was able to create and sustain a populist identity which synthesised socialism and fascism. Replying to one critic he wrote: 'I love my county and people; in fact I am a National Socialist.'[112]

The background of the local activists over the time of Callow's leadership (1936–39) matched the pattern found by Cullen and Linehan. A contemporary letter described the BUF as a 'British worker's movement'[113] and the branch included engineering workers, railwaymen, meter readers and black coated workers. One blackshirt, who worked as a clerk in the Public Assistance department, saw his BUF membership as an expression of left-wing inclinations, remembering the BUF as akin to the ILP in its mission.[114] Another, an engineer, looked back on fascism as promising a 'right-wing workers revolution'.[115]

The activities of the BUF in the town also suggest an ambition to fill the political space occupied by Labour. In the local elections it was 'Northampton's strongest Labour ward' that Callow chose to fight and his election address argued for a 'Britain first' policy to protect the town's boot and shoe industry.[116] His policies for Castle Ward included calls for slum clearance, a not inappropriate message in an area described as the 'most slummy district' of the town.[117] The Blackshirts moved their head-quarters to the ward and continued to court its predominantly working-class inhabitants with activities including a 'New Year's party' and 'a day's outing' for the 'less fortunate children of Castle Ward'.[118]

The Northampton blackshirts are an example of how, as long as 'theory' remained unchallenged by 'practice', quasi-socialist rhetoric could be effective in building a fascist movement around a shared populist identity. This is one reason why a sufficient understanding of a fascist movement cannot avoid considering the functioning of its own discourse. At the same time, this does not preclude a 'critical' approach to the subject.[119] Populist identities forged in fascist political language were not spoken into a vacuum but uttered in the face of the pre-existing premises and agendas of class. Whilst Mosley spoke of the classless nation to come, identities formed in the class-ridden present pushed the movement which claimed to anticipate the 'Greater Britain' in quite a different direction.[120]

Notes

1. A longer version of this chapter originally appeared in *Twentieth Century British History*, 13, 1, 2002, pp. 38–61.

2. R. P. Dutt, *World Politics 1918–1936* (London: Gollancz, 1936), p. 329.
3. Roger Griffin, *The Nature of Fascism* (London: Routledge, 1993).
4. David Renton, *Fascism: Theory and Practice* (London: Pluto, 1999), pp. 3–4.
5. David Renton, *Fascism*, pp. 1, 3.
6. David Renton, *Fascism*, p. 2.
7. Philip M. Coupland, 'The Blackshirted Utopians', *Journal of Contemporary History*, 33, April 1998, pp. 255–72.
8. David Renton, 'Docker and Garment Worker, Railwayman and Cabinet Maker: The Class Memory of Cable Street', in Tony Kushner and Nadia Valman (eds), *Remembering Cable Street: Fascism and Anti-Fascism in British Society* (London: Vallentine Mitchell, 2000), p. 100; original emphases.
9. Dave Renton, *Fascism*, pp. 104–7.
10. John Strachey, *The Menace of Fascism* (London: Gollancz, 1933), pp. 165–6.
11. R. P. Dutt, *Fascism and Social Revolution: A Study of the Economics and Politics of the Last Stages of Capitalism in Decay* (London: Gollancz, 1935), p. 264.
12. John Campbell, *Nye Bevan and the Mirage of British Socialism* (London: Weidenfeld and Nicolson, 1987), pp. 40–4; Hugh Thomas, *John Strachey* (London: Eyre Methuen, 1973), chs 4–7; Michael Newman, *John Strachey* (Manchester: Manchester University Press, 1989), chs 1–2; Paul Davies, A. J. Cook (Manchester: Manchester University Press, 1987).
13. H. G. Wells, *Experiment in Autobiography: Discoveries and Conclusions of a Very Ordinary Brain (Since 1866), Volume II* (London: Gollancz, 1934), p. 782; J. Johnson (President, Birmingham Borough Labour Party), 'Birmingham Labour and the New Party', *The Labour Magazine*, 9, April 1931, pp. 534–6. See also Robert Skidelsky, *Oswald Mosley* (London: Papermac, 1990; first published 1975), chs 7–11; Dan S. White, *Lost Comrades: Socialists of the Front Generation 1918–1945* (Cambridge, MA: Harvard University Press, 1992), passim.
14. George E. G. Catlin, *A Preface to Action* (London: Allen & Unwin, 1934), p. 235.
15. Ellen Wilkinson and Edward Conze, *Why Fascism?* (London: Selwyn & Blount, undated; c.1934), p. 231.
16. Hilda Kean, 'Some Problems of Constructing and Reconstructing a Suffragette's Life: Mary Richardson, Suffragette, Socialist and Fascist', *Women's History Review*, 7, 1998, pp. 475–93.
17. Ellen Wilkinson and Edward Conze, *Why Fascism?* p. 59; University of Sheffield Library, Richard Reynell Bellamy, 'We Marched With Mosley: A British Fascist's View of the Twentieth Century', undated typescript, p. 102; Colin Cross, *The Fascists in Britain* (London: Barrie and Rockliff, 1961), pp. 67–8.
18. Colin Cross, *The Fascists in Britian*, p. 145.
19. Colin Cross, *The Fascists in Britain*, p. 68.
20. John Beckett, 'After My Fashion (Twenty Post-war Years)', unpublished typescript, 1938, p. 350, British Union Collection, University of Sheffield.
21. *The New Clarion*, 4 March 1933.
22. *British Fascism*, Special Summer Propaganda Number, undated; c.1933, p. 11.
23. MSS 127/NU/GS/3/5A, copy of letter signed by Charles Dolan, 9 November 1934.
24. *Blackshirt*, February 1933.
25. Public Records Office (PRO), HO144/20140/97; *Blackshirt*, 23 February–1 March 1934; William Parsons, 'What was FUBW?', *Comrade*, 30, June/August 1991, p. 7.

26. *Blackshirt*, 23–9 March 1934.
27. University of Warwick, Modern Records Centre (MRC), MSS. 127/NU/GS/3/5B, Jack Cutter, 'Takes a Day Off and Reviews the Fascist Forces', *The Labour Organiser*, 165, March 1935, p. 50.
28. *Blackshirt*, 26 January–1 February 1934.
29. FUBW, *Fascism and Trade Unionism*, undated; *c*.1933–34.
30. *Blackshirt*, 19–25 January 1934.
31. *Blackshirt*, 1 June 1934.
32. *Blackshirt*, 2–8 September 1933; 2–8 March 1934; 23–9 March 1934; 30 March–5 April 1934; 6–12 April 1934; 20–6 April 1934.
33. MRC, MSS292/743/6, 'Report by H. R. S. Phillpott on the results of enquiries into the Fascist movement in England and Wales', May 1933, pp. 4, 8; *Blackshirt*, 23–9 March 1934.
34. R. M. White, 'Some Features of the Development of Fascism in England', *The Communist International*, 10, October 1933, pp. 640–6, especially 641.
35. *Blackshirt*, 5–11 January 1934; 19–25 January 1934; 26 January–1 February 1934; 2–8 February 1934; 9–15 February 1934; 23 February–1 March; 1934 9–15 March 1934; 23–9 March 1934; 30 March–5 April 1934; 25–31 May 1934.
36. R. M. White, 'Some Features of the Development of Fascism', p. 645.
37. MRC, MSS126/T&G/4/2/9, TGWU, *The Record*, XII, February 1934, p. 163.
38. R. M. White, 'Some Features of the Development of Fascism', p. 645.
39. Wal Hannington, *The Problem of the Distressed Areas* (London: Gollancz, 1937), p. 240.
40. R. M. White, 'Some Features of the Development of Fascism', p. 645.
41. W. Parsons, 'What was FUBW?', p. 7.
42. *Blackshirt*, March 1933; 30 March–5 April 1934; 6–12 April 1934; 11–17 May 1934; 18–24 May 1934.
43. MRC, MSS 292/743/6, hand-written notes headed 'BUF' and 'Fascist Movement'; Public Record Office (PRO), HO144/20141/155, cutting from *The Daily Telegraph*, 21 January 1934.
44. R. M. White, 'Some Features of the Development of Fascism', p. 645; *Daily Worker*, 14 July 1933; MRC, MSS292/743/6, hand-written notes headed 'BUF' and 'Fascist Movement'; 'The Firestone Strike', *The Communist Review*, 6, October 1933, pp. 384–8; MRC, MSS292/743/11/2, unnamed [Kay Fredericks] typescript memoir.
45. *Blackshirt*, 2–8 February 1934.
46. MRC, MSS126/T&G/4/2/9 TGWU, *The Record*, XII, June 1934, pp. 244, 252.
47. MRC, MSS 127/NU/GS/3/5B, Jack Cutter, *The Labour Organiser*, p. 50.
48. R. M. White, 'Some Features of the Development of Fascism', p. 645.
49. MRC, MSS127/NU/GS/3/5A, 'The Development of the British Union of Fascists', p. 4.
50. Trades Union Congress, *The Menace of Dictatorship: The Debate at the Brighton Trades Union Conference, 1933* (Manchester: TUC, undated; *c*.1933), p. 9.
51. MRC, MSS292/743/11/2, A. C. Miles, 'The Streets Are Still/Mosley in Motley', typescript memoir, undated; *c*.1937. A much-abbreviated account appeared as *Mosley in Motley* (London, undated; *c*.1937).
52. *The Fascist Week*, 22–8 December 1933.
53. Cf. A. C. Miles, *Fascism and Shipping* (BUF Publications, undated; *c*.1934).

54. MRC, MSS126/T&G/1/1/11, Minutes and Record of the General Executive Council and Financial and General Purposes Committee, XI, 1933, Finance and General Purpose Committee, 28 September 1933, minute No. 758, 215.
55. *The Busman's Punch*, October 1933.
56. *The Busman's Punch*, November 1933.
57. FUBW, *London Transport Workers*, undated; *c*.1934; Glatter, 'London Busmen Rise and Fall of a Rank and File Movement', *International Socialism*, No. 74, January 1975 p. 7.
58. *Blackshirt*, 11–17 May 1934.
59. MRC, MSS 292/743/7, 'Report on Replies to Fascist Questionnaire', p. 2.
60. *Daily Worker*, 18 January 1934; 16 February 1934.
61. PRO, HO144/20140/113, Special Branch Report, 30 April 1934; *The Birmingham Mail*, 27 March 1934; John D. Brewer, *Mosley's Men; the British Union of Fascists in the West Midlands* (Aldershot: Gower, *c*.1984), p. 77.
62. MRC, MSS292/743/4, Steward Rainbird (Agent and Secretary East Ham North Labour Party) to the General Secretary of the TUC, 28 September 1934; BUF, *Busmen and Fascism*, undated; *c*.1934.
63. *The Fascist Week*, 6–12 April 1934.
64. See also MRC, MSS292/743/6, 'Report by H. R. S. Phillpott on the results of enquiries into the Fascist movement in England and Wales', May 1933.
65. *Blackshirt*, 26 January–1 February 1934; 16–22 March 1934.
66. PRO, HO144/20145/236, Special Branch Report, 3 July 1935.
67. *Blackshirt*, 31 August 1934.
68. *Blackshirt*, 12–18 August; *The Fascist Week*, 1–7 December 1933.
69. Arthur Marsh and Victoria Ryan, *The Clerks: A History of Apex 1890–1989* (Oxford: Malthouse Publishing, 1997), pp. 61–99.
70. *Church Times*, 29 March 1934.
71. PRO, HO144/2014/114, Special Branch Report, 30 April 1934; *Blackshirt*, 13–17 April 1934.
72. W. Parsons, 'What was FUBW?', p. 7; *Blackshirt*, 1 June 1934.
73. Richard C. Thurlow, *Fascism in Britain: A history, 1918–1985* (Oxford: Basil Blackwell, 1987), pp. 140–3.
74. MRC, MSS292/743/6, cutting from *The Observer*, 21 January 1934.
75. R. R. Bellamy, 'We Marched With Mosley', pp. 50–1.
76. MRC, MSS292/743/11/2, unnamed [Kay Fredericks] typescript memoir.
77. Oswald Mosley, *My Life* (London: Nelson, 1969), pp. 303–6; Keith Simpson, 'The Officers', in Ian F. W. Beckett and Keith Simpson (eds), *A Nation in Arms: A Social Study of the British Army in the First World War* (Manchester: Manchester University Press, 1985).
78. Martin Petter, ' "Temporary Gentlemen" in the Aftermath of the Great War: Rank, Status and the Ex-Officer Problem', *The Historical Journal*, 27, 1994, pp. 127–52.
79. PRO, HO144/20142/81, Special Branch Report, 18 July 1934.
80. J. Beckett, 'After My Fashion', p. 360.
81. PRO, HO144/20140/243, Special Branch Report, 10 October 1934.
82. R. R. Bellamy, 'We Marched With Mosley', pp. 60–1.
83. PRO, HO144/20140/314, Special Branch Report, 17 October 1934.
84. PRO, HO144/20142/241, Special Branch Report, 10 October 1934.
85. *Blackshirt*, 12 October 1934; 19 October 1934.

86. PRO, HO144/20144/236, Special Branch Report, 17 December 1934.
87. *The Fascist Week*, 4–10 May 1934.
88. PRO, HO144/20144/18, Special Branch Report, 17 January 1935.
89. Oswald Mosley, *The Greater Britain* (London: BUF, 1932), p.15.
90. R. R. Bellamy, 'We Marched With Mosley', pp. 61–7.
91. R. R. Bellamy, 'We Marched With Mosley', pp. 74–8.
92. MRC, MSS126/TG/3/Sack6/1, 'What's in a Name?', *Busman's Punch*, October 1934, p. 4.
93. Geoffrey Alderman, 'Document: Dr. Robert Forgan's Resignation from the British Union of Fascists', *Labour History Review*, 57, Spring 1992, pp. 37–41.
94. Miles left the BUF in February or March 1936 and Chester recalled speaking to his informant in May 1936 when the latter had 'just left' the BUF. This person was also described as organising anti-fascist meetings, as Miles did in Hyde Park. Around the same time Special Branch also recorded that Miles was working part-time in London for NUBSO, in which his uncle held 'a good position' (PRO, HO144/20147/142, Special Branch Report, 21 May 1936).
95. NUBSO, *Official Report of the Forty-Sixth Union Conference 1–6 June 1936*, p. 278.
96. John Hope, 'Fascism, the Security Service and the Curious Careers of Maxwell Knight and James McGuirk Hughes', *Lobster*, 22, 1991, pp. 1–5.
97. John Hope, *Lobster*, p. 4; Richard C. Thurlow, 'State Management of the British Union of Fascists in the 1930s', in Mike Cronin (ed.), *The Failure of British Fascism: The Far Right and the Fight for Political Recognition* (London: Macmillan, 1996), pp. 29–52.
98. University of Birmingham, Mosley Papers, Box 8, Forgan to Mosley, 16 June 1934; 'John Christian' Pseud, [John Warburton], 'The South London Reporter', in Leonard Wise *et al.* (eds), *Mosley's Blackshirts: The Inside Story of the British Union of Fascists 1932–1940* (London: Sanctuary Press, 1986), p. 38.
99. Untitled typescript memoir of John Warburton, p. 16.
100. Roy Bean, 'Liverpool Shipping Employers and the Anti-Communist Activities of J. M. Hughes, 1920–25', *Society for the Study of Labour History Bulletin*, 34, 1977, pp. 22–6; John G. Hope, 'Surveillance or Collusion? Maxwell Knight, MI5 and the British Fascisti', *Intelligence and National Security*, 9, October 1994, pp. 651–75, especially 659; Charles M. Dolan, *The Blackshirt Racket: Mosley Exposed* (undated; *c*.1934–35), p. 14.
101. PRO, HO144/20144/164, Special Branch Report, 28 January 1935.
102. Miles' memory of meeting Sir Shadforth Watts must be incorrect as Watts died in 1926. However, a Mrs Watts – of a 'well known shipping family' – was described as 'an ardent Fascist' (*Blackshirt*, 21 September 1934) and in 1935 William Joyce and 'P. G. Taylor' were charged with rewriting Miles' shipping and seaman's leaflet, 'consulting E. H. Watts of the Watts Shipping Company' (PRO, HO144/20145/240, Special Branch Report, 2 July 1935).
103. C. F. Wegg-Prosser, 'The Worker and the State', *Fascist Quarterly*, 2, 1936, pp. 255–66.
104. Cross, *The Fascists in Britain*, p. 173; [Charles Wegg-Prosser], *The BUF and Anti-Semitism (An Exposure)* (undated; *c*.1937–38).
105. W. F. Mandle, 'The Leadership of the British Union of Fascists', *The Australian Journal of Politics and History*, 112, December 1966, 360–83.

106. Stephen M. Cullen, 'The British Union of Fascists, 1932–1940; Ideology, Membership and Meetings' (unpublished MLitt Thesis, University of Oxford, 1987), pp. 42–5.
107. Fenner Brockway, *Inside the Left: Thirty Years of Platform, Press, Prison and Parliament* (London: G. Allen & Unwin, 1942), p. 271; Thomas P. Linehan, *East London For Mosley: the British Union of Fascists in East London and South-West Essex, 1933–40* (London: Frank Cass, 1996), p. 214.
108. Gordon Beckwell, 'British Union's Finest Hour', *Comrade*, 53, June/July 1989, p. 4.
109. Philip M. Coupland, 'The Blackshirts in Northampton, 1933–1940', *Northamptonshire Past and Present*, 53, 2000, pp. 71–82.
110. *Northampton Chronicle and Echo*, 10 April 1939.
111. *Action*, 28 August 1937.
112. *Northampton Chronicle and Echo*, 25 September 1937.
113. *Northampton Chronicle and Echo*, 25 September 1937.
114. Interview with PW, ex-District Treasurer Northampton BUF (*c.*1936–40), 17 May 1997.
115. Undated [1997] letter from WW, ex-Northampton BUF.
116. *Northampton Chronicle and Echo*, 31 October 1938.
117. *Northampton Chronicle and Echo*, 18 October 1937; 1 November 1937; J. Hilton, *English Ways: A Walk from the Pennines to Epsom Downs in 1939* (London: Jonathan Cape, 1940), p. 103; The Boroughs and Horsemarket Living History Project, *In Living Memory: Life in 'The Boroughs'* (Northampton: Northampton Arts Development, 1987).
118. *Northampton Chronicle and Echo*, 10 January 1939, 20 May 1939.
119. David Renton, *Fascism*, pp. 25–9.
120. O. Mosley, *The Greater Britain*, p. 40.

6
Practical Anti-fascism? The 'Aid Spain' Campaigns in North-East England, 1936–39

Lewis H. Mates

'When the fighting broke out on 18 July [1936] it is probable that every anti-Fascist in Europe felt a thrill of hope. For here, at last, apparently, was democracy standing up to Fascism. For years past the so-called democratic countries had been surrendering to Fascism at every step. [...] It seemed – possibly it was – the turning of the tide.'[1] So wrote George Orwell about the Spanish military revolt, backed by two of Europe's fascist powers, Italy and Germany, against the Spanish popular front government.[2] However, the national leadership of the 'official' (i.e. non-communist) British labour movement advocated support for the right-wing 'National' government's policy of non-intervention in Spain. By denying the Republic's right under international law to buy arms for self-defence, this agreement effectively aided the rebels. Though the labour movement eventually reversed its policy, the national leadership took little positive action in support of the Republic.

Those angered at this inactivity organised in numerous 'Aid Spain' campaigns, ostensibly to aid the Republic, which emerged to fill the void. Though often inspired by the formation of an organisation at national level, these campaigns owed their significance to the widespread and energetic work of grass roots activists. The response was impressive. Jim Fyrth claimed that what he deemed the 'Aid Spain movement' was 'the most widespread and representative mass movement in Britain since the mid-nineteenth century days of Chartism and the Anti-Corn Law Leagues, and the most outstanding example of international solidarity in British history'.[3] However, there is surprisingly little published on this important topic and what there is tends to view these campaigns in an uncritical manner.[4]

This chapter aims to redress this, in part, by examining the most important 'Aid Spain' campaigns that emerged in the north-east of

England, a region characterised by a strong (especially in County Durham), traditionally moderate and loyal labour movement.[5] Despite this loyalty, militant anti-fascism was strong in the region, or, more accurately, on Tyneside. The British Union of Fascists (BUF), which made early progress in the North East, was met with strong opposition, both spontaneous and organised by the left, which culminated with the formation of the 'Anti-Fascist League' in summer 1934. The peak of anti-fascist resistance was reached during two days of violence in May 1934. After this time, BUF activities were severely limited and an attempted fascist revival in 1935 proved abortive. Effectively, as Nigel Todd has shown, the BUF threat was eliminated in the region by 1935.[6] There was clearly a strong base of anti-fascist sentiment in the region that could have been capitalised on in order to mount solidarity action for the Spanish Republic. However, it is clear that 'Aid Spain' campaigns were not simply an unequivocal manifestation of practical anti-fascist politics, as many included strong elements of humanitarianism. This chapter aims to isolate the humanitarian strands from the anti-fascism in these campaigns, and then to assess their effects and implications. Of course, there is some blurring between the two concepts, the definitions of which could be eternally debated. However, this overlap has been overemphasised by those wishing to depict all of these campaigns as integral elements of a successful anti-fascist mass movement.

The Spanish Medical Aid committees

As the first group of campaigns to emerge, it is logical to begin by examining the Spanish Medical Aid committees.[7] The national committee was established by socialist and communist doctors in August 1936 and at least 17 similarly named committees emerged in the North East in the ensuing months, mostly based in the larger towns and cities, with a handful of others scattered around the pit villages of County Durham. The first committee in the area was at Newcastle, formed in September 1936. North Shields and Gateshead committees were in existence by the end of 1936 and, in the first six months of 1937, between one and three new committees a month appeared. The last, Morpeth, was formed in September 1937. There was a great deal of diversity amongst the committees in terms of their political complexion. At least six, like that at Gateshead, seem to have been run exclusively by activists from the 'official' labour movement. Three others, including Blaydon committee, had both 'official' labour movement activists and communists working together on them. A further four incorporated individuals from across the political spectrum.[8]

The key difference, though, was the way in which they framed their campaigning message. Ostensibly the issue was clear. The message, surely, had to be 'fight fascism in Spain by supporting the Republic', an unequivocal anti-fascist stance. Some committees did campaign on these terms. Blaydon committee, for example, was explicit in the need to support the 'struggle of Spanish democracy against Fascist intervention'.[9] However, it is striking that some of the other committees did not depict their campaign in this explicit anti-fascist manner. Instead, they chose to emphasise the suffering of innocent women and children in the conflict. Thus, for example, a Newcastle committee appeal in late October 1936 called for medical supplies and clothes for 'the sufferers among the civilian population'.[10] This emphasis on humanitarianism implied that the plight of civilians was somehow separate from the political situation, and that to side with people who were merely the innocent victims of war was not to take a political stance and side with either the Republic or the rebels.

The *Linaria* Strike and the Defence Committee

A second campaign emerged after 23 February 1937, when the north-eastern crew of the SS *Linaria* held a sit-in strike in protest at being ordered to transport a cargo of nitrates from Boston (Massachusetts) to the Franco-held port of Sevilla. The leader of the strike was Alex Robson, an active communist who was clearly acting on anti-fascist motives.[11] Given the rarity of strike action for overtly political motives, especially in Britain in the 1930s, the event was highly significant and potentially full of anti-fascist propaganda possibilities. Although the crew's submission to the captain protested at 'being made a party by the fascists to their suppression of the people of Spain', a Robson quote that simultaneously got equal press coverage made no explicit mention of fascism.[12] Instead, the crew did 'not want to help to deliver nitrate because we do not want to be a party to the killing of women and children by bombs and shells'.[13] In this quote, it sounded as though the crew were acting from anti-war motives (because wars killed the innocent), and that equally it would have gone on strike if the nitrate had been bound for the Republic. As a consequence, the anti-fascist message of the crew's action was somewhat blunted.

Established to support the deported crew, the *Linaria* Defence Committee, like some of the Spanish Medical Aid committees, also included individuals from the right of the labour movement, as well as communists and Labour Party members.[14] And, like the broad-based

Spanish Medical Aid committees, here, too, the campaign to help the men was not as explicitly anti-fascist as it could have been and as the crew's initial complaint to the *Linaria*'s captain clearly was. Thus, the Defence Committee's president (who was also an Independent councillor), commented at a fund-raising meeting in mid-April 1937 that he was 'not concerned so much with the rights and wrongs of the crew of the ship [...] as with ensuring the men had funds when they returned to Liverpool for the court case'.[15] Implicit in the Defence Committee's appeal published in the press was that the need to maintain non-intervention was at least as important a motivation as anti-fascism. Robson himself had also said this. The appeal noted a second motive in the crew's desire to avoid entering a war zone.[16] Though the press reports on the Defence Committee's few meetings were imprecise, the evidence that remains clearly suggests that the anti-fascist politics evident in the crew's strike action were down-played and that *Linaria* Defence Committee meetings were confined largely to raising money for the crew's court case rather than propagandising against fascism.

Finally in court, and charged for impeding the navigation of a vessel, anti-fascism again played a minor role. The crew's defence employed two main arguments, both of which had been prominent before the court case: first, that the crew acted solely to uphold non-intervention. This implied that they would have done the same if the cargo had been destined for a Republican port, as non-intervention theoretically treated both sides the same. The second and ultimately successful argument, in that it achieved a quashing of their earlier conviction, was that the crew had the right to refuse to enter a war zone.[17] Given the significance of the initial strike action, it is noteworthy that the campaign to support the *Linaria* crewmen appeared to have little impact. There were perhaps only three Defence Committee meetings in the region and the action of the crew, once the strike itself was over, appeared to excite remarkably little debate or controversy, which was surprising given the novel nature of the initial action.[18] Perhaps this was partly because so little had been made of the anti-fascist motives of the strike leader, and presumably most of the strikers, of whom only two signed back on the ship and went to Spain. (Of the remaining 17 deportees, it is unclear how many merely did not wish to enter a war zone.)

These considerations temper Don Watson and John Corcoran's claim that the crew's court victory was a 'notable victory for the Aid Spain movement'.[19] As far as the individual crewmen were concerned it was something of a victory as they could eventually return to their jobs, though Robson himself had a considerable fight on his hands before he finally achieved this. Yet in presenting the defence case in this way, tremendous potential anti-fascist political capital was sacrificed. Thus, the outcome of the trial and appeal was far more a victory for the British legal system, and what could be argued was the illegal non-intervention agreement, than it was for the crew. Watson and Corcoran claimed, plausibly, that 'Had more followed their [the crew's] example the government policy of "non-intervention" could have been under real pressure.'[20] Yet more people might have followed the example of the *Linaria* crew if the anti-fascist politics of its action had been made crystal clear before, during and after the trial and appeal.

The campaign to support the Tynemouth Basque Refugee Children's Hostel

The Basque Children's Committee was formed in early May 1937 to support the 4,000 refugee children who came to Britain as victims of the Franco offensive on their homeland (between April and August 1937). A hostel for a group of these children was established in Tynemouth and a campaign mounted to fund it. As with the *Linaria* crew, but in quite a different way, the presence of children who could quite easily and justifiably be presented as the victims of fascist aggression allowed for wide-reaching anti-fascist propaganda opportunities. But once again this potential was not exploited for political purposes. In this case, the Tynemouth Hostel Committee was following instructions from the national Basque Children's Committee, which had been formed from the National Joint Committee for Spanish Relief (an umbrella organisation that co-ordinated 'Aid Spain' activity) and the TUC. However, the Salvation Army, Quakers and the Catholic Church were also involved and this, combined with the express wishes of the Basque government, meant that the fund-raising campaign was conducted on purely humanitarian terms.[21] Thus, whilst anti-fascist motives must have informed the involvement of Nell Badsey, the communist warden of the hostel, and that of ILP members on the hostel's management committee, there were other members of it who were, in the words of communist Charlie Woods, 'actuated by the humanitarian nature of the appeal'.[22]

The Tyneside foodship campaign

The final set of campaigns were the 'foodships', that came as the Republic, in its final months of life, had to deal with an influx of refugees fleeing Franco's rapidly advancing forces. The Tyneside foodship campaign was by far the most widespread and concertedly energetic single 'Aid Spain' campaign in the North East. Whilst 17 Spanish Medical Aid committees emerged in the space of three years, 120 sub-committees of the Newcastle-based central foodship committee sprang up in less than 3 months after the campaign was launched in early December 1938.[23] Indeed, the Tyneside foodship campaign was one of, if not the, largest of the foodship campaigns (in terms of the numbers of sub-committees) and it became a model for others around Britain.[24] It raised £4,500, a 'great deal' from what was an economically depressed area.[25]

As suggested by its considerable size, those involved in the Tyneside foodship campaign were highly diverse in social and political terms. For example, the campaign's two presidents, though both aristocrats, were Labour left winger C. P. Trevelyan and Conservative Viscount Ridley who were, politically speaking, poles apart. This diversity was reflected throughout the campaign, from its patrons to the activists in both the central and sub-committees. There was active involvement from members of trade unions, the Council of Action for Peace and Reconstruction (CAPR, a very small and unorthodox liberal group), Labour, Communist, Liberal and Conservative Parties, Co-operative Guilds, the National Unemployed Workers' Movement, book club groups, boys' clubs, the International Brigade, League of Nations Union (LNU, which included Liberals and Conservatives amongst its membership), the clergy, women's sections of the British Legion and the Town's Women's Guild. Those publicly supporting and donating to the appeal were even more diverse in terms of class, political and religious affiliation, and included a National Liberal PPC, Ex-Servicemen's Association groups and Women's Institutes.[26]

As with several of the other 'Aid Spain' campaigns, the main campaign organisers played down the politics of the conflict. For example, in early January 1939, central campaign organiser Thomas Tindle Anderson wrote: 'We are not concerned with the rights and wrongs of the present conflict in Spain.'[27] It is striking that throughout the campaign the central organisers did not once explicitly present the foodship as a way of combating Franco and fascism. Instead, they were consistently clear that the foodship was 'purely humanitarian' and 'non-political in aims'.[28] Another notable feature of the campaign was that the sub-committees, almost without exception, followed the central committee in the way they framed the campaign. Their message differed only in that some committees called for help to end the starvation of the 'Spanish people', whilst others specified that aid would go to refugees in Republican territory.[29] Only the Labour Party-controlled Gateshead sub-committee partially strayed from this non-political stance, but even there the politics was muted by humanitarianism. Apart from this, some of the speakers at a central foodship public meeting, in Newcastle on 22 January 1939, mentioned the politics of the Spanish conflict in association with the foodship campaign but, again, the overall message was confused and muted.[30] Overall, the constantly repeated humanitarian message from all the main campaign organisers must have had far more of an impact on the general populace.

Why the humanitarian message?

An emphasis on humanitarianism clearly played an important role in many of these campaigns, and there were many reasons for this. The Basque government's request, coupled with involvement of the Catholic Church, explains the humanitarian emphasis in the Basque Hostel campaign, and the desire not to jeopardise the *Linaria* crew's livelihoods meant that anti-fascism was underplayed in their campaign and court case. Clearly, many involved in the 'Aid Spain' campaigns that depicted their activity as a humanitarian mission rather than as a means of combating fascism were themselves involved because they *were* anti-fascists. Nell Badsey, the North Shields communist who ran the Tynemouth Basque Hostel was an obvious example, as were several members of the foodship central committee, who had been anti-fascist activists for some years.[31]

However, humanitarianism also allowed for the involvement of individuals whose motives appeared quite different. A significant example of this was T. T. Anderson, the single most important foodship organiser in the region. With a conservative, middle-class background, Anderson was a grammar school teacher and 'well-known personality' who was involved in a great deal of charitable and social work.[32] A Quaker, Anderson appears to have become involved in the foodship campaign through the same kind of motives that led to his charity work: benevolent humanitarianism rather than anti-fascist politics. Certainly, he made no public anti-fascist statement before or during his involvement in the foodship campaign.

When some involved in the foodship, and other campaigns, emphasised the humanitarian and 'non-political' aims of the campaign, they were merely adhering to a tactical policy decision, presumably taken to minimise opposition to the fund and thereby maximise its financial success. But, when people like Anderson repeated the same mantras, it is likely that this was because they actually saw the campaign in those terms. Did anti-fascists allow the 'humanitarians' to set the agenda and simply acquiesce, or did they take the decision in order to bring human-itarians in, thereby broadening the campaign's base? Without detailed documentation, this question is impossible to answer for certain. The nearest understanding of the process can be gleaned in the foodship campaign, which was the best documented. There, the initiative first came from the Tyneside Joint Peace Council (TJPC), an organisation composed of communists, Labour Party and CAPR members and dedicated to organising anti-fascist and anti-appeasement propaganda.[33] It thus looks likely that the TJPC working group decided to bring in a figure who was not obviously 'political' to head the campaign and to do this must have decided that a 'non-political' humanitarian stance was required. Certainly, the most prominent Labour left and communist TJPC activists were not obviously involved in the foodship campaign, but whether that was by their design, someone else's, or was merely chance remains unclear.[34]

Whatever the process, for the anti-fascists to sacrifice the potential for political propaganda in the pursuit of greater financial success was surely a crucial mistake. Ultimately, the Republic needed arms to defeat fascism and, whilst food helped feed it and medicines helped patch up its wounded, without guns, shells and bullets it was never going to win. It could be argued, with some validity, that this was to misunderstand what the 'Aid Spain' campaigns were for; that the overtly 'political' demonstrations organised by the left parties against non-intervention were for placing this pressure on government, and that the 'Aid Spain' campaigns were more about attempting to show solidarity in a tangible way. There may be some mileage in this argument, but, for the sheer amount of application and hard work put into these campaigns by anti-fascists, the political dividends for their cause appear very meagre. Of course, whether the National government would have changed its policy on Spain in the face of mass demonstrations and resolutions it received from anti-fascists, is another question. But the appeal to liberals in the popular front policy effectively precluded most calls for industrial direct action to force a change in government policy on Spain.

'Humanitarianism' vs 'Politics'

The discussion so far has accepted that 'humanitarianism' and 'politics' are quite distinct. Of course, in reality there is no strict dividing line between the two concepts. In its widest sense, almost any human action or thought could be deemed 'political', but this definition is unhelpful. Moreover, when those keenest to defend the 'Aid Spain' campaigns' achievement provided counter arguments to the claim that they were humanitarian rather than politically based, they were thereby tacitly recognising a valid and significant distinction between the two. Thus, Jim Fyrth argued that

> To collect, or even give food or money for Spain became a political act as well as a humanitarian one, because the collection was probably organised by people of left sympathies on behalf of people with a left-wing government opposed by the British government and abused by most of the Conservative media.[35]

Several points can be made in response. First, a significant number of the organisers of some of the 'Aid Spain' campaigns in the North East clearly did not have 'left wing sympathies'. For example, Viscount Ridley or C. V. H. Vincent, a member of Jarrow foodship sub-committee and chairperson of Jarrow Conservative Association. Though he seemed relatively progressive, Vincent, midway through the foodship campaign, moved a motion conveying Jarrow Conservatives' 'loyal Christmas greetings' to Chamberlain, the arch-appeaser.[36]

Second, as has been shown, it was by no means clear that some of the collections being made were intended for the 'left-wing government' at all. The way the foodship campaign was framed, for example, suggested that it was intended to feed those who merely happened to find themselves in the 'left-wing government's territory' as an accident of war: the aid was never depicted as support for the Republican government itself. Of course, the aid would indirectly help the government's struggle, though by late 1938 only overwhelming military intervention on the Republic's side could have saved it. Third, even if the collection had been organised entirely by the left in aid of a 'left-wing government', if those collecting had said the aid was for a humanitarian fund to help the innocent victims of war, then collecting for that fund was in no sense 'political'. The politics of the conflict that threatened the 'innocents' had been completely disregarded.

Similarly, Fyrth also claimed that the need to defeat fascism in Spain, the political aspect, and the humanitarian, 'were rarely separate in the minds of those taking part'.[37] This might have been the case, but it cannot be shown and seems to be wishful thinking. Those acting on political motives were also likely to have been moved by the human suffering, but the reverse does not follow. For the 'Aid Spain' campaigns that were presented in clear anti-fascist terms, it seems reasonable to assume that the money raised was largely from those who agreed with the analysis. However, the same cannot be said of the motives of those involved in the campaigns presented as humanitarian efforts.

This attempt to completely blend humanitarianism and politics was applied to the motives of donors who, Mike Squires claimed, were showing sympathy with the plight of the hungry in Spain and 'at the same time, although not always in a conscious way, registered their abhorrence of fascism, and their support of democracy'.[38] If by this Squires meant that donating to these appeals objectively aided the Republic's fight against fascism (albeit not greatly) whether the donor knew it or not, then this seems a reasonable, though somewhat futile, statement. If, however, this is a claim that all donors were sub-conscious anti-fascists, then that is another matter. It seems a little desperate, to say the least, to employ arguments based on speculation about the sub-conscious thoughts of large numbers of people. If all the 'Aid Spain' campaigns had been expressed in explicit anti-fascist terms, there would be a reasonable degree of certainty that donors *were* anti-fascist. As this was not always the case, it seems fairly clear that there was an important and relatively clear distinction between those donating to express anti-fascist sentiment and those wanting merely to help starving women and children, a humanitarian reason.

Politicisation?

Given the results of contemporary public opinion polls, many of which showed that the Republic had strong popular support in Britain, it could reasonably be argued that the majority of donors *were* anti-fascist. However, as many of the campaigns they donated to had not supplied an anti-fascist message in their appeals, it would seem that the vast majority of these people must have been anti-fascist anyway. Clearly the 'Aid Spain' campaigns framed in humanitarian terms were highly unlikely to have 'converted' them to anti-fascism. In other words, the level of politicisation brought about by the humanitarian 'Aid Spain' campaigns must have been very low.

If individual cases are examined, it becomes clear that involvement in the humanitarian-based campaigns did not engender any obvious degree of 'politicisation' in the participants. Perhaps the most striking single example is that of T. T. Anderson, the main foodship organiser. His attitude to conscription, expressed in May 1939, revealed that his world view had not altered. Though he wanted a guarantee that the 'conscience clause' would be strictly observed, he echoed statements on Spain when saying that he had no 'corporate view' on the 'rights and wrongs' of conscription and no desire to 'obstruct' it.[39] Anderson was not obviously involved with any overtly 'political' agitation in 1939. That the most high profile and active individual in the foodship campaign was not obviously politicised by his involvement is signifi-cant as it appears that Anderson was representative of both that, and the other, humanitarian campaigns. The same was true of Conservatives such as C. V. H. Vincent of the foodship campaign. They did or said nothing after their involvement in the campaign that suggested their political perspective had altered in an anti-fascist direction. The same applies to those involved from the supposedly 'non political' town's women's guilds, Women's Institutes, women's sections of the Royal British Legion and the various churches. The obvious assumption is that these individuals and groups perceived the issue in the terms in which it was presented: as a 'non-political', benevolent, humanitarian cause and that this did not change.[40]

Though prominent Conservative and 'non-political' individuals involved in these campaigns do not appear to have been politicised, it is possible that similar but unnamed people who carried out door-to-door collections for the humanitarian campaigns were. This was Jim Fyrth's position, as he claimed that political arguments were essential to cam-paigning activities and that this changed individuals' political consciousness.[41] But did political arguments over the Spanish conflict nec-essarily have to enter doorstep discussions? The clearest indication on this came in the foodship campaign, when, in mid-January 1939, Anderson responded in the press to recurrent questions asked of collectors. Anderson cited a LNU report in order to counter the claim that foodship aid was helping the Republic as it was going solely to Republican civilians. The report stated that, due to a huge influx of refugees from Nationalist Spain, conditions in the Republic were both critical and entirely different to those in Franco territory. For this reason, Anderson argued, 'it would be unrea-sonable to treat both sides alike when the needs are different'.[42] The responses to several other questions also emphasised the non-political (i.e. politically neutral) and humanitarian nature of the campaign.

It seems reasonable to suppose that the responses Anderson supplied here were the self-same ones employed by collectors when asked about the partisanship of the campaign. Thus those collecting for humanitarian reasons were unlikely to be inadvertently politicised by their activities by being thrust reluctantly into political debates with prospective donors. If asked why they were collecting for the 'reds', the collector could avoid being compelled to engage in a discussion about the rights and wrongs of Franco and fascism simply by saying that the fund was to help starving and innocent Spanish women and children. Curiously, despite the Spanish Civil War being an ostensibly highly 'political' topic, politics *did not have to enter* the debate if the collector did not wish it to.

Of course, a collector could choose to defend the campaign on anti-fascist terms, but they were surely far more likely to do this if they already regarded the issue in a 'political' manner. And if, for example, the food-ship collectors individually followed the lead of the anti-fascist central organisers who deliberately depicted the foodship as 'non-political', even this would not have happened. Ellen Wilkinson's comment about the national Basque Children's Committee seems apt for all the humanitarian-based 'Aid Spain' campaigns: 'No one has shifted their political or religious affiliations by a hair-breadth by working on that committee, but on big humanitarian issues, British people have some-how learned to co-operate.'[43] Tom Buchanan noted that the 'actual level of politicisation in these ["Aid Spain"] coalitions was very limited, not least due to the sheer, exhausting amount of practical work required'.[44] But *politicisation* could have occurred, despite (or perhaps even because of) the amount of work required, if these campaigns had been framed in explicitly anti-fascist terms.

This is not to argue that no one was politicised by involvement in the humanitarian-based 'Aid Spain' campaigns. Of course, politicisation *can* occur in the most unpromising of circumstances for the obscurest of reasons, but the rhetoric employed by activists to frame their campaigns serves to either maximise or minimise the potential for politicisation. And, given the rhetoric, surely those politicised by the humanitarian 'Aid Spain' campaigns were a minor exception. A considerable element of 'Aid Spain' (the humanitarian) was unlikely to have done much at all to help 'awaken the British people to the nature of fascism'.[45] A final implication of this was that, because fund-raisers could quite easily side-step political discussion, the potential for politicising prospective donors on their doorsteps was also minimal. These considerations throw doubt on Jim Fyrth's claim that the 'Aid Spain' campaigns had a *palpable* political impact in that they made an important contribution to the 1945 Labour election landslide.[46] Surely, if this were the case, there would be at least some evidence of change occurring before war inter-vened to fundamentally alter the political landscape.

The popular front debate

The debates around the humanitarianism of the 'Aid Spain' campaigns and the degree of politicisation within them are relevant to another area of discussion. This is the debate surrounding the popular front, a strategy aimed at an alliance of all anti-fascists that could win political power in democracies and then forge alliances between countries, including Soviet Russia, in order to contain the fascist threat. In Britain, though the 'formal' campaigns for a popular front achieved little, some contemporary commentators saw great potential in the cross-party co-operation apparently achieved in the 'Aid Spain' campaigns. For example, Trevelyan, speaking in March 1939, thought that the popular front was achievable as 'All the local co-operation to help the Spaniards has proved it to be possible.'[47] This was echoed by historians such as Jim Fyrth, who claimed that 'The Aid for Spain Campaign was the nearest thing to a People's Front that came about in Britain.'[48] Implicit in these claims is the idea that the British popular front project had untapped potential because something similar came about 'unofficially' in the course of 'Aid Spain' campaigning work.

Two of the interconnected planks of the case for regarding the 'Aid Spain' campaigns as a de facto popular front were that their 'humanitarian' aspects were inextricable from their politics and that they therefore politicised many. Serious doubt has already been expressed on these claims, but a specific aspect of politicisation requires comment. If the 'Aid Spain' campaigns had represented potential support for the popular front, why was there not even an indication of this in the support that the popular front campaigns themselves garnered? In the North East, the popular front was never well received, with the United Peace Alliance campaign of 1938 rallying very little support. By the time Cripps launched his popular front 'Petition campaign' in January 1939, the foodship campaign was already in full swing. Theoretically, the conditions could hardly have been better, as the foodship campaign was the largest and most significant 'Aid Spain' campaign in the North East. It was not only Trevelyan on the Cripps-supporting Labour left that recognised this potential. Announcing his support for Cripps' popular front memorandum, Arthur Blenkinsop (a Newcastle Labour PPC), argued that those who had recently worked on the foodship campaign 'understand how effective such co-operation can be'.[49] Yet Blenkinsop's name did not figure in the foodship campaign and, more significantly, those involved in the foodship campaign generally did not emerge as Cripps supporters. So, for example, T. T. Anderson does not appear to have supported the Cripps campaign. In fact, the only names that do emerge in relation to both foodship and Cripps campaigns were those of left wingers like Trevelyan himself.

Regarding Liberals, only members of the tiny CAPR were involved in both the 'Aid Spain' and popular front campaigns. An indeterminate number of other liberals collected for the 'Aid Spain' campaigns as individuals, and some of the more prominent regional leaders expressed pro-Republic, anti-Franco views. But there was very little liberal support for the popular front in the North East. Viewing Labour as the main enemy, most liberal activists, and voters, sided with the Conservatives against Labour and liberal involvement in the 'Aid Spain' campaigns, such as it was, had no obvious impact on these attitudes.[50] In an apparent attempt to show that the 'Aid Spain' campaigns *had* fed people into the popular front campaigns, Fyrth claimed that 'Aid Spain' activists were prominent in support of 'people's front' candidates in the elections autumn and winter 1938.[51] But Fyrth made no attempt to show that these individuals had been brought to supporting the popular front by their involvement in humanitarian 'Aid Spain' campaigning. Of course, some 'Aid Spain' campaigners would be expected to be also involved in the popular front, but, certainly in the North East, these individuals were almost exclusively left wingers who would have supported it regardless of their involvement in 'Aid Spain' campaigns.[52]

Other arguments employed regard contemporary perceptions. Fyrth claimed that 'very many of those involved in "Aid Spain" felt that they were also building a "People's Front from below" '.[53] Though no supporting evidence is presented, it seems quite likely that communists and others already favourable to the idea did think that 'Aid Spain' campaigns they were involved in constituted a popular front. But this does not mean that *they were right*. Unfortunately, it is impossible now to ask individuals like T. T. Anderson about their perceptions of the campaigns, but, given the evidence that there is of their words and actions during and after the campaigns, it seems unlikely that they would have agreed with Fyrth's claim.

The perceptions of those who were not involved have also been employed to bolster the 'de facto popular front' argument. Thus, Fyrth claimed that the 'Aid Spain' campaigns were regarded (and feared) by the Labour leadership as 'backdoor' popular fronts that were making communists respectable.[54] It is possible that the leadership felt threatened by these campaigns, because, as Fyrth explained, they brought Labour Party members into contact with communists. However, the threat was not deemed great enough in the North East to actually expel Labour Party members for their involvement.[55] Moreover, if the leadership did fear these campaigns, this can be explained as merely another case of its communist paranoia clouding its judgement. Communists did not appear, for the most part, to have been made 'respectable' by involvement in the humanitarian 'Aid Spain' campaigns, simply because politics were not discussed. As Len Edmondson, an ILP activist, noted, within these campaigns 'none of it [politics] was ever raised then. It didn't interfere with any of the local activity on behalf of aid for Spain.'[56]

In fact, it seems likely that the majority of those involved in the humanitarian campaigns were unaware that they were organising with communists. Certainly, the prominent communists involved were not identified as such in the press. For example, a foodship press appeal signed by Sunderland dignitaries included the name of Frank Graham, but there was no indication that he was a communist or even an ex-International Brigade member. The same can be said of other mentions Graham had in the press in relation to the foodship campaign.[57] Individual communists must surely have gained 'respect' for their energetic activities in these campaigns, but this respect was accorded to them *as individuals*, not as communists. There was, indeed, a tacit recognition of this when communist Hymie Lee, commenting on the north-east situation in March 1939, complained that 'in all the mass activity we are hiding the face of the party. Communists are working everywhere but they don't show that they are communists.'[58] It seems that individual communists only achieved an apparent air of respectability precisely because their party affiliation was not broadcast.

The north-east CP's predicament in March 1939 throws light on another aspect of the claim that the 'Aid Spain' campaigns politicised. Noreen Branson wrote that communists had begun to understand 'that if you can lead people into action on some issue on which they feel strongly, the very experience itself can bring about a change in their ideas [...] whereas you seldom convert anyone to socialism by preaching from the sidelines'.[59] Though ostensibly reasonable, this claim does not explain why the foodship campaign did not bring any direct benefit to the party in the form of new recruits. In fact, far from increasing in early 1939, north-east CP membership actually *decreased* by 10 per cent (50 individuals).[60] This came in the context of CP membership at national level hitting a 'plateau' between January and July 1939.[61] Yet, even by national standards, the decline in Tyneside, a district that already had a low membership, was little short of disastrous. When, in March 1939, Lee complained that the regional party had no profile despite its activity, he added that 'there is no feeling about the party growing', and these two observations surely must have been causally linked.[62] The energetic but anonymous communist activity in the foodship, and other human-itarian campaigns, had, not surprisingly, brought little or no success in converting people to 'socialism'. Of course, the overtly 'political' demonstrations organised by the CP, the campaigns it helped organise that *were* framed in explicitly political terms and its organising of the International Brigade did bring recruits to the party. But the party would surely have gained more by channelling its energies into only those 'Aid Spain' campaigns that were overtly anti-fascist, and eschewing those with a 'non-political', humanitarian-basis.[63]

Ultimately, it is insufficient to remark that, as some of the 'Aid Spain' campaigns looked like popular fronts in action, that is what they must have been. The popular front was a political project. Its two most basic building-blocks were anti-fascism and, one step up from this, a critique of the Chamberlain government's appeasement policy, because it was regarded as pro-fascist. Inspired by David Blaazer's work, this definition of a 'popular front outlook' seems the widest tenable in a British con-text.[64] Yet, even with this inclusive theoretical framework, it is clear that some, often important, individuals in the humanitarian-based 'Aid Spain' campaigns did not share this 'popular front outlook', nor did they adopt one as a result of the politicisation process that any truly 'political' campaign has on a good degree of its participants.

The underlying unifying factor in these cases was humanitarianism. It might be argued that, as these funds went to the Republic, these indi-viduals were acting as unconscious (or 'objective') anti-fascists, but that is simply not enough. The popular front demanded a positive political stand on some of the most pressing issues of the day, and these indi-viduals either did not make one, or, if they did, it was not to side with the popular fronters. All the north-east 'Aid Spain' campaigns that looked like popular fronts in terms of those involved (with perhaps the *Linaria* Defence Committee as a relatively insignificant exception) sacri-ficed the politics of the situation in Spain in order to employ a strictly humanitarian campaigning message. With only a couple of exceptional occasions, none of these campaigns organised meetings with 'speakers from all parties supporting the Republic' and they did not campaign against non-intervention, a clearly political stance.[65] The evidence of 'Aid Spain' campaigns in the North East supports Buchanan's claim that 'there is no evidence that humanitarian work for Spain on a Popular Front basis translated into effective political action'.[66] In fact, it appears that these campaigns only achieved the appearance of a popular front at all precisely *because* the Spanish conflict was *not* depicted in a 'polit-ical' manner. Thus the de facto popular front based around these campaigns was no more than an illusion. If the humanitarian-based 'Aid Spain' campaigns are all that supporters of the popular front strategy can cite in its defence, then it is clear that the strategy was never viable in 1930s Britain.

Final debates: working-class attitudes, the role of communists and the ' "Aid Spain" movement'

Some final areas of the debate between Tom Buchanan and Jim Fyrth require comment. First, is the attitude of the British working class to the conflict. Buchanan pointed out that Fyrth excluded 'discordant experiences', such as working-class internationalism that was pro-Franco.[67] Buchanan also noted that Fyrth did not properly consider the concerns of working-class Catholics, some of whom left the Labour Party over the issue. Whilst Buchanan was right to observe that it was unsatisfactory to represent Catholic opposition as 'aberrant', it appears that he himself may have slightly overstated the Catholic labour movement opposition to the party's stance on Spain. Certainly, in the North East, which had the second largest population of Catholics in England, there is hardly any evidence of open labour movement Catholic hostility to the Republic. Indeed, in places such as Jarrow, with the highest concentration of labour movement Catholics in the region, the party and its MP, Ellen Wilkinson, did a great deal in support of the Republic.[68] In the North East, the working-class movement acted in support of the Republic, through both official and unofficial channels, and seemed to be relatively well supported by ordinary working-class people. Yet the impression given by many of the humanitarian 'Aid Spain' campaigns was that the middle classes spoke from the public platforms and played leading roles in many of the committees, whilst the working classes, who could least afford it, were those who provided the bulk of the donations. Given the minimal political impact that these humanitarian campaigns had (both in Britain and in Spain), the very real sacrifices made by many working-class people in these campaigns were simply not justified.

Second, is the disagreement over the role of communists in the campaigns, Buchanan claiming that they should not necessarily be credited with the 'leading historical role' in 'Aid Spain' activities.[69] Though Fyrth appeared very quick to establish that communists were behind every campaign in his book, his reply to Buchanan was more measured. Whilst communists were not dominant in 'Aid Spain' as a whole, Fyrth argued, they did dominate or were prominent in some organisations and very active in many.[70] In the North-East communists were clearly at the centre of some campaigns, for examples, Alex Robson, the *Linaria* strike leader, Nell Badsey the Tynemouth Basque Hostel warden and Wilf Jobling, in Blaydon Spanish Medical Aid Committee. However, the communists involved in the larger and more popular of the campaigns, such as the foodship, appeared swamped by others who did not share even their broad views on the international situation. If these communists had tried to influence others in a 'left-ward' direction, they had clearly failed to have an impact. Certainly, being prominent in a particular 'Aid Spain' organisation did not necessarily indicate 'political dominance' of it. It is also striking that in, for example, many of the Spanish Medical Aid committees there are no identifiable communists. This must partly be due to the paucity of evidence, but must also indicate that in many of these committees communists were not a force at all. In the North East, what can be safely said is that communists were involved in many (but probably not all) 'Aid Spain' campaigns, that sometimes they were also prominent, but that 'dominance' seems unlikely in the larger campaigns. Certainly, as has been seen, despite this extensive communist activity, the regional Communist Party itself gained very little from all its work.

Finally, there was the question of whether it is legitimate to talk of, in Fyrth's lexicon, an 'Aid Spain movement'. Buchanan complained that Fyrth did not define the 'Aid Spain movement' and asserted that 'Aid Spain' 'did not exist as a national political entity and had no institutional basis'.[71] The 'real hallmark of "Aid Spain" was its very diversity', claimed Buchanan, and that 'this very diversity denies the character of a "mass movement" '.[72] In response, Fyrth asked, quite reasonably, 'Is not diversity an *essential* condition of mass movements in countries with pluralist traditions?'[73] Fyrth's counter argument that movements do not necessarily have a 'formal national existence' was also convincing, and on those terms it seems that there was a case for using the term 'Aid Spain movement'. But the crux of this discussion is in Buchanan's question: 'What *united* these diverse phenomena beyond a broad internationalist sympathy with the people and workers of Spain and hatred of fascism?'[74] Surely, the factors that Buchanan recognised here as uniting the campaigns would be enough to justifiably apply the term 'movement' to them. The problem arises, of course, if we apply this statement to the individuals involved in 'Aid Spain' campaigns. Then, as the case of the North East has shown, the uniting force was not, in many of the most important campaigns, a 'hatred of fascism' at all, rather it was a 'humanitarian sympathy' with the people of Spain.

Conclusions

One of Jim Fyrth's stranger claims, in response to Buchanan's point that the 'Aid Spain' campaigns were 'spectacularly unsuccessful in affecting the politics of the labour movement or government', was that it was 'arguable' that 'the growing support for the Republic, which undoubtedly owed much to the Aid Spain campaigns, prevented the British government from more open support of Franco'.[75] Short of actually supporting Franco militarily, it is difficult to imagine how the British government could have been more pro-Franco, given how the sham of non-intervention effectively supported his forces and weakened the Republic. The British government's attitude was quite clear to most; it did not need spelling out. (And the 'Aid Spain' campaigns surely owed far more to the growing support for the Republic than the other way round.) But the spectacular lack of success of these campaigns (on Buchanan's terms) was at least in part due to the fact that many of them did not even attempt to alter either labour movement politics or the government's attitude. Instead, many aimed at raising the most money they could for suffering civilians in the Republic by framing a 'non-political' campaign. It was not to the left's credit that Franco-supporting Catholics also often neglected to mention who the aid was for.[76]

Tom Buchanan's claim that, whilst consisting of broad coalitions of individuals and institutions both within and without the labour movement, 'Aid Spain' at local level was *not* a 'political project', is partly confirmed by the evidence of the 'Aid Spain' campaigns in the North East.[77] However, as has been seen, it would be wrong to view all the highly diverse 'Aid Spain' campaigns as being essentially the same. Certainly, it is clear that all the campaigns that took on the appearance of popular fronts were humanitarian based, but many of the Spanish Medical Aid committees were not as politically diverse and they expressed the issue in clear anti-fascist terms. This was the most important distinction to be made in the supposed 'Aid Spain movement'. With this in mind, James Klugmann's claim that there were three levels of support for the Republic can be assessed. The highest level, for Klugmann, was fighting in the International Brigade and there was a middle level of political action against non-intervention. The third level was one of 'extraordinarily broad' support for the Republic on the basis of foodships, medicines and so forth that 'involved people of all political opinions [...] It was an extremely broad, humanitarian movement.'[78] In the North East, the majority of those who were involved in these campaigns experienced the third 'humanitarian' level. However, elements of some campaigns, such as Blaydon Spanish Medical Aid committee, seem to have occupied an area that straddled the third and second levels.

Ultimately though, by accident or by design, anti-fascism did not play a significant part in many of the most important of the 'Aid Spain' campaigns, which is a quite striking feature given how 'political' the whole situation in Spain was. At Labour's annual conference in October 1936, one of the most devastating attacks on the leadership's support for non-intervention came from a north-eastern delegate. C. P. Trevelyan told the Labour leadership: 'You are beggared of policy at this moment [...] When the last great war that is looming comes [...] I hope then the Labour Party will have some other policy to offer than sympathy, accompanied by bandages and cigarettes.'[79] It was somewhat ironic that, hamstrung by its support for the popular front, the left that Trevelyan represented could not come up with a better, practical policy for aiding the Republic and fighting fascism during these years.

Notes

1. George Orwell, 'Homage to Catalonia' in George Orwell (ed.) *Orwell in Spain* (London: Penguin, 2001), p. 170.
2. Though Franco himself was no fascist (and neither was a considerable section of the right-wing coalition he forged), it is still legitimate to talk of anti-fascism in relation to this conflict given the support that Franco received from Hitler and Mussolini.
3. Jim Fyrth, *The Signal Was Spain. The Aid Spain Movement in Britain, 1936–39* (London: Lawrence and Wishart, 1986), p. 21.
4. See Hywel Francis, *Miners Against Fascism. Wales and the Spanish Civil War* (London: Lawrence and Wishart, 1984) and Mike Squires, *The Aid to Spain Movement in Battersea, 1936–1939* (London: Elmsfield Publications, 1994).
5. A version of this chapter appeared as 'Britain's De Facto Popular Front? The Case of the Tyneside Foodship Campaign, 1938–1939', *Labour History Review*, 69(1), 2004, pp. 323–45. For the purposes of this chapter 'north-east England' is what is now Northumberland, Tyneside and County Durham, but not Teesside. Though there appears to be no internal records left by any of the part of any 'Aid Spain' campaign in the region, there is a good deal of information on some of these campaigns in the regional press and other sources like trade union minutes. For a comprehensive list of all the material examined for this research, see Lewis H. Mates, 'The United Front and the Popular Front in the North East of England, 1936–1939', unpublished PhD Thesis (Newcastle University, 2002), pp. 291–311.
6. Nigel Todd, *In Excited Times. The People Against the Blackshirts* (Whitley Bay: Bewick Press, 1995), pp. 13, 23, 26, 28–33, 65, 74.
7. The International Brigade Dependant's Aid, British Youth Foodship and Voluntary Industrial Aid campaigns are not discussed as they did not involve significant numbers of people and left little evidence of their activities in the region.

8. Lewis H. Mates, 'United Front', pp. 41–3, 129–33, 274.
9. *Blaydon Courier*, 16 January 1937.

The view that the Spanish struggle was essentially about 'democracy versus fascism' was, partly as a consequence of the popular front policy, the dominant paradigm on the left. However, it was not the only view of the conflict on the left, and some, such as George Orwell, emphasised the revolution that had occurred in many parts of Republican Spain. This had significant implications for the kind of solidarity action that could be contemplated, for the level of working class response and for its effectiveness. (George Orwell, *Orwell in Spain*, p. 188)

10. *Newcastle Evening Chronicle*, 27 October 1936.
11. *North Mail*, 24 February 1937, 5 March 1937; Alec Robson, *Spike: Alec 'Spike' Robson 1895–1979: Class Fighter* (North Shields: North Tyneside TUC, 1987), p. 11.
12. *North Mail*, 24 February 1937.
13. *North Mail*, 22 February 1937.
14. *North Mail*, 19 April 1937; Manchester Labour History Archive (MLHA), CP/CENT/PERS/5/05, Tom O'Byrne autobiography.
15. *North Mail*, 19 April 1937.
16. Tom Buchanan, *The Spanish Civil War and the British Labour Movement* (Cambridge: Cambridge University Press, 1991), p. 212.
17. *North Mail*, 4, 5 May and 7 June 1937.
18. *Shields Gazette*, 13 March, 19 and 27 April 1937.
19. Don Watson and John Corcoran, *An Inspiring Example: The North East of England and the Spanish Civil War, 1936–1939* (London: McGuffin Press, 1996), p. 20.
20. Don Watson and John Corcoran, *An Inspiring Example*, p. 22.
21. Jim Fyrth, 'The Aid Spain Movement in Britain, 1936–39', *History Workshop Journal*, 35, 1993, p. 157; Lewis H. Mates, 'United Front', p. 274.
22. Marx Memorial Library (MML), BoxB-4/M/1, Charlie Woods letter to Jim Fyrth, 18 February 1985; Len Edmondson (b. Gateshead, 1913), Tape-recorded Interview with Lewis Mates, 19 June 1998.
23. It is likely that there were a few more Spanish Medical Aid Committees that left no evidence of their existence, but surely not a hundred more. *North Mail*, 7 February 1939.
24. Lewis H. Mates, 'United Front', pp. 242–3, 251–2.
25. *Spanish Relief*, March 1939.
26. There appear to have been very few Conservatives involved in these campaigns. Lewis H. Mates, 'United Front', pp. 244–7.
27. *Shields Gazette*, 3 January 1939.
28. Shields Gazette, 22 January 1939.
29. Shields Gazette, 17 January 1939; *Heslop's Local Advertiser*, 17 February 1939.
30. Lewis H. Mates, 'United Front', pp. 249–51.
31. Lewis H. Mates, 'United Front', pp. 35, 192–221.
32. *Shields Gazette*, 6 January 1939.
33. Lewis H. Mates, 'United Front', pp. 35–40, 244.
34. Or perhaps they were too busy, supporting Cripps' popular front campaign or running the Basque Tynemouth Hostel.

35. Jim Fyrth, 'The Aid Spain Movement in Britain, 1936–39' *History Workshop Journal*, 35, 1993, p. 162.
36. *Shields Gazette*, 16 December 1938.
37. Jim Fyrth, *History Workshop Journal*, 35, 1993, p. 162.
38. Mike Squires, *Aid to Spain Movement*, p. 40.
39. *Shields Gazette*, 12 May 1939.
40. Lewis H. Mates , 'United Front', pp. 254–9.
41. Jim Fyrth, *History Workshop Journal*, 35, 1993, pp. 162–3.
42. *North Mail*, 19 January 1939.
43. *Sunday Sun*, 20 December 1936.
44. Tom Buchanan, 'Britain's Popular Front? Aid for Spain and the British Labour Movement' *History Workshop Journal*, 31, 1991, p. 71.
45. Jim Fyrth, *History Workshop Journal*, 35, 1993, p. 162.
46. Jim Fyrth, *History Workshop Journal*, pp. 162–3.
47. Newcastle Robinson Library (NRL), CPT184, Notes for speech at Empress Stadium, 12 March 1939.
48. Jim Fyrth, *Signal*, p. 22.
49. *Tribune*, 27 January 1939.
50. Lewis H. Mates, 'United Front', pp. 160–231.
51. Jim Fyrth, *History Workshop Journal*, 35, 1993, p. 161.
52. Lewis H. Mates, 'United Front', pp. 160–91.
53. Jim Fyrth, *History Workshop Journal*, 35, 1993, p. 161.
54. Jim Fyrth, *History Workshop Journal*, p. 160.
55. Lewis H. Mates, 'United Front', pp. 130–1.
56. Len Edmondson Interview, 19 June 1998.
57. Frank Graham, *The Battle of Jarama* (Newcastle: F. Graham, 1987), p. 34.
58. MML, Microfilm, CP Central Committee Minutes, 19 March 1939.
59. Noreen Branson, 'Myths from Right and Left', in Jim Fyrth (ed.), *Britain, Fascism and the Popular Front* (London: Lawrence and Wishart, 1985), p. 127.
60. CP Central Committee Minutes, 19 March 1939.
61. Andrew Thorpe, 'The Membership of the Communist Party of Great Britain, 1920–1945', *Historical Journal*, 43, 3, 2000, p. 783.
62. CP Central Committee Minutes, 19 March 1939.
63. Of course, as indigenous fascism was defeated in the region by 1935, practical anti-fascism for the left could only manifest itself in support for the Spanish Republic and those fighting fascism elsewhere abroad.
64. David Blaazer, *The Popular Front and the Progressive Tradition* (Cambridge: Cambridge University Press, 1992), passim.
65. Jim Fyrth, *History Workshop Journal*, 35, 1993, p. 161.
66. Tom Buchanan, *Spanish Civil War*, p. 139.
67. Tom Buchanan, *History Workshop Journal*, 31, 1991, p. 65.
68. Lewis H. Mates, 'United Front', pp. 79–108.
69. Tom Buchanan, *History Workshop Journal*, 31, 1991, p. 67.
70. Jim Fyrth, *History Workshop Journal*, 35, 1993, p. 160.
71. Tom Buchanan, *History Workshop Journal*, 31, 1991, p. 62.
72. Tom Buchanan, *History Workshop Journal*, p. 71.
73. Jim Fyrth, *History Workshop Journal*, 35, 1993, p. 156.
74. Tom Buchanan, *History Workshop Journal*, 31, 1991, p. 71.

75. Tom Buchanan, *History Workshop Journal*, p. 70; Jim Fyrth, *History Workshop Journal*, 35, 1993, p. 163.
76. For example, in a letter asking for donations to the *Catholic Universe*'s Medical Fund for Spain, G. Keenan claimed that the funds were for the 'sick and wounded in Spain', but did not specify on which side (*Newcastle Journal*, 2 January 1937).
77. Tom Buchanan, *History Workshop Journal*, 31, 1991, p. 71.
78. J. Klugmann, 'The Crisis of the Thirties: A View From the Left', in J. Clark, M. Heinemann, D. Margolies and C. Snee (eds), *Culture and Crisis in Britain in the 30s* (London: Lawrence and Wishart, 1979), p. 19.
79. Report of the Thirty-sixth Annual Labour Party Conference (Edinburgh, 1936), pp. 172–3.

7
Guarding the Barricades: Working-class Anti-fascism 1974–79

David Renton

The 1970s campaign against fascism was one of the largest protest movements that Britain has ever seen.[1] It took place during the fall of the 1974–79 Labour government. The far-right National Front then claimed up to 20,000 members. The party put up 413 candidates in local elections in 1977 and threatened to achieve further breakthroughs in the 1979 general election.[2] National Front slogans against immigration resulted in violence against immigrants and black Britons. Where Front candidates polled well, the number of anti-racist attacks rose. Anti-fascists responded with a wide range of initiatives. The single largest campaign, the Anti-Nazi League (ANL), distributed around nine million leaflets between 1977 and 1979, warning of the danger posed by the far right. Around 250 ANL branches mobilised some 40,000 to 50,000 members. Through individual donations, the League raised £600,000 between 1977 and 1980. Other groups including Rock Against Racism (RAR) also took part in the campaign.[3] Probably around half a million people were involved in anti-racist activity, joining demonstrations, giving out leaflets or painting out graffiti. By the end of the decade, the National Front had been forced into retreat.

The purpose of this chapter is first of all to draw attention to working-class involvement in the anti-fascist campaign. A consensus among recent historians has insisted on the cross-class appeal of racism and fascism.[4] Yet in every recent society, real barriers have existed, which have tended to limit the appeal of these ideas to small groups. For example, Philip Coupland's chapter in this collection studies that minority of workers in the 1930s who briefly identified with Oswald Mosley's British Union of Fascists.[5] Almost without exception, he reports, such figures

141

were driven out. Joining the fascists under the influence of redistributive slogans, such militants soon learned that fascism was not a party for them. Its proclaimed belief in revolution was skin-deep. Fascism's hostility to the trade unions, to welfare, to any idea of equality was more profound. One by one, such proletarian fascists were driven out.

The processes that Coupland describes were the expression, in various individuals' lives, of a more important, general trend. In society as a whole, barriers existed to prevent large numbers of workers from going over to fascism. The organised labour movement trained its members in an ideology of reform. The underlying principles of solidarity were inimical to the tradition of radical inequality on which fascism was based. Of course, barriers could be breached. The ideas of reformism had to be carried by real people, they might be argued in an unconvincing manner, or people might carry contradictory ideas in their heads. So frustrated by the labour movement, motivated sometimes by anti-communism, or influenced by long periods of unemployment, there were trade unionists who joined the fascists. If we view this process from the perspective of an isolated individual, then anyone from any background 'could' become a fascist. But if we look above the level of individuals, towards society as a whole, then some generalisations hold true. Where trade unionism has been strongest, fascism has always been weak. Working-class fascists were a minority compared to the multitudes of trade unionist anti-fascists.

The contribution of working-class militants has been defined deliberately narrowly here. The emphasis is on trade union involvement. That is not to say that other forms of working-class contributions were insignificant. It would be just as feasible to emphasise the role of community activism based on working-class districts in the campaign, or the role of particular women's groups often with a strong socialist-feminist tinge, as I have attempted elsewhere.[6] Yet trade union activity is a particular indicator of class involvement, a sign that any campaign involved some of the central organisation of the British labour movement.

Second, this activity is examined critically. Some emphasis is placed on the contradictions of the campaign, especially the complex relationship between rank-and-file activists and the leadership of the Labour Party. The anti-fascist campaign took place while Labour was in office. The people described in the following sections were working-class anti-fascists. Some were members of the Labour Party. Almost all were members of trade unions affiliated to Labour. Many of them felt that if Labour had been doing its job properly and representing working-class interests, then there would have been little need for anti-fascists to fight this defensive campaign. Without mis-government, unemployment or poverty, there would have been little space for racism to flourish. Anti-fascists openly asked if Labour was responding to its roots?

From the Tiber to Southall

We can begin by summarising briefly the events of the campaign as a whole. For our purposes, the fascism of the late 1970s began with a populist campaign against immigration. On 22 April 1968, Enoch Powell a member of Edward Heath's Shadow Cabinet gave a speech in Birmingham, in which he argued for an end to further migration to Britain.[7] Powell's speech led immediately to an upsurge of popular racism. In London, Dockers and Smithfield market workers downed tools to back his claims.[8] Powell's speech gave publicity to fringe racist groups, including the National Front, which had been established in February 1967. Just 250 people attended the party's inaugural meeting in London, which gives a fair indication of the organisation's entire national membership at that time. Yet under the impact of a series of press scares about racism, the National Front grew. At a by-election in West Bromwich in 1973, one leader of the party Martin Webster secured 16 per cent or just under five thousand votes. In the February 1974 general election, the Front fielded 54 candidates who received a total of 75,000 votes. In October, some 90 National Front candidates received a grand total of 113,000 votes.[9]

The Labour Party had won the two 1974 elections on the back of a profound desire for change, and its manifesto promised the abolition of the House of Lords and the public schools, and increased taxes for the rich to pay for better public services. Trade union left wingers, including the 'terrible twins' Jack Jones and Hugh Scanlon, were brought into close contact with the government. In return for consultation, the unions promised to reduce the strikes that had undermined the previous, Conservative government. Unemployment rose from 600,000 in 1974 to over one million, five years later. There was a sharp fall in the number of strikes. The government reduced spending on public services, even closing hospitals. Within the trade unions the established lefts were confused and demoralised by Labour's lurch to the right. When strikes revived they did so on a section basis, and were bitterly unpopular. The period of the Wilson-Callaghan government was a time of popular disillusionment that prepared the way for the Tories' victory in 1979.

The National Front received 119,000 votes in the May 1977 Greater London Council elections, and almost quarter of a million votes in that year's local elections. The activity of the far right forced its opponents to respond. On 23 April 1977, a twelve hundred-strong National Front march through Wood Green was opposed by some 3,000 anti-racists, including delegations from Haringey Labour Party, trade unionists, the Indian Workers' Association, local West Indians, members of RAR and the Socialist Workers Party (SWP). In May 1977, 23 anti-fascist committees in London came together to form an All London Anti-Racist Anti-Fascist Co-ordinating Committee (ALARAFCC), which adopted *CARF*, the paper of the Kingston Campaign against racism and fascism as its bi-monthly journal.[10]

On 13 August 1977, around five thousand anti-fascists, including large numbers of local Black youths, prevented 800 National Front supporters from marching through Lewisham. Daily and weekly newspapers ran the sensational story of 200 people being arrested and the 50 policemen injured, ignoring the causes of the protest, and portraying the conflict as a senseless battle between two parallel sets of extremists. Journalist Hugo Young, then at the *Sunday Times*, solemnly announced that antifascists were 'a forerunner of the forces of darkness'. Tory leader Margaret Thatcher was interviewed. She informed the press that 'Your Communism is the left foot of Socialism and your Fascism the right foot of it.'[11]

Yet the main effect of the Lewisham protest was actually to boost antiracism. In its aftermath, the Labour Party conference voted to establish a united anti-fascist campaign. Jim Nichol and Paul Holborow of the Socialist Workers Party began the negotiations that led to the formation of the ANL, the largest and most important of the various anti-fascist groups. The League received the support of around forty Labour members of parliament and sections of the broader left. Prominent members of the ANL included Tariq Ali of the International Marxist Group, Arthur Scargill of the National Union of Mineworkers', Peter Hain the anti-apartheid activist, Ernie Roberts of the engineers' union, and Neil Kinnock, then a prominent left winger but later a right-wing leader of the Labour Party.[12]

Through the 1979 election campaign, stories came in of violence between fascists and their opponents. Two hundred police were required to prevent anti-fascist protests in Battersea. Five thousand police were used at Leicester and four thousand at Newham. On 28 April, over a thousand police were employed in West Bromwich, and similar numbers at Bradford on 30 April.[13] At Southall in West London, fighting between police and anti-racists ended with the death of Blair Peach, a left-wing teacher from New Zealand.[14] The constant disturbances disrupted any NF claims of respectability. Confronted every time it met by activists of the left, the Front also lost supporters to Margaret Thatcher's renascent Conservatives. The Front split three ways, and soon found itself outpaced on the ground by smaller, more militant, far-right factions such as Column 88 and the British National Party (BNP). The National Front found itself unable to hold meetings or sell its newspapers. Its candidates no longer received sympathetic press coverage. Membership went into a catastrophic decline. For ten years and more, British fascism was on the retreat.

Rail, school, fire-fighters

We can turn now to our central theme, of working-class involvement in the anti-fascist campaign. The ANL counted 50 local Labour Parties among its affiliates, along with some 30 branches of the engineering workers' union AUEW, 25 trades councils, 13 shop stewards committees, 11 NUM lodges, and similar numbers of branches from other unions including TGWU, CPSA, TASS, NUJ, NUT and NUPE.[15] In November 1978 Bill Dunn of the Communist Party of Great Britain wrote an article for his party's paper the *Morning Star* reporting on the successes of anti-fascists in winning the support of trade unionists for their campaign. Twenty trade union executive committees had voted to back the ANL. Six hundred trade union and workplace organisations were 'in direct contact' with the League. 'Among them are ANL groups working in massive factories like British Leyland Longbridge or Fords of Dagenham, Yorkshire miners, civil servants and local government.' Bill Keys, general secretary of the print union SOGAT, had addressed anti-Nazi rallies in Northern England, as well as marches in London. There were also ANL blocs among the print workers of Fleet Street and among technicians and journalists working on national and regional television.[16]

In Preston, the fire-fighters union and the postal workers' union backed the League, as did the joint shop stewards' committee at Leyland motors. Len Brindle, the convenor at the local Leyland works, backed the ANL. In Nottingham, the League received support from the white-collar union ASTMS. One of the most important members of the League in the city was Don Devin, an activist within the National Union of Hosiery and Knitworkers. In Manchester, supporters included FBU members from New Mills Fire Station. Elsewhere, the technicians' union ACTT worked with the League in arguing that the National Front's broadcasts should be banned. One journalist Francis Wheen rang Alan Sapper, general secretary of the ACTT to suggest that such disruptive action would only make martyrs of the National Front. 'Democracy is threatened', Sapper replied, 'We don't need to bother with philosophical arguments. We can discuss democracy until the concentration camps come in.'[17]

The Preston fire-fighters were not the only members of the union to have contacts with anti-racists. During the national dispute of 1978–79, striking fire-fighters took collections at RAR events all around London. On this occasion, it was undoubtedly trade unionism that gained from the connections made by anti-fascism. 'Dressed in full fire-fighting uniform, they mingled freely with the young punk audience, made a good collection and had a great time.'[18]

One public voice of the anti-fascist campaign was Claudine Eccleston, a 24-year-old plumber and activist in the electrician's union EEPTU, who also took part in activities organised by the black socialist organisation – Flame. She was interviewed for the socialist feminist newspaper *Women's Voice*. Eccleston reminded her colleagues that anti-fascism needed to evolve into a broader campaign. 'It will take the defeat of the white racists at the polls', she argued, 'to get the blacks on the streets. When they see how much can be done through the activity of the Anti-Nazi League – then they will start organising on other issues. Now all our energies go into stopping the National Front. But we have not started attacking the roots of racism.'[19]

Some workplace ANL groups were little more than a badge, while others were able to establish a regular newspaper or magazine. The latter included Rail Against the Nazis, members of the rail union RMT, ASLEF and TSSA. Their banner showed a high-speed train knocking over a gang of Nazis. Members of Kings Cross ASLEF initially set up the branch. One member of this union branch, Leno Carraro was arrested at Lewisham in 1977. His colleagues took round a collection to pay his fine. When the ANL was established, a leading steward Steve Forey took a petition around his colleagues in the branch. Badges were sold and stickers put up. Forty people attended a meeting in the depot, to establish a local group. Members of the Kings Cross branch took part in protests against the National Front at Brick Lane. This activity then led to the formation of a national network. John Robson from Wood Green was a key activist in this campaign. 'One day, I put up a poster saying that at the next meeting we would affiliate to the Anti-Nazi League. About fifty people came, and there was a big row, but we affiliated. After that the branch never looked back.'[20]

One industry where this support was especially important was education. The Front made a series of attempts to recruit school children, culminating in the publication of a Young National Front paper, *Bulldog*. In response, the ANL dedicated resources to the formation of its own Skaters' and School Kids' sections. SKAN had its own 16-page magazine, which featured interviews with reggae bands like Steel Pulse or poems from Leon Rosselson.[21] The group Teachers Against the Nazis wrote education packs against racism and fascism, establishing a tradition of anti-racist education that would continue into the 1990s. An ANL teachers' conference was held in Manchester in May 1978, with John Rowbotham speaking for the NUT.[22] The follow-up conference in June 1979 was organised under the banner of Campaign Against Racism in Education. Speakers included a school student from Soweto and A. Sivanandan of *Race and Class*.[23] The first National Education Conference of Teachers Against the Nazis took place on 23 September 1978, the day before the second Carnival. Many speakers were long-term anti-fascists, including Maurice Ludmer the editor of *Searchlight* and Joan Lestor the Labour MP. Yet alongside traditional anti-fascism there was also space for a discussion of the broader issues of racism in education, with workshops on 'Asian Girls in Schools' and 'Why Schools fail the Black Community.' As well as teachers, other white-collar workers contributed. Following a National Front arson attack on the ANL headquarters in London, the Civil Service Union gave a one-off grant of £500 to the League to pay for repairs to its premises.[24] Ten national trade unions voted to back the League, and several more gave assistance to the anti-racist campaign.[25]

In February 1979, 200 people attended a Miners Against the Nazis conference, held in Barnsley. Speakers included Arthur Scargill, Jonathon Dimbelby, Paul Holborow and Alex Biswas.[26] It has often been said that members of the Socialist Workers Party dominated the ANL. For example, Richard Thurlow writes, 'the decline of the NF was partially due to the successful undermining of it by the ANL. When the latter itself was blatantly taken over by the Socialist Workers Party the organisation folded as the bulk of the membership refused to tolerate being controlled by a notorious factional hard-line Trotskyist group.'[27] The SWP did indeed play an important role in sponsoring and initiating a campaign. Yet the movement could not have grown without the support of rival left-wing forces. The SWP could count several dozen supporters in the mines, but not hundreds. The turnout seen in February 1979 could only have been made possible by co-operation with Communist Party members among the miners in Yorkshire, Derbyshire and elsewhere.

In Manchester, the trades' council and the AUEW-TASS divisional council both affiliated to the ANL. At other times, the Manchester Teachers' Association, ASTMS (Central Manchester) and COHSE (Ladywell Hospital) all gave their support. The National Union of Railwaymen's North West council also affiliated to the League.

The most symbolic campaign took place on the docks. Early on in the campaign, socialist dockers set themselves the task of undoing the defeat they had suffered in 1968, when the dockers marched in support of Powell's 'Rivers of Blood' speech. The port of London shop stewards committee voted to affiliate to the League. Bob Light, Eddie Prevost and Mickey Fenn were key activists. Always at the front of the marches, Fenn was arrested in June 1977 and accused by the police of assaulting fascists. The charge was dropped. In an important move, the London dockers provided the stewards for the first Carnival. They also loaned the ANL their banner, 'Arise Ye Workers'. It was a great turn-around after the defeat of ten years' earlier.

Another notable campaign was the localised general strike that preceded the police riot at Southall in April 1979. Faced with the news that the National Front was planning to hold an election meeting in their area, which was one of the most diverse parts of London, black, white and Asian workers held joint strike actions to protest. With the support of groups such as the Indian Workers' Association, as well as the socialist parties, rank-and-file workers were able to call wildcat strikes at Heathrow airport and Ford's Langley, as well as smaller factories, including the SunBlest bakery, Walls pie factory and Quaker Oats.[28] These were large-scale strikes, uniting black and white workers, to protest against the National Front presence in Southall. More than anything else, these strikes reveal the success of several years' active campaigning by left-wing and black activists. The ANL provided the space to make unity work.

Working-class anti-fascism in the North East

The class character of anti-fascism was most evident in those regions where trade unionism predominated. In the North East, working-class anti-fascism went back to the interwar years.[29] As early as 1972, an Anti-Fascist Committee was formed on South Tyneside with the support of the local Trades Council.[30] In winter 1974, Bernard Appleton of South Shields Trades Council had his face slashed with a razor. This incident followed the count at the October general election. Harry Donkin, a former Labour councillor who had defected to the Front saw Appleton and pointed him out. Thugs then chased Appleton down the street, caught and beat him.[31]

Bob Murdoch came to the North East in 1971, to work at the large C. A. Parson plant.[32] In the early 1970s Murdoch recalls fascism was rarely discussed in union circles, or not in Newcastle anyway. 'At that time, there was no feeling that the National Front was the threat. The enemy was the company, not just for me but for the mass of the work-force, or the enemy was the Heath government.' As the Front started to stand candidates in the region, concerns grew. But even, then, only a minority was interested. 'We first raised it at [Parsons at] a General Meeting in 1974. One or two of the right-wingers raised a rival motion. We put it to the reps committee, which was still 60 strong or even bigger. It represented about 900 members of the clerical staff. Both motions were put, and both rejected. The message was that it wasn't something in which our members wanted to get involved.'[33]

During the 1976 by-election, the BBC regional studios were occupied by anti-fascists, in protest against the corporation for airing interviews with members of the National Front.[34] Bob Bagnall had only recently moved to the North East from the east Midlands. He remembers this as a difficult period. 'For a whole year, we were battling the National Front all over the country. We were very much up against it. People were getting beaten up all over the place. I can remember going to Rotherham for a march against the Front. There were three times more of them than us.' As for the BBC occupation, 'We only just made it. We went in, got the interview cancelled, and then the police were called. We only just got out in time.'[35]

One aspect of this period was the decline of industrial employment. In the North East, the trend was especially acute. In the mid-1970s, a Trade Union Studies Information Unit used to have offices on Queen Street in Newcastle. Three issues of their bulletin from 1976 and 1977, chosen at random, report 700 jobs threatened at John Collier's in South Shields, 1500 staff laid off at Plessey's in Sunderland, 600 jobs to go with the closure of the Jackson the Tailor factory in Gateshead.[36] Is there any sense that such processes as the rise in unemployment, or that the decline in manufacturing industry made life easier for the extreme right?

Bob Murdoch recalls arguments at work. 'There was one NF member on the shop floor. We had a bit of a to do by the turbines.' The levels of popular racism grew, he felt, through 1976, 1977 and 1978. The stewards at Parsons 'tended to have quite a lot of arguments with our members. It wasn't any particular grades. Maybe it was more open on the shop floor and less open among the clerical grades, where the union leadership was associated with a strong anti-racist position. Whether it was actually less, that's a different matter.' One of the worst rows saw Murdoch battling against an older woman worker who argued that immigration actually caused unemployment. 'She said that someone should take a boat out to sea, and sink all the immigrants. I remember having a huge argument with her, there and then. People were watching. It was easier once racism had been confronted.'[37]

The local perception was that anti-fascism worked. Jim Hutchinson worked with the teacher's union caucus, Rank and File. The Newcastle group brought together activists from the Socialist Workers Party, the Communist Party and other left-wing parties. It supported the formation of the ANL. 'We set up our own group, Teachers Against the Nazis. We took people down to London for big anti-racist events, including an education conference addressed by Arthur Scargill. We brought about three hundred people to a meeting and film showing at the News Theatre. After Blair Peach was killed, we organised protest meetings. Amanda Leon spoke at one and we picketed local the Marlin Street police station.'[38]

Under the pressure of a popular mass movement, the supporters of the National Front largely gave up on their previous tactics of standing in elections and seeking widespread, popular support. Instead they turned to more violent manoeuvres. According to Bagnall, 'We were hearing of attacks on anti-racists in Derby. I used to get death-threats all the time.' One particular target was the Socialist Workers Party's full-time organiser John Cowley. 'He lived on a terrace house in the middle of Byker. The Nazis firebombed his house. I can't believe no-one was killed.'[39] Yet horrible as they were such incidents as these tended to confirm the suspicion of anti-fascists, that the far right had been forced onto the defensive, and had given up its previous strategies of mass recruitment. British fascism was on the way out.

After 1979, many activists could now be found working in other campaigns. At Parsons, Bob Murdoch recalls, it felt as if the argument against the racists had largely been won. Stewards voted to support the ANL and its local offshoot, an Engineers Against the Nazis campaign. In the 1980s, support was extended to the Tottenham Three, black victims of the police riot at Broadwater Farm. The stewards also affiliated to the campaign of Moses Mayakiso, a prominent black trade unionist under arrest in apartheid South Africa. 'We tried to make the members proud to see the appearance of black faces on the union notice-board.'[40]

For or against Labour?

Why was there no attempt by anti-fascists to petition the Labour government calling for a ban on fascism? Previous waves of popular anti-fascism had, after all, been based on such demands. In the 1940s, for example, some tens of thousands of workers had besieged the Home Office with letters and petitions calling for the government to act against Mosley.[41] One explanation for this absence begins with the leadership of the campaign. By 1977–78, the key force on the British far left was the Socialist Workers Party. It was far a smaller, angrier organisation than the Communist Party, the most important previous carrier of working-class anti-fascism. The SWP's ascendancy was bound up with a generational shift. Most young workers had lost any faith in the willingness of the Labour Party to deliver change.

There was a gap between official and popular perceptions. According to the jurisprudence of the labour movement, it should have followed that any campaign that succeeded in establishing widespread support among trade unionists would ultimately receive the endorsement of senior labour movement figures, and the Labour Party itself. Peter Sedgwick, had been a member of the Labour and then the Communist Party in the 1950s.[42] The politics of the Labour Party, he later argued, had then still been an expression of values deeply held in the labour movement. Labour's constitution had reflected a relationship between party and class:

> The organisational mythology of the committed Left amounted to the construction of a vast shadow panoply of trade-union structures, manned by conscious militants at branch and district level, and by progressive or reactionary, Left-wing or Right-wing, responsible or autocratic General Secretaries and Executives in their national offices. Like the constitutional map of Soviet Russia projected by Sidney and Beatrice Webb in the 1930s, the initiatives of the rank-and-file were supposed to send countless pressures upwards, channelled and summed in the block vote of six or seven digits that were cast at the annual Trade Union Congress or the Labour Party Conference. As the neurologist's recording equipment marks the gross electrical rhythms of the brain, each stroke on the graph representing the aggregate of millions of tiny voltages from the individual neurons, so the Conference or Congress vote aggregated the voices of invisible throngs: or rather would do so, provided that the recording machinery itself were not spiked by treacherous leaders.

By the 1970s, Sedgwick argued, everything had changed. Marches still happened, but were no longer acknowledged by Labour's leaders. The movement was more antagonistic towards the state. 'The Labour MPs are more prosperous since then, and more remote ... very few workers would have enough faith in Parliament to take a day off and come down to London to waste their time and breath.'[43]

The purpose of this chapter is to see the events of the 1970s 'from below', to describe the events from the perspective of the working-class militants who contributed to the anti-fascist campaign. It would be possible to argue that Labour Party did support the anti-fascist campaign. Certainly by autumn 1976, the Party was willing to dedicate its party political broadcasts to a limited critique of racism. Most of the radicals who took part, however, tended to see events differently. Most felt that Labour contributed little to anti-fascism. Others disputed the extent of Labour's conversion, when it took place. Many interpreted the relative support that some sections of the Labour Party gave to anti-fascism after 1977 as a sign of the party's opportunism, its search for a new generation of supporters.

The campaign was always characterised, then, by a certain tension. The clear majority of those who took part would have voted Labour. Many had canvassed for Labour in 1974. Many others would go on to do the same in 1979. Yet within the literature produced by ANL supporters, and certainly in the memory of prominent activists from the time, there is a strong sense of betrayal by the government. The Front was seen to have gained from the failure of the Labour government and the sequent disillusionment with the left. In July 1976, for example, James Fenton wrote a piece for the *New Statesman*, describing a National Front meeting addressed by Robert Relf in Tilbury, Essex. Fenton asked 'Who speaks against the National Front?' He expressed the frustration of a generation of young anti-racists who were fed up of waiting for Labour to take a lead:

> The Tories talk in a code which yields the argument without the slightest demur. 'Parliamentary language' barely conceals the assumptions which the Tilbury meeting shared. Indeed it is in a way refreshing to go from Westminster to such a gathering and hear people say what they really mean. As for Labour, the issue is fought in the worst possible terms – arguments about numbers, and whether the pool of immigrants will ever dry up. And all the while (it was a constant feature of Monday's immigration debate) there is an air of congratulation – all the participants in the debate, or nearly all of them, are being so responsible. Thank God we can sit down together and discuss the matter in a civilised way.

Fenton concluded, 'if the Front have grown, as they have, to the point where they are no longer treated as a joke, it is not because the Left have sometimes opposed them on the streets; it is because Parliament has been embarrassed to meet them head on.'[44] Such views became a sort of common sense, not just among the left groups, but also in the colleges, among the stewards and with many Labour Party activists.

Nationalising the mustard factories

Those who represented the Labour Party as a hostile entity did not go without challenge. In particular, the Socialist Workers' Party's involvement was attacked from both the left and the right. Smaller far-left groups such as the Revolutionary Communist Group and the Spartacist League maintained that the ANL was not a working-class alliance but an all-class alliance.[45] Indeed there were differences between the classic formulations of socialist tactics, going back to the 1930s, and the actual alliance that took place. Einde O'Callaghan was an activist in London. 'The Anti-Nazi League wasn't a united front, but it was a united front-type organisation. It wasn't a pact between mass organisations, but there was an alliance between reformists and revolutionaries [involving] unity around specific organisation, demands which left the organisations free.'

Meanwhile, Joan Lestor, a former editor of *Searchlight* magazine, was the central figure behind the Joint Committee Against Racialism, which was launched in December 1977.[46] Stan Taylor dubbed this group an 'alternative to the ANL for moderates'. It attracted support from the Labour Party, the Liberal Party, the British Council of Churches, various immigrant organisations, the National Union of Students and despite the protests of Margaret Thatcher, the National Union of Conservative Associations. Another important backer of the Joint Committee Against Racialism was the Board of Deputies of British Jews, which was hostile to the anti-Zionist politics of the Socialist Workers Party, and campaigned against the League, accusing it of being a front dominated by the SWP. Unsurprisingly, with such broad representation, difficulties were encountered in agreeing to policies. 'Activity appears to have largely centred around distribution of anti-racist literature.'[47]

The Joint Committee Against Racialism was criticised in turn by left-wing Labour MPs who accused Lestor of jeopardising the important united work in which the ANL had been engaged. The *New Statesman* magazine, one traditional voice of the Labour left, ran a front page 'In defence of the Anti-Nazis.'

> Its National Secretary, Paul Holborrow [sic], is a member of the SWP. But most of the other members of the steering committee – Peter Hain, Neil Kinnock MP, Audrey Wise MP, Ernie Roberts *et al.* – are scarcely Trots, whatever else they may be. Suppose that Mr. Holborrow and his SWP friends were, with manipulative cunning, to try and turn the Anti-Nazi League away from its simple anti-racialist platform and towards some sinister purpose of their own – nationalising the

mustard-factories perhaps, or substituting Vanessa Redgrave for the Queen – is it really plausible that they should succeed? It is a long time since the Comintern days when 'fronts' really were marched and counter-marched with clockwork precision.[48]

A large number of Labour MPs backed the ANL – not just Kinnock and Wise, but Tony Benn, Dennis Skinner, Martin Flannery and Gwyneth Dunwoody.

The Labour Party nationally went to certain efforts to ensure that it was associated with the anti-racist cause, including militant or street level anti-fascism. *Time Out* ran an advertisement calling for a Labour vote as a vote against racism. Meanwhile, the *Leveller* came out with a back-page advertisement taking a quote from Frank Allaun, chair of the Labour Party, and superimposing it over a photograph of the crowd at an ANL Carnival. This was an unashamed bid for the support of the RAR generation:

> 'If voting could change the system, they wouldn't let you do it ...' Maybe voting isn't everything. Certainly you and me voting Labour won't in itself bring socialism. Campaigning against unemployment, poverty, homelessness, racial and sexual oppression, and the many other evils of the system, needs all our effort all the time. But I believe we need a Labour government – with a socialist programme, a healthy labour movement and a majority of MPs behind it. So I hope you'll not only vote Labour on May 3rd, but you'll come out and work for a Labour victory.[49]

The Labour Party, at its top, was divided between those who wanted to work with the ANL, and those who wanted to ignore it. Even the latter, however, would have sanctioned this bid for the hearts of the movement's young activists.

At the height of anti-fascist campaigning, debates over the role played by the Labour government tended to be postponed, with activists eager not to turn their rival perspectives into points of principle that might leave a floating audience cold. After the defeat of James Callaghan's government, in April 1979, however, there was a sort of open season on the left, in which rival strategies were debated more honestly. In the dying days of Callaghan's government, Rock Against Racism's David Widgery blamed Labour Party for pushing society rightwards,

> Since 1974 the most radical post-war election manifesto and a Cabinet studded with Tribunite heavies has succeeded in bringing back mass

unemployment as a permanent feature of the economy ... The scale of the retreat is difficult to measure with the eye. It isn't socialism but a species of cost-benefit accountancy ... In some senses we've witnessed a 1931 in slow motion. Labour is a National Government and sod the Conference and the backbenchers. This is the real fruit of the Social Contract. Somnambulance, a universal sense of resentful passivity, a nation of Fawlties, barely suppressing hysteria. We're doing what we're told, so it must be someone else's fault things still go wrong: the blacks, the Reds, the queers, the strikers. Those who stand out against the tide of national obedience; the Right to Work marchers with their valiant orange jackets and blistered feet, the fire-fighters in their strike-huts last Christmas, the Fight back committee at the gutted Hounslow Hospital [are] held responsible for the very conditions they protest against.[50]

Following the 1979 election, Widgery wrote, 'We face a new Toryism, frankly elitist, not just making racialism respectable but Reaction itself fashionable.'[51]

From the distance of hindsight, what we really observe is a multiplicity of left strategies. In spring 1980 former Young Liberal Peter Hain, radicalised by his experiences in the ANL, agreed to chair 'the debate of the decade', a two thousand-strong meeting held in Central Hall with representatives of the Labour Party and the extra-parliamentary left. Hain's introduction to the discussion began by contrasting the mood of the late 1960s – when such unions as the engineers' AUEW had seemed capable of transforming society – and of the early 1980s, when the entire left (reformist and revolutionary alike) lacked popular approval. In his words,

> The trade union movement as a whole is in political disarray, unsure of its grass roots base, uncertain about its national direction; the left outside the Labour Party is weaker in terms of its political base; the student movement is passive and middle-of-the road in its politics; and the Labour Party, whilst moving significantly leftwards; still has not shaken off a dominant right-wing leadership. Above all, socialism patently lacks the appeal and allegiance in the working class, which it once had.[52]

In this case, the diagnosis of left weakness was allied to a political argument. Labour could deliver, Hain implied, if only the labour movement was strengthened.

Meanwhile, left academic Stuart Hall told the Communist Party's magazine *Marxism Today* that Mrs Thatcher represented an 'authoritarian populism', which would mean 'a striking weakening of democratic forms and initiatives, but not their suspension'. Hall sought to explain Thatcher's success as a cultural project, using family values and Conservative morality to place its imprint on political, economic and ideological life.[53] If Thatcherism was primarily a form of cultural politics, then it followed that the Tories could best be resisted in the cultural sphere. Hall praised RAR in particular as 'one of the timeliest and best constructed of cultural interventions, repaying serious and extended analysis'. Perhaps the best alternative to Conservatism, would be a revised anti-Nazi-style alliance, perhaps with the name 'Rock Against the Tories', or some other such-like title?

Different voices were struggling to be heard. All implied different approaches for the period beyond the ANL. None succeeded in winning a majority on the left. The downturn in radical politics that began in Britain in 1974 continued after 1979 with a vengeance. The defeat of the steelworkers, the miners and the GLC demoralised the generation that had been part of the ANL, and although many remained part of the movement, there simply was not the space in society for the creation of a mass pole of left-wing sentiment during the Callaghan or certainly the Thatcher years. The criticisms of Labour were blunted over time.

Conclusion

Despite the hard times for working-class politics that followed the 1979 election, the basic success of the anti-fascist campaign still demonstrates a series of points. First, it proves that space existed in society for working-class values to be expressed, if only negatively, in response to the threat from the far right. Second, the campaign demonstrates the ability of the Labour Party to shift leftwards, on particular issues, rather than be outflanked by more radical voices threatening to gain popular support. Third it shows the potential openness of trade unionists to political campaigns, when the ideas motivating these movements were judged relevant. We can also observe the contrast between the forces of British fascism, which lacked the general backing of any group in society, and the anti-fascist majority, rooted as it was in the trade union millions. This episode as a whole demonstrates above all that trade union organisation has acted as a general barrier to fascism, and indeed that this barrier rose, as demands were put upon it. While individuals from working-class backgrounds might have been open to fascistic ideas,[54] there was no danger of fascism becoming a working-class force, while the unions were opposed.

Thirty years later, trade unions are still the largest voluntary organisations in Britain. The basic incompatibility between trade union solidarity and the ideas of racial exclusion remains in place. Although many jobs in mining and manufacturing have been lost, a new generation of workers has emerged in industries that are just beginning to be organised. In this sense, the history of the anti-fascist campaigns represents a stock of experience on which activists can still draw.

Notes

1. D. Widgery, *Beating Time: Riot 'n' Race 'n' Rock and Roll* (London: Chatto and Windus, 1986); P. Gilroy, *There Ain't No Black in the Union Jack: The Cultural Politics of Race and Nation* (London: Routledge, 1987), pp. 114–62, 117–18; J. Savage, *England's Dreaming: Sex Pistols and Punk Rock* (London: Faber and Faber, 1991); P. Alexander, *Racism, Resistance and Revolution* (London: Bookmarks, 1978); N. Copsey, *Anti-Fascism in Britain* (London: Macmillan, 2000); R. Messina, *Race and Party Competition in Britain* (Oxford: Clarendon Press, 1989), pp. 109–25.
2. M. Walker, *The National Front* (Glasgow: Fontana, 1977); R. Thurlow, *Fascism in Britain: From Oswald Mosley's Blackshirts to the National Front* (London: I. B. Tauris, 1998), pp. 245–67; M. Billig, *Fascists: A Social Psychological View of the National Front* (London and New York: Harcourt Brace Jovanovich, 1978); D. Edgar, *Racism, Fascism and the Politics of the National Front* (London: Race and Class, 1977).
3. I. Goodyer, 'The Cultural Politics of Rock Against Racism' (MA Thesis, Sheffield Hallam, 2002), p. 3.
4. C. Fischer, *The Rise of The Nazis* (Manchester: Manchester University Press, 1995); R. Griffin, *Fascism* (Oxford, 1995), p. 7; also R. Griffin (ed.), *International Fascism: Theories, Causes and the New Consensus* (London: Arnold, 1998).
5. P. Coupland, ' "Left-Wing Fascism" in Theory and Practice: The Case of the British Union of Fascists', *Twentieth Century British History*, 13, 1, 2002, pp. 38–61.
6. D. Renton, 'Can the Oppressed Unite? Women and Anti-fascism in Britain 1977–1982', in C. Barker (ed.), *Alternative Futures and Popular Protests 2000* (Manchester: Manchester Metropolitan University, 2000); D. Renton, 'Anti-fascism in the North West 1976–1982', *North West Labour History* 27, 2002, pp. 17–28.
7. *Birmingham Post*, 22 April 1968.
8. F. Lindop, 'Racism and the Working Class: Strikes in Support of Enoch Powell in 1968', *Labour History Review* 66, 1, 2001, pp. 79–100.
9. D. Clark, *We do not want the Earth* (Whitley Bay: Bewick Press, 1992), p. 138.
10. *CARF*, 1 May 1977, p. 4.
11. *Sunday People*, 14 August 1977; *Daily* Mail, 15 August 1977; *Daily Express*, 15 August 1977; *New Statesman and Nation*, 29 September 1978.

12. ANL, 'Founding Statement', leaflet, 1977; for Ernie Robert's support, E. Roberts, *Strike Back* (Orpington: Ernie Roberts, 1994), pp. 251–4.
13. 'The Cost of the NF', *CARF*, 9, Spring 1979, p. 2.
14. D. Widgery, *Beating Time* p. 17; K. Leech, *Struggle in Babylon: Racism in the Cities and Churches of Britain* (London: Sheldon Press, 1988), pp. 84–5; Bethnal Green and Stepney Trades Council, *Blood on the Streets* (London: Bethnal Green and Stepney Trades Council, 1978).
15. R. Messina, *Race and Party Competition in Britain*, p. 118; D. Field, 'Flushing out the Front', *Socialist Review*, May 1978; E. Roberts, *Strike Back* (Orpington: Ernie Roberts, 1994), p. 252; Anti-Nazi League, *Inside the National Front, Sheffield's Nazis Uncovered* (Sheffield: Sheffield ANL, 1979); B. Dunn, 'No to NF', *Morning Star*, 15 November 1978.
16. B. Dunn, 'No to NF', *Morning Star*, 15 November 1978.
17. F. Wheen, 'The National Front's Reptilian Aspects', *New Statesman*, 22 September 1978.
18. Tyne and Wear Anti-Fascist Association, 'Fascism and the Labour Movement', Internal bulletin, 1986, p. 15.
19. C. Eccleston, 'My Roots are Here', *Women's Voice*, August 1978.
20. J. Rose, *Solidarity Forever: One Hundred Years of Kings Cross ASLEF* (London: Kings Cross ASLEF, 1986), pp. 49, 73.
21. *SKAN*, Summer 1978.
22. The same year also witnessed the launching of a parallel anti-racist organisation, All London Teachers Against Racism and Fascism (ALTARF). For their activity, see All London Teachers Against Racism and Fascism, *Challenging Racism* (London: ALTARF, 1978).
23. ANL leaflet, 'NF = No Future for Education', undated.
24. ANL, 'Emergency Appeal', leaflet, Spring 1978?
25. See the leaflets produced by national unions: ASTMS, *Stop Racism at Work!* (London: Community Relations Group, 1976); General and Municipal Workers' Union, *Race Relations at Work* (London: GMWU, 1976?); Trades Union Congress, *Trade Unions and Race Relations* (London: Trades Union Congress, 1977?).
26. *ANL News Letter*, February 1979.
27. R. Thurlow, *Fascism in Britain*, p. 256.
28. SWP, *Southall: The Fight for our Future* (London: SWP, 1979), p. 2.
29. N. Todd, *In Excited Times* (Newcastle: Bewick Press, 1995), pp. 8–11.
30. Grassby, *Unfinished Revolution*, p. 239.
31. 'Attack on South Shields Anti-fascist', *Red Flag*, 7 November 1974.
32. For some of the dynamics of this workplace, see J. Charlton, 'Newcastle Red', *Socialist Review*, June 2001.
33. Interview with Bob Murdoch, 24 September 2003.
34. *Socialist Worker*, 22 May 1976.
35. Interview with Bob Bagnall, 20 October 2003.
36. *Monthly Bulletin*, July 1976, August 1976, February 1977, copies in Tyne and Wear Archives, 948/39.
37. Interview with Bob Murdoch, 24 September 2003.
38. Interview with Jim Hutchinson, 8 October 2003.
39. Interview with Bob Bagnall, 20 October 2003.
40. Interview with Bob Murdoch, 24 September 2003.

41. D. Renton, 'Not just Economics but Politics as well: Trade Unions, Labour Movement Activists and Anti-Fascist Protests 1945–51', *Labour History Review* 65, 2, 2000, pp. 166–80. This paper should also be compared to the accounts which appear in D. Renton, *Fascism, Anti-Fascism and the 1940s* (London: Macmillan Press, 2000); D. Renton, 'The Police and Fascist/ Anti-Fascist Street Conflict 1945–1951', in C. Barker (ed.), *Alternative Futures and Popular Protests 1997* (Manchester: 1997); and D. Renton, 'Fascism and Anti-fascism and Britain in the 1940s', A. L. Morton Memorial Lecture, Socialist History Society, London, 15 September 2001 (published on tape by the Socialist History Society).

42. For Peter Sedgwick's views on fascism, see P. Sedgwick, 'The Problem of Fascism', *International Socialism* 42, 1970, 30–4.

43. N. Harris and J. Palmer (eds), *World Crisis: Essays in Revolutionary Socialism* (London: Hutchinson and Co., 1971), pp. 27, 34.

44. J. Fenton, 'An Evening with Robert Relf', *New Statesman*, 9 July 1976.

45. Revolutionary Communist Group, *The Anti-Nazi League and the Struggle against Racism* (Revolutionary Communist Group: London, 1978).

46. *Labour Weekly*, 'The Fight for our Freedoms', no date, January 1978?

47. *Unity Against Fascism*, 1, 1976; N. Copsey, *Anti-Fascism in Britain*, pp. 148–9.

48. 'In defence of the Anti-Nazis', *New Statesman*, 6 October 1978.

49. *Leveller*, May 1979.

50. 'The Winter of 1979', in D. Widgery (ed.), *Preserving Disorder: Selected Essays 1968–1988* (London: Pluto, 1989), pp. 165–6.

51. 'I'm not going to work on Maggie's Farm', in D. Widgery, *Preserving Disorder*, pp. 171–6.

52. P. Hain (ed.), *The Crisis and Future of the Left: the Debate of the Decade* (London: Pluto, 1980), p. 7.

53. 'The Great Moving Right Show' (1978), reprinted in S. Hall, *The Hard Road to Renewal: Thatcherism and the Crisis of the Left* (London: Verso, 1988), pp. 39–56, especially 40, 42.

54. C. Sparks, 'Fascism in Britain', 'Fascism and the Working Class, part two: the National Front Today', *International Socialism Journal*, 3, 1978, pp. 17–38; Messina, *Race and Party Competition*, p. 110; M. Harrop, J. England and C. T. Husbands, 'The Bases of National Front Support', *Political Studies*, 28, 2, 1980, pp. 272–83, 282; also C. T. Husbands, 'The National Front: A Response to Crisis?', *New Society*, 15 May 1975; S. Taylor, 'The National Front: Backlash or Boot Boys?', *New Society*, 11 August 1977.

8
Whatever Happened to the Labour Movement? Proletarians and the Far Right in Contemporary Britain

Thomas P. Linehan

This chapter has two principal strands. First, it contends that, historically, the British far right, because it sought to mobilise a diverse cross-class support base, as did generic fascist parties and movements in other national contexts, showed a capacity to successfully to draw support from the working class. Second, the chapter posits the view that in the contemporary period, owing to a distinct convergence of structural, ideological and party-political developments which are serving to fundamentally reconfigure the traditional British labour movement, there exists a greater potential for the far right to make inroads into working-class voter constituencies across a wide and varied geographical space. The years since the mid-1980s have been characterised by the structurally induced contraction of the organised working class, the gravitational shift to the right in British politics, the porous nature of political identities, and a waning of traditional proletarian militancy and working class collective self-identity. Now passed over by New Labour and increasingly disorganised, the electoral support of unspecified numbers of workers seems to have been secured by the latest manifestation of Britain's far right, as signified by the recent alarming British National Party (BNP) electoral gains in certain former predominantly working-class Labour strongholds, particularly in the north-west of England.

There are other, more short-term, reasons for the BNP's recent rise to electoral prominence, of course. The BNP's efforts to 'modernise' its image, style and political approach along the lines of Jean-Marie Le Pen's *Front National* (FN) has reaped some electoral benefits by making it appear more mainstream and 'respectable' in the eyes of some voters who, hitherto, may have balked at the prospect of giving support to a neo-fascist party. In a related sense, FN gains in various French elections since the mid-1990s helped raise the general profile of the far right and, with it, that of the BNP in Britain. Additionally, from the late 1990s a barrage of lurid tabloid press accounts of asylum seekers have served to demonise and stereotype the latter, giving some legitimacy to anti-ethnic and racist sentiment, a new mood which has been exploited by the BNP. However, while these short-term factors have undoubtedly played a part in the BNP's resurgence, it is the longer term developments reshaping the British labour movement, as described in the introduction, that are considered more fundamental to the advance of the far right.

The history of the British fascism shows that support for home-grown fascist parties straddled social-class boundaries and that workers were just as liable as members of other social-class groups to succumb to the far right's various messages, however chauvinistic, philistine, elitist, anti-Semitic or racist. Stuart Rawnsley's research into the British Union of Fascists (BUF) in the north of England in the 1930s highlighted the working class presence within the BUF's northern membership. Rawnsley's study showed that the BUF recruited chemical plant operatives and railway workers in Lancaster, mechanics in Blackburn and, a factor that is particularly apposite to the more recent situation in the North West with regard to the BNP, cotton workers, both employed and unemployed, in places like Middleton and Nelson in east Lancashire.[1] The fascist social constituency in east London and south-west Essex also harboured a working-class element. During my own research into the socio-economic and demographic backing of local fascism in that region, I found a range of classic proletarian occupational types within the fascist support network.[2] They included painters and decorators, van drivers, 'navvies', bus conductors, railway porters, dustmen, grocery and milk roundsmen, electricians' mates and electricians, bricklayers, furriers, upholsterers, welders and even an ex-miner, amongst others.

The extreme right's disturbing ability to accumulate a cross-class following that swept up proletarians, as well as other social-class types, is borne out by recent work on interwar fascism and Nazism in continental Europe. In Nazi Germany, according to Stanley Payne, 'workers had constituted about a third of all members when Hitler took power, but their proportion among all new members reached 40 per cent by 1939 and 43 per cent by 1942–44. If master craftsmen were included in the category of workers, the percentages would be distinctly higher.'[3] In the Nazi's electoral constituency, too, voting support for the NSDAP leapt among virtually all social strata, including blue-collar workers, in the pivotal Reichstag election of July 1932, when the Nazis secured 37.4 per cent of the overall vote and 230 seats.[4] As Detlef Mühlberger explained it: 'Acceptance of the fact that irrational political behavior is not the prerogative of any particular class, but of sections of all class groupings, is an essential step to the ultimate understanding of the very complex social response on which Nazism was based.'[5] Even the social physiognomy of Italian fascism, which more closely conformed to the more conventional notion of fascism as a 'middle class' phenomenon, revealed a proletarian side, particularly in its formative phase. Between 1921 and 1922, the PNF's social makeup came very near to representing Italy's overall social structure, with urban and rural workers comprising 39.7 per cent of the party membership, as against constituting 41.4 per cent of the active population.[6]

The recent evidence of a substantial worker presence in the interwar fascist support network, both domestic and overseas, is at variance with the notion of fascism as a predominantly 'middle class' phenomenon, one of the 'classic' paradigmatic models of fascist recruitment. The tendency with this model is to assert the homogeneity of social-class affiliation. One variant of the 'middle class fascism' thesis, which was proclaimed by liberals like Seymour Lipset, casts fascism as an expression of middle class fear and frustration brought on by an adverse economic situation. The contention is that financial insecurity and dread of status loss supposedly brought on by the destabilising processes of economic rationalisation in an era of economic uncertainty and the levelling inclination within socialism impelled the angst-ridden middle classes towards reactionary fascism.[7] 'Third International' Marxism also claimed that fascism was essentially a middle class movement. Fascism is here defined as an offensive by the bourgeoisie against the working class and its representative organisations, an argument that not only assumed middle class support for this anti-proletarian project but saw fascism, eschatologically, as a derivative of capitalism, the latter's final ugly phase.[8] Fascism is thus conceptualised as the direct counterpart to revolutionary proletarian activity, its opposite and antithesis. The drawback of the 'middle class fascism' thesis, then, is that it asserts the essential homogeneity of the fascist social-class profile, whereas the empirical evidence tends to reveal heterogeneity. It thus conceptualises fascism, sociologically, in terms of a single stereotype.

It is essential, at this point to inject an important qualification into the analysis. While the proposition that classical interwar fascism mobilised support from diverse cross-class groupings that included workers holds firm, this support tended to come from dislocated elements of the unorganised proletariat. Thankfully, during the interwar period, in Britain at least, the organised labour movement acted as a barrier against fascism's advance, restricting its political space and, structurally, inhibiting its potential to make more significant encroachments into working-class membership and voter constituencies.[9] It is a matter of historical record that the labour movement, its ancillary organisations and supporting cultural networks effectively hampered the BUF's political progress during the 1930s by denying it moral and political legitimacy and restricting the political space in which it could operate.[10] A string of anti-fascist resolutions emanating from trade unions, trade councils, and constituency Labour parties, Labour local authority bans on fascist indoor meetings, and the mobilisation of an overwhelming mass presence at Oswald Mosley's outdoor rallies ensured that an unremitting pressure was maintained on the BUF throughout its brief life. Other strands of the labour movement, most notably the Communist Party of Great Britain (CPGB) and the National Unemployed Workers' Movement (NUWM), also played a pivotal role in checking the BUF's progress. As the NUWM's National Organiser Wal Hannington explained, 'the British fascists made strenuous efforts at Labour Exchanges and elsewhere to recruit the unemployed into their organisation but they could not break through the powerful opposition of our NUWM branches'.[11] CPGB activists on the ground also worked to hinder fascist progress. When the BUF attempted to force its way into east London in 1934, an area where it previously had no strength, it found its way barred by mass activity instigated by the local Communist Party. The Secretary of the CPGB's Stepney branch in this period, Joe Jacobs, recalled that: 'The fascists no longer appeared in Newby Place, Poplar, or Stepney Green, because whenever there was a rumour to the effect that they would be at these places, thousands of workers who had been called to the streets by the Party were ready to prevent fascist meetings being held.'[12]

Such opposition meant that workers were never likely to be present in overwhelming numbers in fascist formations in this period, particularly organised workers. This was certainly true in the north of England where the BUF made few gains in recruiting members from the highly unionised working class, such as engineering workers and coal miners, and in east London, where proletarian fascists overwhelmingly came from the non-unionised sections of the local labour market.[13] In the east London borough of Stepney, for example, organised trade union opposition would frequently thwart the BUF in its attempts to widen its local support base. Although the BUF managed to secure a high degree of working-class support in some areas of Stepney, such as Duckett Street, Shandy Street and Harford Street in the Mile End Old Town Centre ward, it failed to advance into wards where lived workers who were more likely to have links with the organised labour movement. This certainly applied to Stepney's Wapping and Shadwell wards, where were housed many Irish dockers attached to the Stevedores Union who had 'a long history of working class struggle behind them'.[14] The Stepney Borough Council elections of November 1937 provided an example of how organised labour in the shape of the dock workers could impede fascist progress. When a Mile End fascist named Cecil Hiron, a casual dock worker at the Free Trade Wharf in Shadwell, announced that he would stand as a BUF candidate for one of the Mile End wards in the Council election, the Shadwell dockers acted. Faced with the prospect of sparking an unoffi-cial strike at the Wharf unless he reversed course, Hiron had no choice but to withdraw his candidature.[15] A similar blow by organised labour in Stepney was aimed at another local fascist, a van driver named Arthur Judge, in late 1937. When the Stepney local of the Transport and General Workers' Union discovered that Judge was a member of Mosley's party, it passed a resolution of expulsion against him which effectively barred him from gaining employment in the unionised local transport sector.[16]

If we turn to the post-1945 situation, we again find a proletarian pres-ence in British far-right groups. The most high profile of such groups, at least prior to the BNP's advance, the National Front (NF), contained a proletarian element. Roger Eatwell has estimated that during the 1970s, its period of growth, the NF 'probably attracted somewhere between 60,000 and 70,000 members', most of whom came from two social-class groups, the lower middle class and the working class.[17] Others who have considered the NF's social composition, including Michael Billig and Stan Taylor, also concluded that the bulk of party members came from these two social groups, the lower middle and working class.[18] Following its 1979 General Election disaster, when the NF's 303 candidates aver-aged a measly 1.3 per cent of the poll, the NF adopted a more openly pro-proletarian stance in its proclamations and policy, this 'Strasserite' orientation even inclining it towards support for the miners during the 1984–85 strike. The NF's proletarian side would show itself again in the late 1980s when the 'Flag Group' within the party, composed of work-ing class and lower middle class elements, tussled with the 'Political Soldiers' over ideology. The Flag Group challenged the latter's attempt to orient the NF away from populism towards a more 'esoteric', mysti-cal version of rebirth fascism with a stress on elitism, anti-materialism, anti-urbanism and the supposed benefits of reverting to a simpler, organic, rural way of life.

Christopher Husbands located the principal dynamics of the NF's electoral support of the 1970s even more firmly in the working class, or at least those 'working class communities' in certain urban locations experiencing long and short-term industrial decline, like parts of Leicester, Bradford, Blackburn or Wolverhampton, or inner city areas experiencing marked local neighbourhood deterioration or 'cultural decline', such as Shoreditch, Hackney and the inner East End in London.[19] All these factors would predispose individuals experiencing such conditions to NF sympathy. In regard to perceived local neighbourhood deterioration, for example, in Husbands' survey sample of respondents, over four-fifths of strong NF sympathisers in Hackney's Moorefield ward registered concern about 'local decline', while the figure climbed to 89 per cent among moderate NF sympathisers in Hackney's De Beauvoir ward.[20] According to Husbands, 'some local NF branches discovered during the early 1970s that their greater electoral successes were in run-down inner city wards or among residents of some of the older council estates rather than in the more genteel parts of the electorate'.[21] Another crucial variable determining working-class support for the NF in some localities in this period, for Husbands, was a local political tradition of anti-minority resentment that was usually historical and generational. This nativist 'territorial-cultural' tradition generated a cultural suspicion of outsiders and an inclination towards 'racially exclusionist' politics on the part of some elements of the host community. Shoreditch and the inner East End were adjudged by Husbands to be particularly susceptible to this type of sentiment and political mobilisation. Husbands even referred to 'the English working class's special vulnerability to the politics of racial exclusionism', which he suggested had roots in the apolitical pragmatism, strong 'locality-orientation', parochialism and 'territorial sensitivity' of aspects of working-class culture.[22]

In some respects, working-class support for the NF anticipated later BNP support. As with the NF, the BNP would secure support in areas which had undergone a degree of de-industrialisation, like Blackburn, or were experiencing local neighbourhood deterioration or perceived 'cultural decline', like the Mixenden ward captured by the BNP in Halifax in January 2003. Additionally, as in the NF period, the BNP found that the strong 'locality-orientation' and 'territorial sensitivity' that existed in parts of the white working-class community in places like Oldham was favourable terrain for its anti-minority and anti-asylum propaganda. It would be a mistake, however, to over-emphasise the continuity. The BNP would be operating in a different spatial and time frame, and socio-economic political conjuncture, to that of the NF in the 1970s. In the

NF phase, the British labour movement was still a sizeable presence, while the Labour Party leadership had not yet begun the systematic dismantling of 'labourism' that would be a feature of the BNP period, which, in the 1970s made some areas of Britain attached to the labour tradition seemingly impervious to far right penetration. In Burnley, for example, which in the 1970s exhibited a distinctive working-class political tradition oriented towards labourism, and where the BNP success would be most marked, the NF did not have any local organisation.[23]

To summarise the argument thus far: in the interwar period and during the 1970s with the NF, the social-class backing of the British far right was diverse and included a working-class component. The evidence on the social physiognomy of continental European Nazism and fascism would seem to support this contention. On the other hand, the presence and strength of the organised British labour movement across this period meant that a more significant far right encroachment into working-class constituencies was prevented, which meant that workers were never likely to be present in overwhelming numbers in far-right groupings and which made some working-class areas relatively impervious to far right organisational and electoral penetration. If we move forward to the contemporary period, however, a new configuration of circumstances and conditions has served to reshape traditional working-class occupational patterns, milieux and political and ideological outlooks, generating new opportunities for the far right to attract support from working-class constituencies. As a result, unlike earlier periods, it is highly possible that workers could form the mainstay of the far right's support profile across a wide and varied geographical space, and that certain areas traditionally closed to fascism could now be open to it, all of which would mark a new departure in the history of the extreme right in Britain.

Within this new configuration of circumstances and conditions we can observe structural, ideological and party-political elements. First, structural and socio-economic changes within contemporary post-industrial capitalism induced by recent and current conditions of globalisation, particularly the shift away from the classical post-Fordist production system, has led to a marked contraction of the industrial proletariat in most countries, including Britain. In the advanced capitalist areas industrial employment reached its high-water mark in the mid-1960s, followed by a rapid process of de-industrialisation during the 1980s. 'Between 1965 and 1990', according to Göran Therborn, 'industrial employment as a proportion of world employment declined, from 19 to 17 per cent; among the "industrial countries", from 37 to 26 per cent'.[24] Even as the 1980s began, thoughtful observers sensed that the historical ground was shifting.

André Gorz, for example, bid 'farewell to the working class' in his influential 1982 book of the same name and claimed that in the era of 'post-industrial' capitalism the 'traditional working class is now no more than a privileged minority'.[25] Other contemporary commentators were also of the opinion that the advanced economies were about to enter a new era, one significantly different to that which preceded it. Writing almost at the same time as Gorz, though from a different perspective, in a well-known commentary on the state of the British labour movement at the beginning of the 1980s, Eric Hobsbawm proclaimed that after a century of steady progress the 'forward march of labour' had halted.[26]

In Eric Hobsbawm's Britain, the industrial proletariat would reach the pinnacle of its size and political influence during the 1970s. The percentage of workers in traditional manufacturing would remain relatively stable during the period 1951 and 1971 (from 37.2 per cent to 34.9 per cent).[27] Between 1974 and 1989, however, UK industrial employment in the UK decreased by 12.6 per cent.[28] The diminution of the organised proletariat in Britain was reflected in the figures for trade union membership. In 1979, trade union membership stood at an impressive 12,639,000, over half the workforce, but by 1998 had dropped sharply to 7,155,000, a fall of around 40 per cent that was unprecedented in the history of the British trade union movement.[29] Although there has been a slight upturn in membership through 1999 and 2000, the figure dipped again in 2001 to settle at 7,295,000. As de-industrialisation and the contraction of organised labour set in, certain well-known features associated with the great historical moment of the industrial working-class movement began to recede from the industrial and political landscape, most notably the solidaristic work cultures, the impressive support networks of traditional working-class milieux, and the 'classical irreverent collectivism' of organised labour. With regard to the latter, organised proletarian militancy, in the 1970s the average number of working days lost as a result of strike action was 12.9 million, whereas in the 1990s it was just 666,000.[30]

Another important feature associated with the great epoch of the industrial labour movement would also change as a consequence of these structural developments, the traditional milieux of class politics based around the old axis of 'capital versus labour' and the related idea of the working class as a subject transcending its members. In the era of de-industrialisation, declared André Gorz, where the traditional proletariat has only minority status, a new post-industrial neo-proletariat comprising the majority of the population has emerged which has no 'definite class identity'.[31] Further, and anticipating post-modernism, 'the non-class

engendered by the decomposition of present-day society' has emerged
at a time when the long-standing idea of History as a transcendent cause
with meaning, that would ultimately reward those who sacrificed themselves for it, was itself in crisis. 'The crisis of the Industrial system heralds
no new world', Gorz lamented.

> Nothing in it is indicative of a redeeming transformation. The present
> does not receive any meaning from the future. The silence of history
> therefore returns individuals to themselves. Forced back upon their
> own subjectivity, they have to take the floor on their own behalf. No
> future society speaks through their mouth, since the society disinte-
> grating before our eyes heralds no new order.[32]

Parallel occurrences in the political-ideological sphere would also undermine and weaken traditional class politics, once cohesive class identities, and the principle of working-class self-identity. The first was the
collapse of the communist developmental model in the early 1990s.
This event not only rendered the possibility of creating a viable, non-
capitalist society in the short or medium term virtually redundant but
it spelt the end of the classical revolutionary tradition and invalidated
the eschatological idea of the proletariat as the 'coming class' entrusted by
history to move society to higher stages of development. The second
occurrence was the gravitational shift to the right in British politics
initiated by the Thatcherite neo-liberal project of the 1980s and then
continued and deepened during the 1990s by the 'Third Way' narrative
of New Labour. The ethos surrounding this bi-partisan neo-liberal project
have now seeped into the pores of British life and politics and tilted the
political co-ordinates further and further to the right and away from the
collective ideals and essentially class-based preoccupations that animated
the traditional labour movement. I have in mind the self-indulgent individualism consecrated in the worship of success and wealth, the increasing
privatisation of production and public services, the sale of assets from
the public to the private sector, the creation of a new share-holding
class, the privileging of the consumer at the expense of the producer at
the point of production, and the exalting of the principle of private over
public ownership in the spheres of both the economy and housing. In
regard to the latter, local authority housing was ruthlessly sold off to
sitting tenants, or transferred to Housing Associations. Between 1979
and 1997 around two million council homes were sold to tenants under
Conservative governments' 'right to buy' programme, an astute, politically

driven initiative that cut a great swathe through one of the most recognisably collective aspects of working-class life and culture.[33]

In terms of the focus of this study, the propensity of the far right in the contemporary period to secure working-class support, the neo-liberal project of New Labour is deemed to be most significant. Since 1994, when this project began to gain momentum, there has been a calculated reluctance on the part of New Labour to use the rhetoric of class, acknowledge the party's working-class roots, continue its long-standing institutional ties with the trade unions, reverse the Tories anti-labour legislation, endorse the Party's 'interventionist' past, or shape its policies with primarily a working-class electorate in mind. This reorientation reached its apogee in Tony Blair's address to the 1999 Labour Party annual conference when he proclaimed that: 'The class war is over ... The 21st century will not be about the battle between capitalism and socialism but between the forces of progress and the forces of conservatism.'[34] A silence has fallen over the language that edified generations of earlier Labour Party activists, such as the references to public ownership, wealth taxation, property iniquities, recurring cycles of poverty and deprivation, the uneven distribution of wealth and 'cultural capital', the goal of equality, and the 'Clarion' cry to build the socialist 'Jerusalem'.

The attack by New Labour on the ethos which this outlook represented, 'labourism', has been relentless. In relation to the trade unions alone, there has been a reduction in the weight of the trade unions' block vote at party conferences, an end to union sponsorship of MPs and the adoption of a more varied system of party fundraising to end what was perceived to be an over-reliance on union contributions and, as stated, a disinclination to restore the unions' legal immunities.[35] Redistributionist and egalitarian principles would be undermined by 'think-tank' driven policy initiatives in other areas of society. High rates of personal taxation for the wealthy were ruled out of court, the party's traditional tax-and-spend outlook was abandoned, the comprehensive principle in secondary school education was jettisoned and a process of 'creeping privatisation' was to be visited upon the National Health Service. The most fundamental attack on the redistributionist and egalitarian canon was in April 1995, when Clause IV of the Party constitution committing the Party to public ownership of the means of production was thrown overboard, to be replaced by a nebulous commitment to a range of other values that included support for a 'just society', the market, rigorous competition and a thriving private sector.

At the same time it was systematically dismantling labourism, New Labour offered its traditional supporters a new discourse to replace the old labourist discourse of class. Underpinned by the mind-numbingly uninspiring concepts of 'social exclusion' and the 'stake-holder' society, it suggested to those trapped in conditions of periodic unemployment, de-industrialisation, low pay, bad housing, poor health, family break-down and living in high crime environments, that it was possible to escape these circumstances through a firm personal and moral commit-ment to society and its system of values. The aim was to achieve an inclusive, cohesive society by cultivating a sense of individual responsi-bility, civic duty, moral uprightness and a new work ethic in the 'socially excluded'. Harriet Harman, then Minister for Social Security, outlined the supposed benefits of the latter in 1997: 'Work is central to the Government's attack on social exclusion. ... Work is not just about earning a living. It is a way of life ... Work helps to fulfill our aspira-tions. It is the key to independence, self-respect and opportunities for advancement ... Work brings a sense of order that is missing from the lives of many unemployed young men ...'[36] The message was clear. Apparently, there was nothing inherently wrong with contemporary society. It just needed to be made more inclusive by the excluded and the government entering into an obligatory contract. While the excluded were told that they needed to come to an arrangement with the *status quo*, accommodate themselves to the 'natural order' created by free market liberalism, the duty of the government was to maximise oppor-tunity by creating a dynamic economic environment and enterprise culture within which the excluded could flourish. It should come as no surprise that enthusiasm for the new philosophy on the part of its sup-posed beneficiaries was somewhat muted. The neo-liberal metaphor of the 'rising tide of the market lifting all boats' remains a fallacious one and, despite the Blairites' attempts to tinker with the 'invisible hand' of the market through its 'social inclusion-stake holder' policy, New Labour has presided over a deeply divided society of winners and losers.

This ideological repositioning has been reflected in the shifting social-class composition of the Labour Party's membership during the 1990s. Between 1990 and 1997, the proportion of party members classified as working class dropped from one quarter to one-seventh, while the pro-portion of members in the 'middle class salariat' climbed from one-half to two-thirds.[37] Even more striking, is the declining numbers of trade unionists in the membership ranks of New Labour. Before 1993 it was a constitutional requirement for all individual Labour Party members to belong to a trade union. By 1997, with the constitutional rule long jettisoned, individual party members belonging to a trade union had plummeted to one-third of the total membership.[38] Clearly, as New Labour moved towards the millennium, its membership profile was becoming increasingly middle class and markedly less proletarian. The same shrinking working-class presence can be discerned with regard to voters. The 2001 general election revealed a contraction of working-class support for the Labour Party, a trend that had carried forward from the previous general election in 1997. In 2001, the Labour Party's share of the vote in its 289 safest seats, the seats which housed its traditional working-class supporters, dropped by 3.9 per cent since the 1997 election, which was accompanied by a decline in turnout of 13.6 per cent.[39] It seemed, then, that by 2001, many of the Labour Party's traditional core supporters were abandoning the party and turning their back on the Third Way. The questions that invariably arise from this seismic profile change taking place within one of Europe's oldest social democratic parties are: how many of these disillusioned working-class voters have gone over to the far right, and how many more of them are likely to go over in the future?

Although this mutual parting of the ways by New Labour and its core electoral constituency primarily stems from New Labour's ideological and tactical reorientation away from the politics of class to the politics of individualism and the market-place, it should also be understood as an aspect of a more general change within the electoral process. Recent electoral trends show higher voter volatility and a less ideological, partisan and emotional attachment to parties, which has served to further decompose traditional class-based political affiliations and allegiances.[40] If the recent evidence suggesting the decline of party identification and ties is to be believed, post-industrial political parties are some distance removed from the idea of parties as, in the words of Raphael Samuel, 'concentrated expressions of class being'.[41] As we have seen in relation to New Labour and its shrinking proletarian voter support base, another indicator of a waning of party identification and bonds and a further sign of shifting political orientations within hitherto relatively stable, socially structured electoral constituencies, including that of the working class, is voter apathy. In the 2001 general election the turnout was just 59.1 per cent, compared to 76.2 in 1979, 71.9 in 1970 and 84.1 per cent in 1950.[42]

One could make the reasonable assumption that that the disillusioned working-class voters who have deserted New Labour and decided to abstain from participating in recent general elections, would find solace and a home in the new forms of Left politics that have emerged contemporaneous with the structural, ideological and party-political developments outlined earlier. The more wealthy Western states, it seems, have mutated into 'post-material' societies which have favoured the emergence of new forms of values and politics centred on issues relating to life style, participation, self-realisation and social and cultural liberalisation, rather than the more conventional politics relating to jobs, unemployment and other forms of economic insecurity.[43] This 'silent revolution' in values and political attitudes, according to Ronald Inglehart's early 1977 definition, has had most impact on the left side of the political spectrum.[44] A kaleidoscope of new political forms, the women's movement, sexual politics, life politics, global protest, the green movement, issue politics, deconstruction, post-modernism and identity politics, have indeed emerged in the last three decades to challenge the hegemony of conventional modes of working-class collective action as embraced by the traditional labour movement. For many sections of the European Left, the old class-based, 'material' concerns and issues that still preoccupy many working-class people simply do not figure in their deliberations. Moreover, there are many in the working class in Britain, and across Europe, who seem mystified and excluded by much of the language of the new left and alienated by its agendas, particularly less-skilled young white males.[45] Some analysts have even argued that the far right has astutely appropriated aspects of this new left rhetoric and, in so doing, has secured for itself a white working-class audience. The new left discourse of identity politics, for example, according to this perspective, with its stress on the virtue of difference and the inviolability of rights for all cultural groups within the nation, is seen to have handed an advantage to a far right that is only too keen to assert the difference of the white working class and champion its 'rights'. 'Assertions of "difference" ', runs this argument, 'are easily translated into an assertion of the "difference" between "our" national group and their "otherness"; the affirmation and pride in being black or gay is replicated in the affirmation and pride in being white and straight'.[46]

It is in this new, re-configured post-industrial political space that the British far right is now operating in the new millennium. We can add to the factors referred to earlier, too, the population displacements and world migration movements that have been stimulated by developments such as capitalist globalisation and regional wars, which have fuelled home-grown xenophobia and provided the far right with an opportunity to peddle anti-immigrant propaganda. As a consequence of this broad convergence of circumstances, the BNP, the most significant of the extreme-right groups, has considerable potential to attract a level of support that includes a much higher proportion of workers than was even the case during the NF phase and across a wider and more varied geographical space. Alarmingly, much of the evidence on the social background characteristics of the rising far-right vote in continental Europe during the 1990s would seem to support this hypothesis concerning rising working-class support.[47] In the 1995 French Presidential elections, for example, when Jean-Marie Le Pen's FN polled around 4.8 million votes in the first round, representing a 16.86 per cent share of a 78 per cent turnout, it attracted more working-class votes than any other candidate, including the Socialist Prime Minister Lionel Jospin.[48] It has been estimated by Mark Neocleous and Nick Startin that those residing in urban, socio-economically deprived areas belonging to 'a working class and de-Christianised milieu' are the largest category within Le Pen's 'core electorate'.[49] Even more striking, in the second ballot of the 2002 legislative elections, Le Pen's greatest gains were recorded in former communist (PCF) strongholds, areas that had undergone a process of de-industrialisation, such as the port of Dunkerque and the northern mining towns of Lens and Henin Beaumont.[50] Jörg Haider's Freedom Party (FPÖ) in Austria was also attracting substantial working-class support, 47 per cent by 1999 according to Roger Eatwell, encouraging Haider to assert in February 2000 that the FPÖ had displaced the Social Democrats as the legitimate defenders of the Austrian working class.[51] The working-class component in the contemporary German far right vote is particularly marked and has led some scholars to conclude that 'the German extreme Right is a distinctly working class and lower social status' movement.[52] In the Baden-Würtemberg state elections in 1992, for example, the German far-right *Republikaner* (REP) received 19.4 per cent of the workers' vote.[53] In line with this chapter's argument, studies of Republikaner 'blue-collar' voters suggest that they tend to be unaffiliated workers adversely experiencing the fall-out from the 'modernisation' process in the transition to more 'knowledge-intensive postindustrial economies'.[54]

Based on existing studies of the contemporary European far right, it is possible to build up a composite sociological picture of the typical working-class far-right supporter in the millennium, taking into account that any such construction is invariably stereotypical and schematic. This supporter would tend to be young, male, poorly educated, secular rather than religious, possesses few skills or obsolete skills, works in industries that struggle to compete in the new global market, and lives in a large metropolitan area experiencing de-industrialisation rather than in a small town. This sociological type would also be disillusioned with mainstream politics and parties, have no political or cultural ties to traditional labour organisations, be ethnocentric and xenophobic, culturally parochial and lives in an area where he perceives that he is in competition with immigrants or other ethnic groups over access to scarce resources.

If data were available to explore the social background characteristics of the rising BNP vote in Britain empirically, we should not be surprised to find the presence of this sociological 'type' voting in some numbers for the BNP. Considered in geographical terms, it would seem that the BNP is indeed building a clear support base in areas which contain a high proportion of working-class residents. The north-west of England is a case in point. In two of the three Oldham constituencies in the 2001 general election, Oldham West and Royton and Oldham East and Saddleworth, both Labour constituencies, the BNP, although only finishing third and fourth respectively, managed to scoop up 11,643 votes. In the Oldham West and Royton constituency, a Labour stronghold, the 6,552 votes and 16.4 per cent total poll share for the BNP Leader Nick Griffin represented the largest vote ever for a far-right candidate in a British Parliamentary election.[55] In the nearby Burnley constituency, another Labour stronghold, where the NF failed to make an impact, the BNP polled 11.25 per cent of the vote in the 2001 general election, a seemingly core electoral base that it would build on in the 2002 Council elections when it won three seats on Burnley Council. The May 2003 Council elections would bring more success for the BNP in Burnley. At the close of the day's poll it ended up with eight seats, forcing the Liberal Democrats into third place with only seven seats and emerging as the official opposition to Labour.[56] Again in the North West, the BNP also won a seat on Darwen Borough Council in Blackburn in November 2002 after topping the poll in the Mill Hill ward.[57]

The BNP has also made its mark in other locations in Britain which have traditionally been linked to Labour or which have a relatively high working-class presence. In the October 2002 Mayoral election in Stoke-on-Trent, the BNP candidate managed to notch up 8,215 votes.[58] The BNP followed this up by snatching a seat on Stoke-on-Trent Council in the May 2003 elections. That the British far right believed that local politics had entered a new, and more favourable, conjuncture could be seen in the BNP's recent audacious attempts to challenge Labour's long-standing hegemony in the North East. In the 2002 local elections, the far-right party secured over 10 per cent of the vote in Gateshead, and achieved a similar level in three wards in Sunderland. In the May 2003 Council elections, the BNP fielded 54 candidates across the North East, compared to just 9, 4 years previously, which included contesting seats on councils in Newcastle, Gateshead, Stockton-on-Tees and Sunderland.[59] Although comfort should be gained from the BNP's failure to capture a single seat in the region, it would be naïve to be complacent. In Sunderland, for example, although the BNP was kept out of all the 25 Sunderland wards it contested in the 2003 elections, it still managed to amass 13,652 votes from a total of 99,288.[60] While the local media mentioned local anxieties regarding crime, public services, local government malpractice and the inevitable bogey of asylum seekers as reasons why the BNP decided to contest Sunderland, it is not without significance in terms of this study that the BNP's organiser for the North East, Kevin Scott, also cited 'Labour's "betrayal" of its traditional supporters' as a potential vote winner for his party.[61]

An attempt to keep the far right out of another previously safe Labour area further south, however, was less successful. A by-election in the Grays Riverside ward in Thurrock, Essex, in September 2003 witnessed another BNP victory, bringing the party its eighteenth council seat. There is clear evidence from these recent electoral advances by the BNP that it had been consciously targeting disgruntled Labour voters.[62] It was in recognition of these attempts by the far right to move into its traditional heartlands that prompted New Labour to open a campaign 'academy' designed to advise its local parties on how to counter the BNP during council elections.[63]

This is not to argue that the electoral pattern is uniform and that other social-class types did not figure in the BNP vote. The extreme right's ability throughout its history, and in a variety of national contexts, to garner support from all social-class groups has already been mentioned. Thus, it should not surprise us that that the new far right has also picked up seats where the centre-right, Tory vote traditionally holds sway. This has happened, for example, in Kirklees, west Yorkshire, where the BNP gained representation on the Council in August 2003. Griffin's party also grabbed a seat at Broxbourne, Hertfordshire, a small rural Tory-controlled council, in the May 2003 Council elections.

It should be mentioned in regard to recent BNP local election victories, and it is a sobering thought, that the BUF, the most prominent and well-resourced far-right party in Britain prior to the BNP's arrival, only managed to win one local government seat. This single victory was registered in the Suffolk Council elections in 1938, when the Mosleyite Suffolk landowner Ronald Creasy topped the poll in Eye. There was to be no electoral breakthrough in other parts of Britain, however. Even in the BUF's east London heartlands where, despite intense campaigning and high expectations on the part of the fascist leadership, it was unable to dislodge Labour. The BUF's best electoral showing was in its Bethnal Green north-east stronghold when it sought representation to the London County Council (LCC) in March 1937 and the Borough Council the following November, but even here its candidates finished some distance behind the winning Labour candidates.[64] In the LCC elections, the two BUF candidates in Bethnal Green north-east did manage to muster 3,000 votes each, or 23.17 per cent of the total poll. Although this was enough to push the Liberals into third place, it fell some way short of the 7,700 votes recorded by the Labour candidates. In the November elections, the highest votes recorded by the fascists were in north and east Bethnal Green: North ward: Labour 2,272; BUF 731; Liberals 630. East ward: Labour 4,474; BUF 1,805; Liberals 1,603. As in the LCC election, the Mosleyite vote pushed the Liberals into third place in the poll. The most significant feature, however, from the point of view of an important aspect of this study, the propensity of the BNP to overtake New Labour in local elections, is that the interwar Labour vote held up when challenged by the far right. It should be of concern that, in the present period, the vote of the re-configured New Labour Party seems far more brittle in the face of electoral challenges from the far right.

On a more optimistic note, although the structural, or 'demand' side, conditions described in this chapter provide the BNP, or a mutation of it, with a greater potential to secure wider working-class support, the political advance of the extreme right is not inevitable. There is an absence of other crucial variables, which suggest that the BNP may not find it easy to make a decisive impact on the national political stage. A contemporary far-right party is more likely to succeed, according to the latest research, if it possesses a charismatic leader, a viable politico-economic programme beyond xenophobia and anti-immigrant rhetoric, a membership and financial capacity large enough to enable it to mount an effective national campaign and a credible political image to help off-set the perception that a vote cast for it is not a wasted vote. Thankfully, most of these features are absent from the BNP's repertoire at this point in time, despite its recent electoral successes. Additionally, in the wider politico-economic picture, there is as yet no major economic crisis which the BNP can feed off, nor is Britain suffering from a deep cultural, 'palingenetic' crisis which would give some resonance to the far right's generic obsession with the myth of national regeneration. Britain also has a commendable, long-standing tradition of anti-fascist opposition, both 'organised' and 'passive', including that emanating from the liberal political culture, which remains healthy and continues to deny the far right political legitimacy by making apparent the odium of racism, anti-semitism, residual Nazism, Holocaust-denial and violence with which it has always been associated.[65]

The disparity between the BNP's recent feats at the polls and its membership strength contemporaneous to these electoral advances should also be stressed, with the latter at an unimpressive 3,000–4,000 failing to match the performances of the former. Some comfort should be gained from the fact that the BNP has, as yet, failed to find a formula to turn more passive voters into more ideologically driven active members. A future dip in the BNP's local electoral fortunes may also bring a return of the chronic internal feuds and petty in-fighting that have always bedevilled fascist and neo-fascist parties and constrained their growth, including the NF. Finally, the experience of many of the BNP's recent local and general election successes suggests that it can be defeated when a larger number of voters are persuaded or encouraged to participate in the electoral process. The electoral evidence shows that the BNP performs better when the poll turnout is low, with defeat usually following when the turnout is high. In the BNP's by-election victory in Thurrock, Essex, for example, only one in five voters turned out. In the May 2003 Council elections in Sunderland, on the other hand, the opposition was able to beat off the BNP challenge relatively comfortably because the overall turnout had more than doubled compared to the 2002 elections, from 22 per cent to 46 per cent.

On a less reassuring note, however, analysts of contemporary European far-right parties warn that, although there has been an absence of serious crises in recent years which might 'de-legitimise capitalism', a major crisis or a serious economic downturn may well see a sharp growth in the 'authoritarian extremist constituency'.[66] 'If overall background political conditions should change dramatically', warned Roger Karapin, 'through economic crisis or regional war, the far right would become a much more effective conduit for the transmission of anti-system ideas and political forces into the political mainstream'.[67] There is another point to be made in relation to Britain. The organised anti-fascist opposition is likely to be significantly weaker if the structural, political and ideological trends outlined in this chapter continue to re-shape, disorganise and shrink the British labour movement. While the former, structural, trends were probably inevitable and irreversible, the latter political and ideological developments were not. All those ideologues, Thatcherite and Blairite, who either conspired to dismantle the organised labour movement, or luxuriated over the prospect of its imminent passing, should pause to reflect on the implications of this should the far right emerge as a significant force in British politics at some stage in the future. For with the passing of the organised labour movement as it was conventionally conceived and understood, will disappear one of the great historic barriers, political and moral, to the advance of the far right.

Notes

1. S. J. Rawnsley, 'Fascism and Fascists in the North of England in the 1930s' (PhD Thesis, University of Bradford, 1983) and S. J. Rawnsley, 'The Membership of the British Union of Fascists' in K. Lunn and R. Thurlow (eds), *British Fascism* (London: Croom Helm, 1980), pp. 150–65.
2. See T. Linehan, *East London for Mosley. The British Union of Fascists in East London and South-West Essex, 1933–40* (London: Frank Cass, 1996).
3. S. Payne, *A History of Fascism 1914–45* (London: UCL Press, 1995), p. 182.
4. S. Payne, *A History of Fascism*, pp. 168–9. The NSDAP captured over 11 million votes in the July 1932 election, the highpoint of its electoral effort, which marked a decisive political breakthrough for Hitler.
5. D. Mühlberger, *Hitler's Followers. Studies in the Sociology of the Nazi Movement* (London: Routledge, 1991), p. 209.
6. S. Payne, *A History of Fascism*, pp. 103–4.
7. S. M. Lipset, ' "Fascism" – Left, Right and Centre', in S. M. Lipset (ed.), *Political Man* (London, Heinemann: 1983), pp. 131–7.
8. For the famous Comintern analysis which spawned numerous derivatives, see the extract from 13th Enlarged Executive of the Communist International (ECCI) Plenum (held in December 1933) on 'Fascism, the War Danger, and the Tasks of the Communist Parties', reprinted under the title 'The Terrorist Dictatorship of Finance Capital, in R. Griffin (ed.), *International Fascism. Theories, Causes and the New Consensus* (London: Arnold, 1998), pp. 59–66.
9. In Germany, too, Hitler failed to make inroads into the working-class support network of the SPD (Sozialdemokratische Partei Deutschlands: Social Democratic Party of Germany).
10. See N. Copsey, *Anti-Fascism in Britain* (Basingstoke: Macmillan, 2000), pp. 12–15.
11. W. Hannington, *Never On Our Knees* (London: Lawrence & Wishart, 1967), p. 331.
12. J. Jacobs, *Out of the Ghetto. My Youth in the East End: Communism and Fascism 1913–1939* (London: Janet Simon, 1978), p. 281.
13. S. J. Rawnsley, 'The Membership of the British Union of Fascists', p. 160; T. Linehan, *East London for Mosley*, pp. 195–236; See also, T. Linehan, *British Fascism 1918–39. Parties, Ideology and Culture* (Manchester: Manchester University Press, 2000), pp. 164–5.
14. J. Jacobs, *Out of the Ghetto*, p. 88.
15. T. Linehan, *East London for Mosley*, pp. 88–9.
16. T. Linehan, *East London for Mosley*, p. 89.
17. R. Eatwell, 'The Esoteric Ideology of the NF in the 1980s', in M. Cronin (ed.), *The Failure of British Fascism. The Far Right and the Fight for Political Recognition* (London: Macmillan, 1996), p. 102.
18. M. Billig, *Fascists: A Social Psychological View of the National Front* (London: Harcourt Brace Jovanovich, 1979); S. Taylor, *The National Front in English*

Politics (London: Macmillan, 1982). See also, M. Hanna, 'The National Front and Other Right-Wing Organisations', *New Community*, 111, 1974, 49–55; D. Scott, 'The National Front in Local Politics: Some Interpretations', in I. Crewe (ed.), *British Political Sociology Yearbook, Volume 2* (London: Croom Helm, 1976), pp. 214–38.

19. 'Studies of aggregate NF electoral support', Husbands' writes, 'have repeatedly demonstrated that areas of NF strength tend to be "working class communities" '. C. Husbands, *Racial Exclusionism and the City. The Urban Support of the National Front* (London: George Allen & Unwin, 1983), p. 141.

20. C. Husbands, *Racial Exclusionism and the City*, p. 117.

21. C. Husbands, *Racial Exclusionism and the City*, p. 7.

22. C. Husbands, *Racial Exclusionism and the City*, pp. 142–3.

23. C. Husbands, *Racial Exclusionism and the City*, p. 94.

24. G. Therborn, 'Into the 21st Century. The New Parameters of Global Politics', *New Left Review*, 10, July–August 2001, p. 99.

25. A. Gorz, *Farewell to the Working Class. An Essay on Post-Industrial Socialism* (London: Pluto Press, 1982), p. 69.

26. E. Hobsbawm, 'The Forward March of Labour Halted?', in M. Jacques and F. Mulhern (eds), *The Forward March of Labour Halted?* (London, Verso: 1981), pp. 1–19.

27. M. Savage, 'Sociology, Class and Male Manual Work Cultures', in J. McIlroy, N. Fishman and A. Campbell (eds), *British Trade Unions and Industrial Politics. The High Tide of Trade Unionism, 1964–79* (Aldershot: Ashgate, 1999), p. 26.

28. G. Therborn, *European Modernity and Beyond. The Trajectory of European Societies 1945–2000* (London: Sage Publications, 1995), p. 71.

29. C. Wrigley, *British Trade Unions Since 1933* (Cambridge: Cambridge University Press, 2002), pp. 19–20, 27. See also J. McIlroy, *Trade Unions in Britain Today* (Manchester: Manchester University Press, 1995, second edition).

30. Wrigley, British Trade Unions Since 1933, p. 42.

31. A. Gorz, *Farewell to the Working Class*, p. 69.

32. A. Gorz, *Farewell to the Working Class*, p. 75.

33. A. Heath, R. Jowell and J. Curtice, *The Rise of New Labour. Party Policies and Voter Choices* (Oxford: Oxford University Press, 2001), p. 14.

34. Cited in P. Seyd and P. Whitely, *New Labour's Grassroots. The Transformation of the Labour Party Membership* (London: Palgrave MacMillan, 2002), p. 13.

35. L. Panitch and C. Leys, *The End of Parliamentary Socialism. From New Left to New Labour* (London, Verso: 1997), pp. 230, 236.

36. Cited in N. Fairclough, *New Labour, New Language?* (London: Routledge, 2000), p. 57.

37. P. Seyd and P. Whitely, *New Labour's Grassroots*, p. 37.

38. P. Seyd and P. Whitely, *New Labour's Grassroots*, p. 43.

39. P. Seyd and P. Whitely, *New Labour's Grassroots*, pp. 177–8.

40. See for example, S. Flanagan and R. Dalton, 'Parties Under Stress: Realignment and Dealignment in Advanced Industrial Societies', *West European Politics*, 7, 1984, pp. 7–23 and P. Mair, 'Continuity, Change and the Vulnerability of Party', *West European Politics*, 12, 1989, pp. 169–86.

41. R. Samuel, 'Class Politics: The Lost World of British Communism, Part Three', *New Left Review*, 165, September/October 1987, p. 56.

42. D. Denver, *Elections and Voters in Britain* (Hampshire: Palgrave Macmillan, 2003), p. 29.

180   Thomas P. Linehan

43. On the 'post-material' societies, see R. Eatwell, 'Ten Theories of the Extreme Right', in P. Merkl and L. Weinberg (eds), *Right-Wing Extremism in the Twenty-First Century* (London: Frank Cass, 2003), pp. 6–7.
44. R. Inglehart, *The Silent Revolution* (Princeton: Princeton University Press, 1977).
45. P. Eatwell, 'Ten Theories of the Extreme Right', p. 6.
46. M. Neocleous and N. Startin, ' "Protest" and Fail to Survive: Le Pen and the Great Moving Right Show', *Politics*, 23, 2003, p. 152. For another version of this argument, see N. Moss and M. Neocleous, 'The Poor Against the Poor? Race, Class and Anti-Fascism', *Radical Philosophy*, 112, March/April 2002, pp. 6–8.
47. For a sample of writings on this new phenomenon, see P. Ignazi, 'The Silent Counter-Revolution. Hypotheses on the Emergence of Extreme Right-Wing Parties in Europe', *European Journal of Political Research*, 22, 1992, pp. 3–34; C. Mudde, 'The War of Words Defining the Extreme Right Party Family', *West European Politics*, 19, 1996, pp. 225–48 and M. Lubbers, M. Gijsberts and P. Scheepers, 'Extreme Right-Wing Voting in Western Europe', *European Journal of Political Research*, 41, 2002, pp. 345–78.
48. R. Eatwell, 'Ten Theories of the Extreme Right', p. 5.
49. M. Neocleous and N. Startin, ' "Protest" and Fail to Survive: Le Pen and the Great Moving Right Show', pp. 145–55.
50. M. Neocleous and N. Startin, ' "Protest" and Fail to Survive: Le Pen and the Great Moving Right Show', p. 150.
51. R. Eatwell, 'Ten Theories of the Extreme Right', pp. 5, 7.
52. H. Kitschelt, *The Radical Right in Western Europe. A Comparative Analysis* (Ann Arbor: University of Michigan Press, 1995), p. 232.
53. H. Kitschelt, *The Radical Right in Western Europe*, p. 232. This figure was determined by exit polls.
54. H. Kitschelt, *The Radical Right in Western Europe*, pp. 229, 234.
55. In the neighbouring, and more middle-class, Oldham East and Saddleworth constituency, the BNP candidate's vote of 5,091 represented 11.2 per cent of the total poll.
56. More recent evidence suggests that the BNP surge in Burnley may have been stemmed. In February 2004, one of its councillors, Maureen Stowe, resigned to become an independent councillor. The party has also lost two by-elections and experienced internal problems and much negative local media publicity after another BNP councilor, Luke Smith, resigned from the Council after he was involved in a violent brawl at a BNP party gathering. The recent poll evidence shows that it is the Liberal Democrats, rather than Labour, that has halted the far right surge in Burnley. In the seat vacated by Luke Smith, the replacement BNP candidate's 357 votes only netted him third place, a figure that was well adrift of the 1,070 votes of the winning Liberal Democrat candidate. On the BNP's difficulties in Burnley, see *Searchlight*, November 2003, at http://www.searchlightmagazine.com
57. Far right ambitions also extended across the Pennines. In a January 2003 by-election, the BNP gained its first seat on Calderdale Council in Halifax, west Yorkshire, after winning the Mixenden ward. This was followed up in May with a victory in Calderdale's Illingworth ward to give the party its second Council seat. In August 2003, the BNP also won a seat on Kirklees Council in west Yorkshire.

58. *Guardian*, 24 January 2003, p. 14.
59. http://www.durham21.co.uk/archive.
60. http://www. news.bbc.co.uk.
61. http://www.timesonline.co.uk.
62. *Independent*, 3 October 2003, p. 9.
63. The BNP first served notice that it could make inroads into the Labour vote in the early 1990s. In the May 1990 local elections in Tower Hamlets, east London, the BNP candidate secured 9.71 per cent of the poll from a 50 per cent turnout in the Holy Trinity ward. The BNP followed this up with a by-election victory in Tower Hamlets' Millwall ward, when Derek Beackon became the party's first ever local councillor when he captured 34 per cent of the poll.
64. On the BUF's campaign in Bethnal Green, see T. Linehan, *East London for Mosley*, pp. 57–77.
65. N. Copsey, *Anti-Fascism in Britain*, pp. 189–93.
66. R. Eatwell, 'Ten Theories of the Extreme Right', p. 17.
67. Roger Karapin, 'Radical Right and Neo-Fascist Political Parties in Western Europe', *Comparative Politics*, 30, 2 January 1998, p. 230. A broadly similar point has been made by Roger Eatwell. See R. Eatwell, 'Ten Theories of the Extreme Right', p. 17.

9
Meeting the Challenge of Contemporary British Fascism? The Labour Party's Response to the National Front and the British National Party

Nigel Copsey

The Labour Party's response to the electoral rise of the National Front (NF) in the 1970s and to the recent emergence of the British National Party (BNP) is the subject of the final chapter in this volume. We start with the 1970s, when popular support for the NF came in two waves: 1972–73 and 1976–77. As we shall see, in countering the NF, the Labour Party was at its most active during the second wave, that is to say, from 1976 onwards. The form that this opposition took and what motivated it is our opening concern. We then move on to the present day and consider at both national and local levels New Labour's response to the BNP. Burnley, branded by one local newspaper in 2003 as the BNP's 'capital of Britain', will serve as our case study.[1] What similarities and differences can we identify between the approaches of old Labour and New Labour? As the final point of reflection, this chapter asks whether New Labour's response to the BNP has contributed to, rather than countered, the electoral success of contemporary British fascism.

Old Labour and the National Front in the 1970s

In 1967, under the banner of the NF, Britain's fascists were united for the first time in a generation. This unity did not deliver instant success however; it was 1972–73 before the Front gained meaningful ground. The Ugandan Asians crisis was the decisive factor. Cashing in on white concerns that Britain was about to accept a mass influx of Ugandan Asians, the NF saw its membership double between October 1972 and

July 1973. Now it could count something like 15,000 members.[2] At local elections in 1973, with its candidates averaging 13 per cent of the vote in Leicester and close to 20 per cent in Blackburn, the Front notched up some notable electoral successes. The most significant occurred in May 1973 when at West Bromwich a deposit was saved in a parliamentary election for the first (and only) time. By 1974 the Front had sufficient strength to contest 54 seats at the February general election and 90 seats by the general election in October.

Prior to 1976, the emergence of the NF occasioned little response from the Labour Party. The radical left – the International Marxist Group and the International Socialists – occupied the foreground of early opposition to the Front. This manifested itself most spectacularly in Red Lion Square in June 1974 when Kevin Gately, a 21-year-old student from Warwick University, received fatal injuries.[3] As far as the mainstream labour movement was concerned, it was the Transport and General Workers' Union (TGWU) that expressed most unease about the activities of the Front. The TGWU, the largest union in the country, had been a target for infiltration by right-wing extremists since London dockers had demonstrated their support for Powell in the late 1960s.[4] When the Smithfield meat porters, organised in the TGWU, had demonstrated against the influx of Ugandan Asians in 1972, they had criticised their union's 'silence' over the immigration issue as well as the 'threat to the living standards of the British working class' posed by the Ugandan Asians.[5]

Attentive to the possibilities of racist mobilisation on the shop floor, the September 1972 issue of the NF's magazine *Spearhead* called on its readers to prepare for propaganda work among the trade unions. This prompted the formation of an *ad-hoc* group known as 'Trade Unionists Against Fascism', which first drew attention to attempts, by fascists, to acquire a foothold in the unions in December 1972.[6] By November 1973, the General Executive Council of the TGWU had responded. The TUC and the Labour Party should mount a campaign exposing the NF as a fascist organisation, it declared.[7] The following October the TGWU published a pamphlet, *Racialism, Fascism and the Trade Unions*. Authored by Brian Nicholson of the TGWU's Docks Group and carrying a forward by Jack Jones, the TGWU's general secretary, it was no doubt a response to the announcement in July 1974 that the NF intended to establish its own Trade Unionists' Association.[8]

Whilst the Labour Party viewed NF activity on the shop floor with some concern, the stand taken by the TGWU was judged sufficiently robust that no further action was necessary.[9] In fact, compared to conflicts over industrial relations, the three-day week and incomes policy, the

Labour Party leadership considered the NF a minor issue. Besides there was a rather complacent assumption amongst Labour Party circles that the NF was stealing its votes not from Labour but from the ranks of disaffected Conservatives who were furious at Heath's 'cowardly' stance on immigration and Britain's entry to the EEC. Yet it would be wrong to suggest that the Labour Party was entirely indifferent to the NF. At the October 1974 general election for instance, Labour's National Executive Committee (NEC) advised its candidates not to take part in any joint platforms with NF candidates and not to appear on any radio or television programmes where a Front candidate was to participate.[10] Accordingly, the Labour Party refused to appear on the BBC's *Nationwide* programmes transmitted from London and Birmingham on 1 October 1974 due to the presence of representatives from the NF.[11] For the moment at least, the low-key nature of Labour's response seemed appropriate. The results of the October 1974 general election bore this out: the NF lost all 90 deposits. Moreover, the following year a major split debilitated the NF and its advance faltered.

A turning point came in 1976. In that year the NF staged a comeback. In a re-run of the Ugandan Asians crisis, the far right once again capitalised on fears that Asian immigrants would flood Britain. This time the refugees were from Malawi, whom the national press sensationalised as the '£600 per week Hotel Asians'. During the first six months of 1976 the NF recruited 2,096 new members.[12] At local elections in Leicester, Bradford and West Bromwich, Front candidates captured around 20 to 25 per cent of the white vote. In one ward in Leicester, a NF candidate came within 62 votes of election. Altogether, 176 National Front candidates obtained almost 50,000 votes and the indications were that the Front had garnered much of its support from working-class constituencies.[13] Meanwhile in Blackburn, two candidates from the NF offshoot, the National Party, were elected. More than 30 attacks on Asian property took place in Blackburn in the immediate wake of these elections. And as racial tensions rose, so Barbara Castle, the local Labour MP and member of the party's NEC, demanded action.[14] Then, on 1 July 1976, at a local council by-election in the traditional Labour stronghold of Deptford, in South London, the combined National Front/National Party vote totalled more than 44 per cent. Extreme-right parties had taken the largest share of the poll.[15]

Labour's leadership quickly reconsidered its position. Closer investigations revealed that significant numbers of inner-city working-class voters were becoming susceptible to the far right. Labour Party strategists identified 21 marginal seats that could possibly fall to the Conservatives in the event of NF intervention.[16] Since Labour had won the October 1974 general election with a 'knife-edge' majority of just three seats, the challenge that the Front seemed to present could no longer be taken lightly, especially since now it was threatening to put up 318 candidates at the next general election.[17] The key to the far right's electoral advance – Labour strategists rightly concluded – was racism. Only at this point did the Labour Party's traditional supporters with racist sympathies give it grounds for real concern.[18] As one speaker candidly remarked at the party's annual conference in 1976, Labour and the trade union movement 'had been pussyfooting about with the issue of racialism for far too long. It took the National Front and neo-fascist parties to galvanise some of our comrades into action.'[19]

In launching its anti-racism campaign, the Labour Party sought co-operation from the TUC and endorsement from the Archbishop of Canterbury, but it was not interested in all-party collaboration. As far as the Labour Party was concerned, it had to deal with its own situation and deal with it quickly.[20] The campaign would direct itself first and foremost towards the party's own rank and file members, trade unionists and traditional Labour Party supporters. Male blue-collar workers, over the age of 35, who saw black workers as a threat to their jobs, were one specific target group. Another was working class and lower middle class people aged over 35 who often had little contact with black people.[21] But as research by academics at the University of Essex would later suggest, Labour had most likely misread its targets. The typical NF supporter was described as working-class, younger (aged under 35) with minimum qualifications.[22]

Disingenuously, the NF welcomed Labour's campaign as 'an important breakthrough'. It was finally forcing the established political parties into an open debate on immigration, the Front claimed.[23] However, Labour's primary objective was not to debate with the Front but to demolish the myths about race and immigration that were being spread by it. Labour's strategy was thus an educative one. Accordingly, the form that its campaign took consisted of anti-racist leaflets, information notes and speakers' notes, local party meetings, articles for trade union journals, a dedicated party political broadcast and a joint Labour–TUC demonstration. Screened on 14 September 1976, Labour's broadcast featured Tom Jackson, general secretary of the Union of Post Office Workers and senior Labour Party figure, Michael Foot. While Jackson challenged the myth that immigrants were not 'pulling their full weight in our society', Foot reassured viewers that immigration policy under Labour remained strictly controlled and that Britain was not overflowing with immigrants. By stressing the need for stringent controls, it could be countered that Foot's position did little to challenge racist attitudes. Yet his condemnation of racism was unequivocal: 'racial hatred creates no jobs, builds no homes, does nothing to solve any problem whatever. It merely feeds the most debased instincts in search for a scapegoat.'[24] As for the joint Labour Party–TUC demonstration against racism, even though there were concerns that it might attract a counter-demonstration by right-wing extremists – a fear voiced by the Labour Party in particular[25] – over 10,000 marched from Hyde Park to Trafalgar Square on 21 November 1976. There were representatives there from every regional Labour Party and over 20 trade unions.[26]

If the Labour Party had called on its branches to assist in the development of the network of anti-racist/anti-fascist committees that sprung up across the country during the mid-1970s, Labour's NEC had no wish to provoke physical confrontations with the NF. Since this allowed right-wing politicians and the media to present a picture of two sets of 'extremists', the party cautioned against combative forms of opposition. Responding to the NF with violence only served to portray the left as irresponsible. Alternatively, Labour looked to deny racists the space to propagate their ideology by inviting Labour-controlled local authorities to 'think twice' and consider not letting public halls to racist organisations.[27] But what the Labour Party faced, of course, was a developing situation and in 1977 the question of how the party should best respond to the challenge of the NF had to be revisited.

Two key developments account for this: the first was the NF's growing intervention in the electoral arena. At the 1977 Greater London Council elections the Front had polled some 119,000 votes and pushed the Liberals into fourth place in 32 seats. The Front had performed best in safe Labour seats in the east and north of London where turnout had been below average. Second, there had been a notable increase in violent disturbances at NF marches and meetings. In some cases, NF activists had instigated attacks on Labour Party meetings and offices. In Tower Hamlets for instance, after the local party called on the Director of Public Prosecutions to prosecute the NF for inciting racial hatred in the area, windows of the Labour Party's office had been smashed, the building had been covered by slogans celebrating Hitler's birthday and most alarmingly, a. 22 bullet was fired through one of the windows.[28]

Not surprisingly, by the time of the Labour Party conference in September 1977, held in the immediate aftermath of violent clashes at a NF demonstration in Lewisham, the rank and file demanded that the party and the government take serious action. A number of resolutions were put forward: a ban on all NF marches; a ban on using public facilities for NF meetings; demands for the Labour government to oppose any fascist demonstrations and for the mobilisation of counter-demonstrations; prohibition of the Union Jack in racist propaganda; special help to be given to Labour candidates where a fascist candidate was standing and out-and-out opposition to common platforms. From London, Hornsey Constituency Labour Party congratulated those Labour councillors that had attended an anti-NF rally at Wood Green in April 1977 (it had ended in serious disorder)[29] but perhaps the most radical demands came from Brighton Labour Party. It blamed the violence at Lewisham on the Labour government's failure to ban the march, called for a repeal of the 'conspiracy immigration laws', insisted on a labour movement inquiry into the role of the police at Lewisham, and demanded that the anti-racist campaign be turned into active defence of minority communities.[30]

Rather than appeasing racism by calling for further curbs on immigration,[31] Labour's NEC responded to pressure by stepping up its anti-racism campaign. In the first place, it devoted a party political broadcast to attacking the NF in December 1977. Narrated by Joe Ashton, MP for Bassetlaw, the NF was condemned as racist and anti-democratic. Disguised as a television journalist, and interspersed with footage of Hitler and Mussolini, Joe Ashton interviewed young football supporters who saw the NF as an outlet for violence. This broadcast was so critical of the Front that the BBC had to censor parts of it. BBC lawyers had suggested at least five modifications to the text and yet the cut version was still hard-hitting. According to one press report, 'observers could not recall such an explosive broadcast being made in Britain before'.[32] And whilst some sections in the media and a number of Tory MPs claimed that it had been counter-productive, the tabloids praised it for exposing the Front's true nature.[33]

That same month, acting on a suggestion by the Board of Deputies of British Jews, a broad-based campaign group, the 'Joint Committee Against Racialism' (JCAR) was launched. This initiative reflected a belief on Labour's part that it could make its anti-racism campaign more efficient and effective by harnessing the resources of organisations outside the labour movement.[34] Thus, whilst Labour anti-racist campaigner Joan Lestor co-chaired this,[35] it also included representatives from the Liberal Party, the Conservative Party, the British Council of Churches, the National Union of Students, the Board of Deputies and various other ethnic minority organisations. However, rather than the industrious body that Labour had anticipated, it turned out to be bureaucratic and slow to react. Hence, its main focus of activity – a national campaign against racism – did not commence until July 1978.[36]

Coinciding with the formation of the JCAR, the Anti-Nazi League (ANL) was launched. Its provenance came from the grassroots of the anti-fascist movement and as a result, Labour's national organisation seemed unaware that any steps were being taken to form it[37] (even though many Tribunite Labour Party MPs were sponsors). Since the Socialist Workers' Party had first initiated the ANL, the Labour Party stopped short of official endorsement. Those Labour Party MPs that sponsored it did so in a personal capacity.[38] But by the summer of 1978, as the ANL grew to between 40,000 and 50,000 members, including many thousands of ordinary Labour Party supporters, its value in terms of thwarting the NF at the ballot box became increasingly apparent to Labour's tacticians.[39] Consequently, accusations from the Board of Deputies of British Jews and the Federation of Conservative Students that the Socialist Workers' Party was unduly influencing the League largely fell on deaf ears.[40]

With the intention of isolating the Front, the NEC once again repeated its advice to Labour candidates not to share platforms with Front candidates although following the local elections in 1977 this policy had been subject to some debate – Labour feared under-exposure of its candidates should the NF stand a large number of candidates at the next general election.[41] The NEC also called on local authorities to refuse to let premises to the NF outside election periods. In a new departure, it recommended that its candidates issue joint statements on 'race' with candidates of the other major political parties and in order to deter the NF from fielding candidates, it proposed that deposits in parliamentary elections be raised from £150 (a figure set in 1918, comparable with £1,250 in 1978) to £500.[42] As well as these recommendations, the NEC's response to the NF also included a call for major legislative changes. Above all, it wanted to see NF marches banned through recourse to amended Race Relations legislation. Rather than rely on the existing Public Order Act, which all too often resulted in 'blanket bans' and also required the police to take the initiative,[43] the NEC proposed that the racial incitement clause in the Race Relations Act be tightened. It suggested a re-wording in such a way that the public expression of racial 'hostility' or 'prejudice' could be prohibited.[44]

As it turned out, however, and despite support from the Trades Union Congress (TUC) which after Lewisham had called for a ban on all marches by the NF and other extreme-right groups,[45] this suggestion fell on stony ground. Labour Home Secretary Merlyn Rees insisted that the NF would circumvent such legislation. All it had to do was simply claim that a march was ostensibly about other issues, such as crime or freedom of speech. Moreover, if demonstrations were banned, Rees argued, so election meetings would have to be banned as well. This would, in effect, constitute a ban on the NF and this precedent would be too dangerous to set.[46] For Rees, the answer was 'not to ban them, but to beat them. Beating racialism by argument is a job for democrats.'[47] A further practical problem was securing passage of fresh legislation given that by this time Labour was a minority government and with a general election fast approaching, there was insufficient time. Needless to say, no such legislation was passed. In any case, by the winter of 1978–79 popular support for the NF was on the wane.

What followed next is well known. After taking a derisory 1.3 per cent of the poll at the 1979 general election, the Front tore itself apart. Within months, therefore, no further action was necessary. The electoral challenge of the NF had foundered. Had Labour's anti-racist campaign played a significant part in triggering the NF's electoral demise at the end of the 1970s? What can be said with little doubt is that where it exposed the Front's 'Nazi side' it helped denude the NF of social and political respectability. In this respect, Labour's 1977 broadcast almost certainly cut the most ice although educative leaflets such as *The National Front is a Nazi Front: The TUC and Labour Party United Against Racialism* also played their part. All the same, Labour's campaign should not be viewed in isolation. The extent of opposition to the NF during the mid-to-late 1970s was impressive, ranging from the radical Left to the Young Conservatives with the churches, various ethnic minority groups, all-party campaign groups and the media also drawn in.[48] We would be wise, therefore, not to overstate Labour's lone contribution. What is more, with racism being continually reproduced in British society, there was little chance that Labour's campaign would encourage a wider anti-racist perspective to take root. Not many would argue that the collapse of the NF vote at the end of the 1970s was due to diminishing racism. Quite the opposite, racism in British society was alive and well. This was exposed by Margaret Thatcher's now infamous use of the 'race card' on Granada TV's *World in Action* programme in January 1978 – a cynical move, which as even the most ardent anti-fascist activist would have to accept, ultimately sealed the electoral fate of the NF.

New Labour and the British National Party

Over two decades later, the spectre of the far right has returned. Originally launched in 1982, the BNP was led by the NF's former chairman, John Tyndall, until Nick Griffin deposed him in a leadership election in 1999. Tyndall's tenure as BNP Chairman had been remarkably unsuccessful – the high point was a solitary local council by-election victory in Tower Hamlets in September 1993. But under Griffin the party's fortunes changed dramatically. With three scores over 10 per cent and five saved deposits, the 2001 general election was the best ever for a far-right party in British political history. At local elections in 2002, the BNP won three council seats. In May 2003, after collecting an average vote of 17.3 per cent across the seats contested, the BNP could lay claim to no fewer than 16 local councillors. The sights were raised higher still when Griffin confidently predicted that the BNP would break through into the British political mainstream in 2004. Whilst the party failed to fulfil these expectations, the BNP still captured over 808,000 votes in the European elections. At the same time, in local elections, the total number of its representatives elected to public office increased to 21 councillors. Neither the British Union of Fascists (BUF) in the 1930s nor the NF in the 1970s achieved anything like this level of electoral success. And whilst the chances of the BNP ever gaining representation in Westminster are slight, the party presents a significant challenge nonetheless – not least because where it does win representation at the local level it invariably brings with it a deleterious effect on 'race' relations.[49]

A number of factors have made the BNP's recent electoral advance possible. Griffin's 'modernisation' of the BNP is certainly one; disaffection with the mainstream parties and protest voting another. But (as it was in the 1970s) the single most important driver has been racism. One survey showed, for instance, that of those who voted BNP in Burnley in May 2003, 8 out of 9 voters gave 'immigration and asylum' as the major issue that determined their choice of vote. 'Many BNP voters are simply racist', the survey concluded.[50] From 2001 onwards, wherever the politicisation of 'race' occurred, be it through Asian-on-white crime in Oldham, 'positive discrimination' in Burnley, post 9/11 anti-Islamic sentiment, or most crucial of all, through populist rhetoric on asylum-seekers, political space opened up for the BNP. At first this space was restricted to its breakthrough zone in north-west England. Yet in no time at all, as the wider climate of hostility towards asylum-seekers gave a free rein to racism, it had spread to other areas.[51]

At the national level, we need only track back to the summer of 2002 to find the moment when New Labour's response to the BNP was decided. During the weekend of 15/16 June, at a specially convened meeting, senior Labour strategists, in particular the focus-group pollster Philip Gould, advised Tony Blair that thousands of 'angry young working-class men' were about to desert Labour for the BNP. Gould insisted that many working-class voters felt increasingly abandoned by New Labour, that they regarded themselves as very British, not European, and that they sharply resented the rising numbers of asylum-seekers entering Britain. If Labour were to avoid losing many of its core voters to the BNP, especially in its northern heartlands, Gould suggested that it should embrace their concerns on asylum and immigration.[52]

The strategy was dubbed 'triangulation'. A former campaign advisor to Bill Clinton had pioneered it during the mid-1990s. Across the Atlantic it had involved occupying the political space held by the Republicans, forcing them further to the right and away from the centre. In the case of the BNP, it meant depriving the far right of its core issues. Yet in so doing, even if New Labour thought in terms of trans-Atlantic 'triangulation', the reality was closer to home and far less inspiring. What New Labour was doing was following Thatcher's example set in the late 1970s. The contrast with its response to the NF in the 1970s could not have been more striking. Then, Labour had campaigned against racism and it had at least tried to take the arguments to its core voters. Despite the 1974–79 Labour government seeking to reassure voters that it had a firm grip over immigration policy, the party's rank and file called for less rather than more immigration controls and Thatcher's 'swamping' speech drew vocal criticism from many, including the Prime Minister James Callaghan who sought a national approach to immigration that avoided distorting 'our community with hatred'.[53] Admittedly, Thatcher's 'swamping' comments did dispossess the NF of support but when, just prior to the 2002 local elections, Home Secretary David Blunkett borrowed from Thatcher's phraseology and declared that children of asylum-seekers were 'swamping' Britain's schools, New Labour's questionable attempts at appearing tough on immigration and asylum seemed to have the opposite effect.

The reasons why are not difficult to find. First of all, with the tabloids railing against Labour over the asylum issue, the electorate had little trust in the Blair government to deliver on asylum. Second, Griffin's BNP was not a carbon copy of the 1970s NF. This time around Britain's far right had comparatively more respectability, more credibility and more professionalism.[54] Bitter experience had taught the BNP that rather than holding NF-style public meetings and demonstrations – activity which would typically invite confrontation with anti-fascists that placed it outside the norms of the liberal-democratic tradition – it should invest more time in doorstep politics. Besides, street confrontation gave life to those militant opposition groups, such as Anti-Fascist Action, that over the years had become a thorn in the side of the extreme right.[55] As Nick Griffin said, 'the idea that we might turn back to slugging it out with unwashed dropouts and sociology students is as unthinkable as it is absolute'.[56] With this change of tactic, not only did it remove militant anti-fascists from the streets it also denied Labour the possibility of using the law to isolate the BNP as a threat to public order, or 'race' relations.[57] Furthermore, whilst an undercurrent of Hitler-worship, hard-line racism and criminality remained, the BNP's image had visibly departed from 'the leather and swastikas school of British fascism'.[58] Hence Burnley's three newly elected BNP councillors could justifiably declare in May 2002: 'We're just normal people.'[59]

When the BNP was last elected to public office, in Millwall in September 1993, the 'crisis' had been short-lived – the seat was lost the following May. The election of three councillors in Burnley in May 2002, however – a town traditionally dominated by Labour – was no flash in the pan. A year later, the BNP could boast eight seats and for a moment it was the second largest group on Burnley Council. This was an unprecedented course of events. To make matters worse, local history could offer little guide as to how Burnley Labour Party should best respond either. Of the two National Party councillors that had won seats in 1976 in neighbouring Blackburn, one had resigned before his first full council meeting and within a year the National Party had disintegrated. Perhaps not surprisingly then, when faced with such an exceptional situation, Burnley Labour Party struggled to formulate a coherent response.

What complicated the issue further was that long before the BNP had established a foothold in the town, Labour had failed to confront the racist vote. This particular problem was partly one of its own making. During the 1990s some Labour councillors in Burnley had been pandering to racism by applying pressure on housing officers in order to make certain that ethnic minorities were not housed in their wards. When this was exposed, those expelled from the Labour Party stood as Independents. They found a local champion in Harry Brooks, a former Labour Party member turned Independent. Brooks attacked the Labour Party's 'political correctness' and supported by the local press, the charismatic Brooks publicised the argument that Burnley Council favoured ethnic minorities in their allocation of resources. On the defensive, Burnley Labour Party was not sure which way to turn. And when the Independents failed to offer a candidate at the 2001 general election, the BNP simply stepped in and seized its opportunity. The immediate response of the Labour leader of the Council, Stuart Caddy, to a BNP candidate polling over 11 per cent of the vote in the Burnley parliamentary constituency, was to deny that the BNP's voters were racist. In his mind, Burnley was not a racist town. Rather than racism it had been Labour's failure to win an argument in relation to the allocation of resources that lay at the root of the problem, Caddy thought.[60]

Prophecy Public Relations, the firm that was asked by the Task Force to monitor the local media's role in the 2001 summer riots in Burnley, had suggested that frequent references to the BNP might create a platform for it. Taking this on board, Burnley Labour Party paid little attention to the BNP in the approach to the 2002 local elections. This did, however, run counter to advice from Labour's regional HQ in the north-west of England, which advocated the use of campaign literature that carried an all-out assault on the BNP. In truth, most public activity against the BNP in Burnley was being organised by the Anti-Nazi League (ANL) at this time. The League had first protested at the BNP's presence in the town at local elections in May 2000[61] and had called on the BNP's prospective parliamentary candidate, Steve Smith, to withdraw his nomination at the 2001 general election.[62] But many local Labour activists had no time for the League. In the immediate wake of the riots in Burnley in June 2001 there were concerns that a possible influx of 'outside agitators' might stir up further unrest. Hence a proposed ANL rally in the town was banned in August 2001.

Set at ease by the failure of the BNP to have any of its candidates elected at a series of by-elections in Burnley in November 2001, the local Labour Party felt confident that the BNP would not win any seats at all in 2002. Frank Dobson, former Secretary of State for Health, who had organised Labour's response to the BNP in Tower Hamlets in 1994, had urged the party to put a real effort into these November 2001 by-elections.[63] Consequently, outside help was brought in – TV personality Tony Robinson made an appearance – and the BNP was kept at bay. Second, the share of the vote for both Labour and Independents had increased (although the Liberal Democrats had decided not to field any candidates in two wards in order to minimise the risk of a BNP victory).[64] Third, the Independents had ruled out any possibility of an election pact with the BNP for the 2002 local elections and this seemed to diminish the threat even further.[65]

Unsurprisingly, when the May 2002 election results were announced, Burnley Labour Party was taken aback. The message from the Labour leadership in London was clear: in no circumstance should it co-operate with the BNP. The local party was told that whilst it should always avoid demonising BNP voters (otherwise it runs the risk of never winning them back), the BNP itself was beyond the pale.[66] 'We will not work with the BNP, a fascist organisation. This is a disaster', Caddy promised at once.[67] Yet behind the rhetoric, Caddy believed (along with other local

Labour activists) that the BNP's councillors were not really fascists at all but politically naïve Independents, ordinary Burnley folk who had been caught up in the tide of anti-Labour protest. Therefore, although attempts were made to isolate them in the Chamber itself, various forms of contact were still maintained in the hope that defections might be secured in the near future.

The first challenge to the BNP in the Chamber occurred in July 2002 when Labour deliberately passed a motion applauding the stance of the town's Football Club in taking action to ban supporters from matches for racial chanting and re-affirmed Council policy to promote racial harmony. This was clearly intended to marginalise the BNP and Carol Hughes, the one BNP councillor in attendance, did abstain.[68] At a full council meeting in August 2003, a motion defied the BNP to tell the people of Burnley what it stood for and during the last council meeting before the 10 June 2004 elections, Labour challenged the BNP with a further motion accusing them of spreading lies about funding.[69] Yet at other times, some Labour councillors have been to known to adopt a far more cordial approach.[70] In one early incident, Caddy was photographed in the local press in a discussion with local residents alongside BNP councillor Carol Hughes.[71] Whilst this has made it easier for the BNP to normalise itself, it finally delivered a result when Maureen Stowe, a BNP councillor elected in 2003, defected to Labour in 2004. This does not mean, however, that everyone within Burnley Labour Party favoured such a tactic. It is fair to say that it has had its critics.[72]

With the 2003 local elections looming, the local Labour Party finally convened a special all-members' meeting. Its purpose was to examine the role that the Labour Party had played in bringing about the emergence of the BNP in Burnley and how an effective anti-BNP campaign strategy might be devised. This meeting was proposed not by the national leadership (which increasingly despaired at the local party)[73] but by members from the Rosehill/Burnley Wood ward. Held on the 25 November 2002, some 52 members split into seven workshops. According to the report of this meeting, most participants said little about tactical relationships or the merits of attacking the BNP in a traditional anti-Nazi manner. Given the perception of the BNP as ordinary folk, it was widely felt that anti-Nazi campaigns did not resonate.[74] Little was said about racism either – an issue that, as we have seen, the party lacked the confidence to confront. Across the entire period since the 2001 riots there had not been a single major anti-racist event organised in Burnley. Caddy had recently refused to allow the ANL use of one of the Council's parks to hold a 'Love Music – Hate Racism' carnival.[75] The focus instead was on practical campaigning issues and the need to re-connect with the electorate.[76] Regrettably, the report of this 25 November meeting was leaked to the Burnley branch of the BNP. Word of this leak reached the local press in January 2003 leading Peter Pike, local Labour MP, to admit that there 'could be racist elements within his own party'.[77]

In line with the recommendations of this meeting, few Labour Party leaflets at the 2003 local elections attacked the BNP outright.[78] During the 2003 local elections, this thinking prevailed throughout the Labour Party's national organisation as well.[79] The general perception within Burnley Labour Party was that the local party was doing a lot of good work but it was not getting the credit for it because of various myths circulated by the BNP, either in conversation in pubs and clubs (a favoured tactic) or within their literature. As a result, Peter Kenyon, the local Labour Party agent, drew up a myth-busting document for activists. This did not tackle racism per se, but sought to counter the BNP's tactics by reassuring voters that Burnley was not being swamped with people of Asian origin, that only 1 in 890 local residents was an asylum-seeker, that the Council was not subsidising the building of a mosque, and that any money spent in the predominantly Asian Daneshouse ward was the consequence of this ward being ranked in the top 1 per cent of the most deprived wards in the country.[80] Yet in so far as it had developed a coherent strategy that could unite the 'lead-players' like Caddy and Pike with ordinary activists, Burnley Labour Party still fell short. Thus, two Labour councillors – Paul Moore and Alice Thornber – were criticised by Caddy and Pike after they removed a wreath laid by a BNP councillor at a Holocaust Memorial Service in Burnley on 26 January 2003.[81] Moore wanted a debate in the local press in order to expose BNP hypocrisy. However, it backfired. The case was referred to the Standards Board for England, which found that both councillors had behaved in an unacceptable manner that had brought their offices into disrepute.[82]

If Burnley Labour Party had been shocked by the election of three BNP councillors, the following year they were distraught. As the BNP increased its local representation by five more councillors, the local party was all at sea. Caddy even admitted to the local press that he did not know why people were voting for the BNP.[83] Ominously for Labour, with two fewer candidates, the BNP had polled as many votes as Labour and 'For the first time in British electoral history' as *Searchlight*'s Nick Lowles tells it, 'people were seriously thinking that both the council and the parliamentary seat were vulnerable to a far right party'.[84] Not surprisingly, therefore, when it came to a council by-election in Burnley's Hapton ward in June 2003 the regional Labour Party intervened. To emphasise its local patriotism, the regional party decided on a new tactic: it would put a Union Jack on claret and blue leaflets (the colours of Burnley Football Club). But after running a strong anti-Labour and anti-BNP campaign it was the Liberal Democrats that emerged victorious. A further local by-election, this time in the town's Lanehead ward in October 2003 saw Labour dispense with its Union Jack tactic. Nonetheless, the Liberal Democrats still won the seat after running yet another effective anti-BNP campaign. Several Liberal Democrat leaflets had drawn attention to BNP criminality, helped by the fact that the election had been precipitated by the resignation of Luke Smith, a 21-year-old BNP councillor who had attacked another BNP activist with a bottle at the party's annual summer festival.

At long last, as the 2004 local and European elections approached, the local Labour Party's response to the BNP became far more cohesive. One key factor here was the selection of Kitty Ussher as the Labour Party's prospective parliamentary candidate.[85] She had addressed the special all-party members' meeting in November 2002 where her position had been that it was the BNP that constituted the 'real enemy' and not the Tories (who had become a local irrelevance). This fastened on the mind despite the fact that the fortunes of Burnley Liberal Democrats had revived in the intervening period. By 26 February 2004 the Liberal Democrats could claim three more council seats than the BNP and therefore offered voters a more credible alternative to Labour. With Ussher providing the lead, and supported by the local party agent, Mike Nelson, a sustained attack on the BNP was carried in the party's election literature. Labour Party activists also helped distribute over 40,000 pieces of third-party anti-fascist material in a town of 37,000 households.[86] The appalling record of Burnley's BNP councillors – dubbed by Caddy as the 'elected group of silence' – undoubtedly helped Labour's cause. They had regularly failed to attend Council meetings – in the case of Carol Hughes for instance, just 45 per cent of all meetings between 30 April 2003 and 1 June 2004 and even when they did attend, their input had been negligible.[87] Fortuitously for Labour, it could also make use of former BNP councillor Maureen Stowe, a well-respected 62-year-old grandmother who quit the party once her eyes were opened to its true character.[88] And with the BNP's share of the poll falling significantly, and its number of Burnley councillors remaining static, few could doubt that Labour's campaign was more effective this time. All the same, with the BNP unfit for office as its main line of attack, the thorny issue of racism still went largely unchallenged.

It need hardly be added, of course, that by focusing on Burnley we lose sight of the fuller picture especially since the BNP has polled well in a number of different areas (including staunch Tory areas) and its candidates have been elected to other local councils. Unfortunately, it is not possible to cover all these cases here. Nevertheless, a broadening of the perspective would find that the pattern of Labour Party response has been subject to some variation. As a rule, where local Labour MPs have been alive to the threat and where there has been a strong trades council presence, party activists have been quick to respond to the BNP threat in their localities. This has been encouraged by Frank Dobson, head of the anti-BNP section of Labour's parliamentary campaign team.[89] At the national level, meanwhile, in order to minimise the chance of Griffin winning a seat in the European elections, all-postal voting was extended to the north-west of England in 2004. The use of an all-postal ballot had helped prevent BNP candidates from being elected in Sunderland in 2003 and Nick Raynsford, the Local Government Minister had taken note: 'The BNP thrives in areas of low turnout', he remarked, 'If you increase turnout there is a better chance that they won't get through.'[90] Moreover, senior Labour Party strategists also participated in a meeting organised by the Joseph Rowntree Reform Trust in January 2004 where strategies for thwarting the BNP were discussed by all the three main parties. As part of this process, New Labour generally welcomed Michael Howard's speech in Burnley the following month in which he underscored the Tory commitment to a tougher stand on immigration and asylum whilst condemning BNP as 'a bunch of thugs dressed up as a political party'.[91] Clearly Tory weakness was encouraging white working-class voters to switch to the BNP, New Labour's strategists thought.

While such responses by the Labour Party at both the local and national level have certainly been a factor in the failure of the BNP to engineer a major electoral breakthrough in 2004, this should not detract us from the fact that Labour's response played a significant part in the emergence of the BNP in the first place.[92] As late as December 2003, Blunkett was telling readers of the *Observer* that, 'I can't back down on asylum.' It was significant that he drew attention to a recent report that had shown that for the first time in nearly two decades, the numbers of people who regard themselves as racist had increased.[93] What Blunkett refused to appreciate was the very obvious connection between New Labour's policies and the fuelling of racism. Others were only too aware of what was happening. The TUC, for instance, had passed a motion at its 2003 annual Congress condemning the Labour government for immigration and asylum policies that pandered to racism and racist organisations, like the BNP.[94] This criticism, unimaginable during the 1970s, once more demonstrates the distance New Labour had travelled from its traditional moorings. Forget, for one moment, its broad acceptance of the neo-liberal Thatcherite project – even in terms of its response to contemporary British fascism, New Labour is clearly not the party it once was.

Conclusion

Drawing this final chapter to its close, two main points need to be made. The first is that Labour's leaders see the BNP in much the same way as they saw the NF in the 1970s, that is to say, as an electoral challenge to their own particular constituency. The reality, however, is that this challenge has been somewhat overstated. In Burnley, for instance, although local surveys indicated a significant shift in votes from Labour to the BNP between 2002 and 2003, the proportion of former Tory voters who had moved to the BNP was higher.[95] However, and this is our second point, the nature of Labour's response today differs noticeably from the 1970s. In that decade, in conjunction with the TUC, Labour campaigned against the attitudinal racism of its own traditional constituency and launched a major attack on the political racism of the NF. In sharp contrast, New Labour responded to the rise of the BNP with ever-tougher language and policies on immigration and asylum – a response that drew only condemnation from the trade unions. To date, New Labour has not devoted any party political broadcast to an onslaught against the BNP and neither has it organised any major anti-racist demonstration.

Yet this does not mean to say that Labour activists have not been involved in anti-BNP campaigns. Nor is it true that Tony Blair and other leading Labour politicians have not condemned the BNP. Just prior to the November 2002 Mill Hill by-election in Blackburn for instance, Tony Blair was featured on the front page of the *Lancashire Evening Telegraph* making a plea to readers not to vote BNP. And as we have seen, one particular challenge that the Labour Party did not have to face in the 1970s was the possibility that a council, if not a parliamentary seat, might be vulnerable to far right capture. This was an entirely unique situation and Labour Party activists in Burnley understandably struggled to come up with a coherent response. It required a co-ordinated strategy but this was not immediately forthcoming not least because the local Labour Party was not confident in addressing racism as a problem and its 'lead-players' saw the BNP councillors as ordinary people caught up in anti-Labour protest. But by 2004, a more effective local campaign strategy had been forged and all the indications are that the onward march of the BNP has ground to a halt in Burnley. This gives us cause for optimism. Moreover, the BNP's tendency to exaggerate its electoral progress does threaten to destabilise it. Squeezed by UKIP, it failed to win any representation to the European Parliament – a breakthrough that Griffin had promised his followers would happen. And having had its glossy image as a 'respectable' political party blown apart in a hard-hitting TV documentary in July 2004,[96] it would come as no surprise if the advance of the BNP came to an end. Nonetheless, with more than 20 councillors, the challenge still remains. It is far too early to write it off. As John Bean, the current editor of the BNP's monthly put it: 'when the transient flame of the febrile UKIP has burnt out, the British National Party will still be here and so will I, unless I am in my box first'.[97]

Notes

1. *Lancashire Evening Telegraph*, 2 May 2003.
2. The anti-fascist magazine *Searchlight* goes as high as 17,500. Tyndall talks about a quadrupling of members from a base figure of only 2,000.
3. On events in Red Lion Square, see *The Red Lion Square Disorders of 15 June 1974, Report of Inquiry by the Rt. Hon Justice Scarman* (London: HMSO, 1975).
4. See Fred Lindorp, 'Racism and the Working Class: Strikes in Support of Enoch Powell in 1968', *Labour History Review*, 4, 66, Spring 2001, pp. 79–95.
5. See *The Times*, 8 September 1972.
6. See Trade Unionists Against Fascism, Against Fascism: A Report on Extreme Right-Wing and Fascist Activities Currently Directed at the Trade Union Movement (December 1972).
7. See *Record*, paper of the TGWU, November 1973, p. 14.
8. Fascist infiltration of the trade unions continued throughout the 1970s although it never amounted to a serious problem.
9. See Labour Party Research Department, Information Paper No. 26, September 1974.
10. National Museum of Labour History Archives (NMLH): National Executive Committee, National Front: An Office Note, September 1977.
11. *The Times*, 3 October 1974.
12. According to *National Front Members' Bulletin*, July–August 1976.
13. Based on analysis by the Board of Deputies of British Jews, see *The Times*, 1 June 1976.
14. See *The Times*, 17 June 1976.
15. See *The Times*, 2 July 1976.
16. M. Walker, *The National Front*, 2nd rev. edn (London: Fontana Collins, 1978), p. 200.
17. *The Times*, 2 July 1976.
18. See NMLH Archives: Labour Party Home Policy Sub-Committee Minutes, 7 July 1976.

19. Tom Jackson, general secretary of the Union of Post Office Workers, see *The Times*, 30 September 1976.
20. See NMLH Archives: Notes of meeting held at Lambeth Palace with the Archbishop of Canterbury, 22 September 1976.
21. NMLH Archives: National Executive Committee: Campaign on Racialism, 25 July 1976.
22. See *The Times*, 6 July 1977.
23. See *The Times*, 4 September 1976.
24. NMLH Archives: Transcript of Labour Party Broadcast, 14 September 1976.
25. See University of Warwick Modern Records Centre (MRC): MSS. 292D/805.99, Box 1955.
26. *The Times*, 22 November 1976.
27. An early example was in Blackburn in 1973, see Board of Deputies of British Jews: Jewish Defence and Group Relations Committee, Current Notes on Municipal Elections, July 1973, p. 11.
28. See *Searchlight*, No. 25, 1977, p. 16.
29. See the London Socialist Historians Group, *The Battle of Wood Green* (London: Harringey Trades Council and London Socialist Historians Group, n.d.).
30. See NMLH Archives: National Executive Committee, National Front: An Office Note, September 1977.
31. See *The Times*, 18 November 1976.
32. *The Times*, 8 December 1977.
33. *The Sun* and *Daily Mirror* praised the Labour Party although *The Times* was more critical.
34. NMLH Archives: National Executive Committee: Anti-Racialism Campaign, 15 January 1978.
35. A former editor of *Searchlight* in the 1960s, Joan Lestor (with Shirley Williams) was a founder of the Labour Party's Race Relations Group. This was first established in 1973.
36. Hundreds of thousands of leaflets declaring: 'Unity is our future. Don't let racialism destroy it' were distributed. See *The Times*, 10 July 1978.
37. NMLH Archives: National Executive Committee Anti-Racialism Campaign, 15 January 1978.
38. Peter Hain, Joe Ashton, Neil Kinnock, Audrey Wise, Frank Allaun, Sid Bidwell and Ian Mikardo for example.
39. See N. Copsey, *Anti-Fascism in Britain* (Basingstoke: Macmillan, 2000), p. 133.
40. See *The Times*, 16 September 1978.
41. See *The Times*, 14 May 1977.
42. The level of the deposit remained at £150 until it was increased to the current level of £500 in 1985. The proportion of votes required to retain the deposit was also reduced from one-eighth to one-twentieth.
43. Neither the Home Secretary nor a local council can originate a ban under the terms of the Public Order Act.
44. See NMLH Archives: Labour Party Home Policy Committee, Response to the National Front, May 1978 and NEC Response to the National Front, September 1978. The problem with incitement to racial hatred is that juries are unlikely to convict since hatred is too strong a word. In 13 months after the 1976 Act became law, over 70 cases were referred to the DPP for prosecutions, but only six prosecutions were authorised, see R. Darlington, 'The

Law on Racialist Activities', *Labour Research*, 67, 9, September 1978. The 1976 Act had resulted from criticism of the shortcomings of the existing Act and was not a response to the NF per se.
45. See MRC MSS 292D/805.99: TUC Race Relations Advisory Committee Minutes, 24 August 1977.
46. See NMLH Archives: Rt. Hon. Merlyn Rees, Secretary of State for Home Affairs to NEC, 10 March 1978.
47. *Runnymede Trust Bulletin*, No. 92, November 1977.
48. See N. Copsey, *Anti-Fascism in Britain*, pp. 115–52.
49. In Burnley for example, 237 racist attacks were recorded between April 2002 and March 2003. This represents an increase of 149 per cent on the period between April 2000 and March 2001. This rise is consistent with increased BNP activity in the area.
50. Greg Deacon, Ahmed Keita and Ken Ritchie, *Burnley and the BNP and the Case for Electoral Reform* (London: Electoral Reform Society, 2004), p. 20.
51. See N. Copsey, *Contemporary British Fascism: the British National Party and the Quest for Legitimacy* (Basingstoke: Palgrave-Macmillan, 2004), pp. 124–50.
52. See *Identity*, 23, August 2002, p. 3.
53. At the 1977 Labour Party conference, a resolution was passed for the repeal of both the 1968 Commonwealth Immigrants Act and 1971 Immigrants Act. For Callaghan's critical response to Thatcher, see *The Times*, 15 February 1978.
54. On Nick Griffin and the 'modernisation' of the BNP, see N. Copsey, *Contemporary British Fascism*, pp. 100–23.
55. On Anti-Fascist Action 'from the inside', see K. Bullstreet, *Bash the Fash: Anti-Fascist Recollections 1984–93* (London: Kate Sharpley Library, 2001) and Dave Hann and Steve Tilzey, *No Retreat: The Secret War Between Britain's Anti-Fascists and the Far Right* (Lytham: Milo Books, 2003).
56. *Identity*, 42, February 2004, p. 6.
57. That said, Blunkett's desire to introduce a new law on incitement to religious hatred was based in part on a recognition that post-9/11, 'Islamophobia has become a refuge for racists', as *The Guardian's* Jeremy Seabrook put it. See *The Guardian*, 23 July 2004.
58. Greg Deacon, Ahmed Keita and Ken Ritchie, *Burnley and the BNP and the Case for Electoral Reform*, p. 8.
59. *Burnley Express*, 7 May 2002.
60. See *The Guardian*, 30 June 2001.
61. See *Burnley Express*, 12 May 2000.
62. See *The Burnley Express*, 25 May 2001.
63. Rt. Hon. Frank Dobson MP to author, 15 July 2004.
64. See *Burnley Express*, 20 November 2001.
65. See *Lancashire Evening Telegraph*, 27 December 2001.
66. Rt. Hon. Frank Dobson MP to author, 15 July 2004.
67. *The Guardian*, 4 May 2002.
68. See Burnley Borough Council: Full Council minutes, 10 July 2002.
69. See Burnley Borough Council: Full Council minutes, 2 August 2003 (motion: 'That this Council: recognising that the British National Party is one of the two largest opposition parties on the Council now has the responsibility to put their policies for this Council to the test of debate ...') and 19 May 2004 (motion: 'That this Council: with increasing concern the continuing

misinformation disseminating throughout the Borough regarding the allocation of regeneration funding ...').

70. Former Labour councillor Paul Moore to author, 30 June 2004.
71. See *Searchlight*, No. 324, June 2002, p. 12.
72. Paul Moore to author, 30 June 2004.
73. Frank Dobson had visited Burnley Labour Group in the approach to the 2002 local elections and advised it to do more to address local concerns. However, he found the local Labour Party complacent. Rt. Hon. Frank Dobson to author, 27 July 2004.
74. Paul Moore to author, 30 June 2004.
75. The carnival was held in Manchester's Platt Fields Park instead. It attracted some 30,000 people. See *Searchlight*, No. 328, October 2002, p. 7.
76. A report by Burnley Labour Party. 'Only Connect': The Special All-Members Meeting of the 25 November 2002.
77. See *Lancashire Evening Telegraph*, 27 January 2003.
78. Jason Hunter, Unison official, to author, 29 June 2004.
79. *Searchlight*, June 2003, p. 6.
80. Labour Party document: 'Myths and Reality'.
81. Paul Moore to author, 30 June 2004.
82. See The Standards Board for England, Case Summary: Case numbers: SBE2517.03; SBE2518.03; SBE2661.03 and SBE26662.03.
83. See *Lancashire Evening Telegraph*, 6 May 2003.
84. The Joseph Rowntree Charitable Trust, *539 Voter's Views: A Voting Behaviour Study in Three Northern Towns* (York: Joseph Rowntree Charitable Trust, 2004), p. 15.
85. Policy Advisor to Patricia Hewitt, Secretary of State for Trade and Industry.
86. See *Searchlight*, No. 349, July 2004, p. 14.
87. See Burnley Borough Council: Return of Attendance of Members, 30 April 2003–1 June 2004.
88. On Maureen Stowe, see *Searchlight*, No. 346, April 2004, pp. 6–7.
89. Rt. Hon. Frank Dobson MP to author, 15 July 2004.
90. See *The Observer*, 4 May 2003.
91. See *The Guardian*, 19 February 2004.
92. See especially David Renton, 'Examining the Success of the British National Party, 1999–2003', *Race and Class*, 45, 2, 2003, pp. 75–85.
93. See *The Observer*, 14 December 2003.
94. See *Searchlight*, No. 340, October 2003, p. 11.
95. See Greg Deacon, Ahmed Keita and Ken Ritchie, *Burnley and the BNP and the Case for Electoral Reform*, p. 17.
96. *Secret Agent*, BBC1, 15 July 2004. This documentary revealed BNP members openly admitting to racially motivated crime. For a useful report, see *The Sunday Telegraph*, 18 July 2004.
97. *Identity*, 45, July 2004, p. 3.

Index